Ethics
DeMYSTiFieD®

D1122724

DeMYSTiFieD® Series

Accounting Demystified	Logic Demystified
Advanced Calculus Demystified	Macroeconomics Demystified
Advanced Physics Demystified	Management Accounting Demystified
Advanced Statistics Demystified	Math Proofs Demystified
Algebra Demystified	Math Word Problems Demystified
Alternative Energy Demystified	MATLAB® Demystified
Anatomy Demystified	Medical Billing and Coding Demystified
asp.net 2.0 Demystified	Medical Terminology Demystified
Astronomy Demystified	Meteorology Demystified
Audio Demystified	Microbiology Demystified
Biology Demystified	Microeconomics Demystified
Biotechnology Demystified	Nanotechnology Demystified
Business Calculus Demystified	Nurse Management Demystified
Business Math Demystified	OOP Demystified
Business Statistics Demystified	Options Demystified
C++ Demystified	Organic Chemistry Demystified
Calculus Demystified	Personal Computing Demystified
Chemistry Demystified	Philosophy Demsytified
Circuit Analysis Demystified	Pharmacology Demystified
College Algebra Demystified	Physics Demystified
Corporate Finance Demystified	Physiology Demystified
Databases Demystified	Pre-Algebra Demystified
Data Structures Demystified	Precalculus Demystified
Differential Equations Demystified	Probability Demystified
Digital Electronics Demystified	Project Management Demystified
Earth Science Demystified	Psychology Demystified
Electricity Demystified	Quality Management Demystified
Electronics Demystified	Quantum Mechanics Demystified
Engineering Statistics Demystified	Real Estate Math Demystified
Environmental Science Demystified	Relativity Demystified
European History Demystified	Robotics Demystified
Everyday Math Demystified	Sales Management Demystified
Fertility Demystified	Signals and Systems Demystified
Financial Planning Demystified	Six Sigma Demystified
Forensics Demystified	Spanish Demystified
French Demystified	sql Demystified
Genetics Demystified	Statics and Dynamics Demystified
Geometry Demystified	Statistics Demystified
German Demystified	Technical Analysis Demystified
Home Networking Demystified	Technical Math Demystified
Investing Demystified	Trigonometry Demystified
Italian Demystified	uml Demystified
Java Demystified	Visual Basic 2005 Demystified
JavaScript Demystified	Visual C# 2005 Demystified
Lean Six Sigma Demystified	xml Demystified
Linear Algebra Demystified	World History Demystified

Ethics
DeMYSTiFieD®

Micah Newman

McGraw Hill

New York Chicago San Francisco Lisbon London Madrid Mexico City
Milan New Delhi San Juan Seoul Singapore Sydney Toronto

The **McGraw·Hill** *Companies*

Copyright © 2011 by The McGraw-Hill Companies, Inc. All rights reserved. Printed in the United States of America. Except as permitted under the United States Copyright Act of 1976, no part of this publication may be reproduced or distributed in any form or by any means, or stored in a database or retrieval system, without the prior written permission of the publisher.

1 2 3 4 5 6 7 8 9 10 11 12 13 14 15 16 17   QFR/QFR   1 9 8 7 6 5 4 3 2 1

ISBN   978-0-07-176275-5
MHID   0-07-176275-2

e-ISBN   978-0-07-176276-2
e-MHID   0-07-176276-0

Library of Congress Control Number   2010941614

Trademarks: McGraw-Hill, the McGraw-Hill Publishing logo, Demystified, and related trade dress are trademarks or registered trademarks of The McGraw-Hill Companies and/or its affiliates in the United States and other countries and may not be used without written permission. All other trademarks are the property of their respective owners. The McGraw-Hill Companies is not associated with any product or vendor mentioned in this book.

McGraw-Hill books are available at special quantity discounts to use as premiums and sales promotions or for use in corporate training programs. To contact a representative, please e-mail us at bulksales@mcgraw-hill.com.

This book is printed on acid-free paper.

Contents

Preface

This book provides an overview of the philosophical subject of ethics and explains how and why philosophers think about certain topics in this area. Ethics itself, of course, is about right and wrong, the so-called subject matter of morality. Traditionally, the word *ethics* has had a broader connotation than *morality*, often denoting something that can be approached in terms of appropriateness, or fittingness. *Morality*, on the other hand, is a more recent addition to the English language and more stringent in its subject matter. Something that is immoral is probably something that elicits outrage from many people; morality is simply doing what is considered minimally decent. But in contemporary usage, the two words usually mean the same thing; when people refer to ethics, they mean morality and vice versa. Accordingly, throughout this book, the two terms are used interchangeably, where *ethics* now means the same as what we mean by *morality*.

The first section of this book deals with the general subject of philosophy itself. Coming to understand what philosophy is about in a general sense will help you get a handle on how ethics is done. You need to understand the role that logic plays in philosophy, specifically in philosophical arguments. Philosophers today are usually not satisfied with simply asserting their beliefs (nor are they content when another philosopher simply states his or her beliefs). Rather, there has to be a reasoning process behind a conclusion, and the role of a formal argument is to make that reasoning process as transparent as possible. This is how philosophers meaningfully engage with others who do not already agree with them on everything (that is, with "almost all other philosophers").

Once that groundwork is established, the book moves on to the two major kinds of topics within ethics: *ethical theory*, which deals with the most general and abstract kinds of ethical questions, including those about the nature of ethics itself; and *applied ethics*, in which arguments are applied to some relevant contemporary moral dilemmas and controversies.

For Further Reading

The subject matter of ethics alone covers quite a vast territory. But a single book has to stop somewhere, even though for any topic in a book like this, there is always much more to be said about it. An introduction to ethics would therefore be incomplete without at least pointing you toward additional resources to deepen your understanding and appreciation for this fascinating subject. The bibliography at the end of this book lists all the works cited in the chapters. Some of these resources are somewhat difficult for the beginner. Many of the most readable and nontechnical essays discussed in this book, which constitute essential primary reading in ethics, are found in the anthology *The Ethical Life: Fundamental Readings in Ethics and Moral Problems* (Shafer-Landau 2010b). Another anthology, *Ethics: The Essential Writings* (Marino 2010), contains some of the same essays, as well as a sampling of ancient and medieval works. Another collection of essential ethics writings that is somewhat broader in scope is the volume edited by Peter Singer titled *Ethics* (Singer 1994). Simon Blackburn's *Being Good: A Short Introduction to Ethics* (Blackburn 2003) is a very engaging and readable introduction to the subject. Further discussion of topics in ethical theory can be found in John Deigh's approachable *An Introduction to Ethics* (Deigh 2010).

There are also podcasts that feature introductions to philosophical topics. Each episode of *Ethics Bites* and *Philosophy Bites* is a ten- to fifteen-minute interview with a leading philosopher on some ethical or other philosophical topic. The discussions are instructive and intelligent but down-to-earth and accessible to the average interested listener. These resources offer a rich variety of material for those who like to learn by listening.

How to Use This Book

Ethics is a major branch of the general discipline of philosophy. Philosophy is unfamiliar to many people, so part of the aim of this book is to convey what philosophers try to do and how they go about doing it. The chapters cover a variety of topics—some of them general and theoretical, others specific and applied. To get the most out of this book, you will need to think about the ideas presented in a certain way. When you read about what positions philosophers have taken on this or that ethical topic, don't treat it as information to be summarized in bullet points, as you might with class notes on another subject. Such summaries do not promote any understanding of the philosophy behind the ideas. The "isms" in ethical theory and the arguments given in applied ethics give examples of how philosophical thought works. The important thing is not so much *what* or *who*, but *why*.

This book contains an abundance of practice quizzes, tests, and exam questions, which are all multiple choice. There is a short quiz at the end of each chapter, which you should take to check your understanding of the material. These are "open-book" quizzes, so you may (and should) refer to the chapter text when taking them. Check your answers against the Answer Key at the end of the book; if you get any wrong, make sure you understand *why* the correct answer is correct. Reread the relevant material as needed. You should try to get at least eight out of ten answers right before moving on to the next chapter.

At the end of each major section of this book is a test to be taken when you're done with all the chapters in that section and have taken all the quizzes. The section tests are "closed book." Don't look back at the text when taking them. Again, answers are in the back of the book, and you should check any incorrect answers against the chapter text. Try to achieve a score of 75 percent or better before moving on to the next section.

The final exam at the end of this book contains questions drawn from all of the chapters. Take this exam when you have finished all the sections and their respective tests.

Do not simply memorize the correct answers to the quizzes, tests, and exam. If you do, you may not really understand why the answers are correct and will not really learn the material. If you do simply memorize answers and you go on to take a class in ethics, even if the quizzes or tests in that class ask essentially the same questions, you may not be able to carry over your answers if those questions are worded differently. Again, make sure you understand *why* the answers are what they are.

In addition to the chapter material and tests, this book has resources at the end of the book to help you learn the material. Ethics, like any branch of philosophy, uses some special terminology, because the subject matter deals with things at a different level from that of ordinary discussions. This book has a glossary that lists important vocabulary that may be unfamiliar (vocabulary terms are also defined as they are introduced in the text). The Appendix gives you some pointers on how to write about philosophy. If you are taking a philosophy class, you will likely be asked to show your knowledge by writing an essay that explains, in your own words, what you have learned. The Appendix will give you a good idea of "what the instructor is looking for" in such an essay. Finally, the book as a whole can be used as a reference for any future ethics studies you may undertake.

Acknowledgments

Thanks are due first and foremost to Paul Bloomfield, Rik Hine, and Michael Lynch of the University of Connecticut. This book could not have been written without the experience I gained teaching introductory philosophy and ethics under their direction. I am very grateful to B. J. Strawser for helpful feedback on some of the original ideas incorporated in this book, which helped me prevent some major blunders. (Any remaining blunders are, of course, purely my own responsibility.) I also thank Jesse Eaton for introducing me to Barbara Herman's refreshing views on Kant, in which I am now a believer.

I am also grateful for the gracious tolerance and generous support of my family, during the periods of time I was holed up writing this book. This includes, but is not limited to, my parents, Jot, Martha, Deidra, Laurel, John, Allie, Matt, Emma, Daylen, Christie, Josh, Elisabeth, Kyle, Evangeline, Elias, Jonathan, Larry, Nancy, Richard, and Tibbie.

Finally, I am very thankful to Mollie Ledwith and Martha Currise for giving me the opportunity to write this book and serving as my liaisons to McGraw-Hill. I owe them big time!

Ethics
DeMYSTiFieD®

Part One

What Philosophy Is and How to Do It

chapter **1**

Philosophy: The Intellectual Pursuit and Social Activity

CHAPTER OBJECTIVES

In this chapter, you will learn the following:

- What philosophy is as an intellectual discipline
- How philosophy is done
- What ethics is as a branch of philosophy

Ethics is one of the major branches of philosophy, so to understand it, you must first be clear on what philosophy is. This first chapter, therefore, addresses the essential questions of what philosophy is and what you need to learn about it. This is especially important if you have never studied philosophy before. This chapter gives you a road map to understanding the nature of philosophy as well as the methodology used to explore philosophical questions. Finally, an overview of the nature of ethics and the subdisciplines within ethics itself helps you get a general idea of how ethical questions are explored philosophically.

What Philosophy Is

Many people, perhaps even you, associate philosophy with an image of bearded men in togas discussing deep thoughts. There were such people in fact, and our Western intellectual heritage owes a lot to the ancient Greeks (which is why we have this mental picture). But it wasn't just the ancient Greeks who did philosophy. Philosophy is a basic human intellectual activity that has been pursued in every advanced culture since time immemorial. Its universality and timeless appeal should tell you something about it right off the bat: the doing of philosophy does not depend on any particular body of outside knowledge. This distinguishes it from any of the other "social sciences." For example, in history, it is absolutely necessary to know specific facts about events. You can't study history just by reasoning or by thinking about ideas. Likewise, you can't do psychology without having a certain scientific view toward human nature and observing actual patterns in human behavior (this is why psychology is, in fact, a relatively recently developed discipline).

What sets philosophy apart is its generality. It deals with the most general intellectual questions possible, such as "Why does anything exist at all?" "What makes an action morally right or wrong?" or "What do I really know?" You can imagine any person from any culture at any point in time asking questions like these (as indeed, they have).

Ethics—the study of the good, or right—is one of the main branches of philosophy. The others, as shown in Figure 1.1, are *metaphysics*, which deals with questions relating to being and existence, and *epistemology*, which deals with the nature of knowledge.

Any philosophical inquiry is going to be involved in ethical, metaphysical, or epistemological questions. For example, in metaphysics, philosophers work on questions such as "What are the most fundamental kinds of things that exist?" "What does it take for something to be destroyed instead of merely changed?"

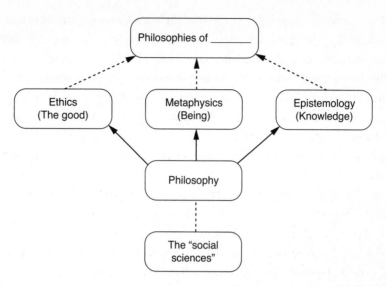

FIGURE 1.1 Philosophy, the most general form of intellectual inquiry, asks questions about three major areas: goodness, being, and knowledge. Philosophy also has many sub-disciplines (each called "philosophy of _____") that ask questions from all three of the major philosophical areas about a given topic (fill in the blank).

"Do things like fictional characters and numbers exist?" In epistemology, philosophers ask things like "What does it take for someone to 'know' something?" and "Is knowledge undermined by things independent of the knower?" In ethics, philosophers approach moral dilemmas and questions of right conduct by trying to find out what general principle applies and how it applies.

Philosophical inquiry starts and ends with principles. What all areas of philosophy have in common is that they set out to answer questions that are basically of the form "What's the principle at work here?" This kind of question can be applied to any area whatsoever, which is why philosophy can be thought of as the most general kind of inquiry.

As also shown in Figure 1.1, there are subdisciplines within philosophy that ask characteristically philosophical questions about some specific area. For example, there is the philosophy of mind, philosophy of language, philosophy of science, philosophy of chemistry—even the philosophy of sport! Each of these "philosophies of" is concerned with ethical, metaphysical, or epistemological questions about its subject matter. Actually, you can plug any sufficiently general topic into the blank in "philosophy of _____" and presto! You have a philosophical subdiscipline.

In an ethics course, you study specific views and arguments that have been put forth by specific individuals. But by and large, anyone could have thought of the same things, and if they had, you would still be learning about the same things, only under different names. To be sure, a philosopher's historical and cultural situation does have an impact on his or her doing of philosophy. (For example, the philosopher may be responding in some way to the needs and issues of a specific time and place.) But keep in mind that it's not nearly so important to memorize who said what as it is to understand the significance of what was said.

In philosophy, what's most crucial is to understand the principles at work, and the reasoning processes that lead to certain views. Memorizing facts and bullet points will not do it. You will have a good understanding of the subject when you can re-create, in your own words, the same reasoning processes that philosophers before you have used. Remembering this throughout your study should help you immensely in getting a handle on the material.

Still Struggling

Like science, philosophy seeks to answer questions. But the kinds of questions philosophy asks cannot be answered based on results of experiments. Instead, you must think carefully about the issues and use reason to come to the most plausible conclusion.

How Philosophy Is Done

This section explains what professional philosophers do and how they do it. In studying philosophy, you will undoubtedly read a good deal of primary material (that is, actual philosophical essays as opposed to writings about philosophy or certain philosophers). As you do, you will encounter numerous examples of the kinds of things discussed in this section; you may even want to refer back to it to see how the information is exemplified in your reading. In subsequent chapters of this book, when particular philosophical views and issues are explained, the principles and arguments that are being used will be spelled out. The general picture given here of how philosophy is done should serve as a basis for understanding how specific issues are dealt with philosophically.

It's All About the Principles

Here is how philosophers begin thinking about the principles they are dealing with. A principle is always of a general form; it is supposed to apply to certain types of things across the board. For example, it may be of the form "Any action that meets conditions A, B, and C is immoral." When most people think of principles, they think first of ethical principles, which naturally enough are those dealt with in ethical philosophy. In philosophy generally, though, it is whatever principle that applies to the subject matter that is important. A going principle in metaphysics, for example, might be "A thing cannot begin to exist at two different times"; in epistemology, it might be "You can be said to know x only if you have formed a justified belief that x is true."

Philosophers both spell out and argue for certain principles. Reasoning plays a crucial role in this process, but it has to start somewhere. You can't argue for a principle out of nowhere. In philosophy, you use reason and logic to show how, *if* you start with a certain principle, it naturally leads to or entails another principle. (Chapter 2 examines the workings of this reasoning process in detail.) This chapter gives an overview of this process in terms of the bigger picture of how philosophy is done so that, when you read philosophical writings, you can have a general sense of what is going on. This is important groundwork, because philosophical writings are more challenging to understand than almost anything else you may be asked to read. The intellectual demands it places on readers are considerably higher than in most other fields. The rest of this section will explain why.

Philosophy: The Social Activity

A philosopher starts by trying to make sense of the data of experience in systematic ways so as to find out what principles govern whatever the area of inquiry is. As you read in the previous section, this can be done by anyone, anywhere, at any time. Some people may be content to "philosophize" within the friendly confines of their own mind without communicating their thoughts to others. In a way, this is perfectly legitimate: the nature of philosophy is such that it can be done without recourse to any particular tools. But no matter how earth-shattering the conclusions reached in this way may be, you cannot be a philosopher in the full sense if no one ever hears about them!

An essential part of the philosophical enterprise, then, is its social nature. To at least "compare notes" with other philosophically interested people adds something crucial to the practice of philosophy itself and not just because it's important to make your ideas more widely known. Rather, it helps you hone your ideas to greater quality. Part of this is making sure that your ideas and reasoning process are as clearly spelled out as possible; ensuring that they're clear to someone else helps make them clearer to yourself. This is how a philosopher ensures that he or she is really making sense and using valid reasoning processes. If you are challenged by someone who seems to disagree, this forces you to be as clear as possible about what principles you are starting with and exactly how you are reasoning to a given conclusion. This gives both participants in a philosophical exchange an indispensable opportunity to hone their ideas and reasoning skills. Thus, the social component of philosophy is an essential part of the doing of philosophy itself.

You may now be able to get a sense of why, when you read a philosophical essay or book, there seems to be so much going on. A philosopher has a lot of tasks to accomplish in his or her writing. First of all, the philosopher has to be clear exactly what he or she is writing about. Along the way, he or she has to anticipate questions or objections that might arise in the mind of someone reading critically (which is part of doing philosophy well). This is another way in which philosophy's social dimension plays out—"keeping the target audience in mind." The heavy load borne by the philosopher is multiplied by the fact that he or she is dealing with abstract and often complex ideas. So, to successfully navigate philosophical material, remember these goals that the philosopher is trying to meet in his or her writing.

Clarity and Explicitness

Now, a bit more about what it means to argue for a conclusion in philosophy. It was mentioned earlier that you can't just reason your way to a conclusion out of thin air; you have to start somewhere. Not only do philosophers have to explain what it is they are arguing *for*, but they lay most of the groundwork by spelling out exactly where they are arguing *from*. This can make it seem like philosophical writing moves along very slowly, and so it does; this is, in fact, the best way to do philosophy. (For example, does this text seem to be proceeding rather slowly? That's largely because it is an instance of "the philosophy of philosophy"!) Many will prefer to write in a way that's rhetorically snappy; the results are certainly easier to read than philosophy is, and can be more straightforwardly effective in convincing many people of the writer's conclusion. But philosophers aren't content with that: they want to know exactly what the reasoning process is and what assumptions are at work in getting from first principles to the conclusion. That way, they can be as clear as possible about what they think and *why*, and they can take each other to task about the principles they use in their arguments.

Taking time to think through and unpack your starting assumptions, then, is a crucial requisite to putting forth an argument for a conclusion. It takes patience and discipline to do this, but the payoff is knowing exactly how you can validly proceed from point A to B to C. The alternative is to rely on rhetoric and on saying things that are going to sound plausible mostly to those who already agree with your conclusion. The difference is that in philosophy, you can show how (if the given argument succeeds) certain starting principles have to lead to others. This is what makes the difference between arguments that boil down to merely "Yes, it is," or "No, it isn't," and philosophical arguments that are meant to force the participants to weigh their principles carefully against other principles (how this works will be explained in detail in the next chapter).

In the process of spelling out your background assumptions, probably the most difficult thing to learn is to recognize that they are there. In ordinary types of communication, we rely on tons of implicit assumptions about ourselves and others that don't have to be stated in advance because they're taken for granted. If they weren't taken for granted, and we had to state all our background assumptions explicitly, ordinary communication would be rendered cumbersome indeed. But, of course, philosophy is a kind of communication that is outside the ordinary. It deals with a level of abstraction that is a step or two removed from the concrete sorts of transactions that are commonplace in our daily interactions. This is why, in philosophy, you must be extra careful that what you are saying and why is clearly understood. A philosopher's skills in this discipline can always stand improvement; it is actually only in the last century or so that a special premium has been placed on clarity. (In studies of much of philosophy from centuries ago, debates still rage about what, precisely, some philosophers were saying.)

Since philosophy is drastically incomplete without the aspects of communication and social interaction, use of language is unavoidable in doing philosophy. But human language wasn't made for philosophizing, so to proceed at all in philosophy, use of language has to be adapted carefully for that purpose. To paraphrase one well-known philosopher, philosophy is like a dog walking on its hind legs; it is not done well, but we are impressed that it is done at all (Van Inwagen 2002: 12).

Commitments and Consistency

As already stated, in philosophy, you argue from certain principles to others; this is what is meant by *argument* in this field. When you use principles in arguments, you make a commitment and are willing to say, "I believe this principle holds true across the board to whatever it applies to." Holding to a principle means that you can't just pick and choose where to invoke it. If you do that, it just indicates that when push comes to shove, you think every situation should be treated differently from any other. In that case, there's no point in the pretense of holding to a principle at all. If you do hold to a principle, however, you have to be held accountable for it. If you make ad hoc (that is, by your own whim) decisions as to where it applies and where it doesn't, you contradict yourself if you say the principle holds generally.

Remember that in philosophy, you are trying to explain things through a process of reasoning, which you can't do without figuring out what principles apply and holding to them consistently. Just as you would do in science, you make explanatory progress in philosophy when you can say, "Oh, I see now that fact A and fact B hold true because they're both instances of principle C, which governs things of this kind." But in making a commitment to a principle, you have to be careful to sort out the rest of your beliefs and commitments to make sure they're consistent with that principle. You can think of it in terms of an analogy to the commitments you make on your calendar. When you mark down that you will do something at a certain time, you make a commitment. If you didn't make any commitments at all, you would just be flying by the seat of your pants every day, and few of us can get away with this. But when you do make commitments, you open yourself up to the possibility of making multiple commitments for the same time, thereby committing yourself to being in different places at the same time—a contradiction. Therefore, when you commit to being in a certain place at a certain time in the future, you have to check your commitments to make sure there are no conflicts. Similarly, when you commit yourself to a principle in philosophy, you have to be held accountable to make sure it doesn't conflict with anything else you are committed to—and if it does, you have to choose between one or the other.

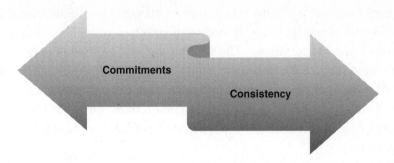

FIGURE 1.2 When you are committed to certain principles, you have to weigh the benefits of their explanatory power with the cost of their conclusions. Most importantly, your commitments must be tested for their consistency with one another—if there's a contradiction between any of them, you have to choose between them to ensure consistency.

All in all, as is represented in Figure 1.2, a tension plays out between stating your commitments and making sure that they're applied consistently and are consistent with each other. With regard to these connections and their ramifications, a large part of philosophy consists of untangling the knots in them and ensuring that an overall position remains stable once the resulting slack is taken out of them.

Remaining consistently committed to your stated principles defines the whole framework in which philosophy is done. You can think of the doing of philosophy, in fact, as the systematic means of avoiding hypocrisy. Hypocrisy, of course, is just being governed by a principle in some instances but not in others. A hypocrite says his or her actions are governed by certain principles but really just does whatever he or she pleases and then justifies it after the fact by finding some principle that seems to fit. If this sort of putting the cart before the horse (or having the tail wag the dog) seems egregious to you, then you will understand what motivates philosophers' careful weighing of principles and commitments. Of course, this systematic avoidance of hypocrisy is especially pertinent to ethics, since outside of philosophy itself, hypocrites are faulted first and foremost for being unethical in their inconsistency.

As you'll see, logic and arguments play a crucial role in sorting out your commitments in philosophy. The role of an argument is to lay out—given certain facts and principles—what other principles you will be committed to if you want to remain consistent. Then you choose between accepting the conclusion, rejecting one of the starting principles, or finding something wrong with the argument's logic. It's a process that never ends, because unlike in mathematics, you can never definitively prove an answer to a philosophical question. Rather, the point is to say, "If you are committed to such and such principles, here's what has to follow." The weighing of commitments against their logical consequences is a process that never ends, because each philosopher will think a different set of starting principles does the best explanatory work. And each philosopher will be able to give good reasons for his or her chosen set of principles—this is where the science (logic) gives way to art (giving voice to intuitions).

In any case, careful study of philosophy can give you the satisfaction of having explored all sides of questions that people have grappled with for centuries. And having come to a thoughtful, reasoned conclusion on your own, you will be in the best position for your reasoning to influence others.

Still Struggling

The philosophical methodology discussed in this section may become clearer with the help of examples: that's the work of Parts Two and Three. Discussion of specific topics will return to the general themes discussed in this chapter, explaining how these themes are exemplified. Overall, when you are reading philosophy, keep in mind that what the author is trying to tell you is not only the conclusion he or she is arguing for, but how he or she is getting there.

Ethical Philosophy

Within ethics itself, different general areas of inquiry vary in their levels of abstraction. It is worthwhile to sort out what's what in advance, so when you consider certain ethical issues, you can keep in mind the scope of a question by understanding into what subdiscipline it falls. Parts Two and Three of this book are organized according to the major division of subdisciplines within ethics: ethical theory and applied ethics. The rest of this section describes each of these subdisciplines and what kinds of questions they deal with.

Ethical Theory

Within ethics, philosophers can ask questions about the nature of ethics itself, separate from any particular ethical issue. These theoretical matters fall under a fairly broad umbrella known, naturally enough, as *ethical theory*. As far as their purpose, ethical theories are like scientific theories: they seek to give explanations of things in whatever way seems to make the best sense of available data. Topics within ethical theory can fall into any of three main subdivisions—value theory, metaethics, and normative ethics.

Value Theory

Value theory, as its name implies, is about the nature of values and asks the most fundamental questions about what is to be valued. This is an area of ethics partly because the fundamental values that we pursue shape the choices we make, and choosing between different courses of action is part of the subject matter of ethics. The value theory question "What is to be valued?" has an "ought" component to it; the question is really "What ought we to value?" Exploring how to tell which of any available values are good—good in an objective sense and not just an "I like it" sense—is also an ethical concern. Most fundamentally, value theory deals with the question of the nature of goodness, which is what makes it an ethical subdiscipline.

We may choose to pursue a variety of fundamental values. They include happiness (whatever that means), pleasure, getting what we want, duties to various other entities, or virtue. Choosing any of these as a supreme value over any other and conscientiously pursuing it has far-reaching consequences, so thinking about these matters is of crucial importance to a thinking person. Chapter 3 gives an overview of some positions offered by value theory and how philosophers think about them.

Normative Ethics

Another family of questions in ethical theory asks what makes actions right in general, whatever the particular issue at hand may be. This is known as *normative ethics*, which seeks to find whatever may fill in the blank in the statement "An action is morally right just when it is _____." The word *normative* means "obligatory" in the moral sense. Our actions are, or at least should be, guided by the set of standards to which we are committed and that dictate when a given action is obligatory, permissible, or impermissible. These standards are referred to as moral norms. The word *norm* is the root of the more familiar word *normal*, which apparently once had a normative connotation, referring to the standards that make an action morally right; the word *normal* is now used in a strictly statistical sense. However, when you hear the word *norm* in the ethical context, keep in mind that it is meant in the ethical, not statistical, sense. Norms are not supposed to be just conventional standards that most of us follow, but standards that reliably point us to right actions.

For example, one theory of normative ethics says that an action is obligatory only if its consequences enhance the greatest possible happiness for the greatest number of beings, no matter what the action is or how it is carried out. Another (diametrically opposed) theory says that an action is right only if it is done according to a person's proper duty, regardless of the consequences. Various theories in normative ethics are discussed in Chapter 4 of this book.

Metaethics

Metaethics seeks to understand the nature of ethical facts, beliefs, and judgments. The prefix *meta-* means "about," so metaethics looks at the subject matter of ethics as a whole to determine what it is, what it is about, and how we come to know about it. In other words, metaethics may be thought of as the philosophy of ethics, asking metaphysical and epistemological (and perhaps even ethical) questions about ethics. One pressing matter in metaethics, for example, is the status of ethical facts. We make ethical judgments we think are correct, which would seem to require facts of some sort for our judgments to refer to in order to be correct. But what sorts of facts could these be, and how do we come to know them? Since purported ethical facts seem to be unlike uncontroversial, objective facts, they could be thought of as fictions of our imagination instead. Or philosophers can come up with metaethical theories that try to make sense of how, as most of us tend to assume, there can be such things as moral facts and in what sense they really exist. Chapter 5 discusses a number of theories in the field of metaethics.

Applied Ethics

The realm of ethics that might be more familiar in terms of discussions and thoughts you have already had is *applied ethics*: specific ethical issues where the rubber meets the road, such as abortion, euthanasia, and war. In applied ethics, any kind of principle and fact relevant to the specific issue is brought into consideration. So although principles are certainly used in arguments in applied ethics, the choice of principles and considerations hinges on what is applicable to the issue at hand. As you learn about some of the different positions on a variety of topics, such as those covered in Part Three, you will understand, from a broader point of view, how ethical arguments are made in philosophy. You may want to use similar strategies when you find yourself arguing for your own point of view on an issue.

In the chapters that follow, ethical theory is discussed first because it may help you understand certain arguments and views that you will encounter in applied ethics. These subdisciplines are not completely independent of each other. In applied ethics, philosophers might argue for a certain conclusion just because it seems the best one for that particular issue. But quite often, when philosophers argue for a certain conclusion on an issue in applied ethics, they are coming at it from a specific standpoint in ethical theory. They assume a position in value theory according to which happiness is the supreme good; they may come from the normative standpoint that acts should be judged solely in terms of their consequences; or they may take the metaethical position that there are ethical facts that apply equally to everyone.

Recognizing these theoretical stances from which philosophers argue can clarify the starting principles of their argument. In an ethics course, you may not be required to look at an ethical issue from more than one theoretical point of view, for example, identifying both the normative standpoint as well as the metaethical position of a philosopher. But it may help you to think of ethics, not in terms of a list of separate subtopics, but as a single discipline that ultimately deals with questions that are pertinent to everyday concerns.

Chapter Summary

Philosophy is an intellectual exercise that anyone can engage in at any time. It seeks to find answers to the most general questions about goodness, existence, and the nature of knowledge. Philosophers have to learn to carefully explain the principles they use in their arguments, so it is as clear as possible why they think that one principle or set of principles commits them to another. Ethics is one of the major areas within philosophy and is concerned with a broad range of questions about what is to be valued, the nature of moral judgments, the principles at work behind right conduct, and the best answers to ethical dilemmas.

QUIZ

1. **Which of the following is a philosophical question?**
   a. When did the universe begin to exist?
   b. Why did the Allies win World War II?
   c. What do grown children owe their parents?
   d. When is the best time to get married?

2. **Why is it important, in philosophy, to be committed to certain principles?**
   a. Because philosophers like to be as moral as possible
   b. So things can be explained in a unified way
   c. To avoid contradicting yourself
   d. To avoid having to change your mind

3. **Why is it important, in philosophy, to think through the logical conclusions of certain principles?**
   a. To ensure overall consistency
   b. To find out whether you are ethical or not
   c. To make sure that your principles are not false
   d. Because it is important to use logic in arguing for a conclusion

4. **What is the role of logic in philosophy?**
   a. To aid in arguing persuasively
   b. To find out what the best principles are
   c. To determine the right answer to an ethical dilemma
   d. To determine what you are committed to as a result of other commitments

5. **Which of the following is *not* an ethical question?**
   a. Is it permissible to steal to feed my family?
   b. Does capital punishment help reduce the crime rate?
   c. Should abortion be permitted under any circumstance?
   d. How much should I give to charity?

6. **Normative ethics is the subdiscipline within ethics that is concerned with which of the following?**
   a. The nature of ethical facts
   b. Requirements for right conduct in general
   c. What is most important in life
   d. The right approach to a particular ethical issue

7. **Applied ethics is the subdiscipline within ethics that is concerned with which of the following?**
   a. The nature of ethical facts
   b. Requirements for right conduct in general
   c. What is most important in life
   d. The right approach to a particular ethical issue

8. **Value theory is the subdiscipline within ethics that is concerned with which of the following?**
   a. The nature of ethical facts
   b. Requirements for right conduct in general
   c. What is most important in life
   d. The right approach to a particular ethical issue

9. **Metaethics is the subdiscipline within ethics that is concerned with which of the following?**
   a. The nature of ethical facts
   b. Requirements for right conduct in general
   c. What kinds of things should be valued
   d. The right approach to a particular ethical issue

10. **Which of the following questions would be asked within the subdiscipline of applied ethics?**
    a. Should torture ever be permitted?
    b. Is getting what you want the most important thing in life?
    c. Do the ends justify the means?
    d. Is morality relative to the observer?

chapter 2

Logic and Arguments in Philosophy

CHAPTER OBJECTIVES

In this chapter, you will learn the following:

- What logic is
- What arguments are supposed to do
- What logical fallacies are

As you saw in Chapter 1, logic and arguments play a crucial role in philosophy. This role has to be considered carefully on its own, since it is one of the aspects that make philosophy unique as well as challenging. When you take the time and care to learn how arguments work and what they do, you will have a powerful tool that can be used in any discussion. Most people who engage in informal arguments and reasoning are not well versed in even the basics of logic, so understanding how logic works can give you a decided advantage in your critical thinking.

Being able to propose a logical, valid argument is particularly invaluable to getting a discussion past a stalemate. Recall that in philosophy, arguments are not supposed to boil down to just "Yes, it is!" on one side and "No, it isn't!" on the other. The way you get past this is, first, to find some potentially common ground in the form of a general principle that you think will be shared by many, even by those who do not agree with your conclusion on the contended issue. If you can then show how being committed to the general principle on independent grounds entails being committed to the conclusion you've drawn about the given issue, you may have the means to convince others that they should accept that conclusion.

This is what an argument does. The role of logic is to clarify the relationship of entailment between the truth of one statement and the truth of another. So a logically solid argument shows how *if* you are committed to a certain principle, you *must*—in order to remain consistent and avoid hypocrisy—also be committed to whatever is entailed by it. Thus, if you put forth a successful argument, the participants in a discussion must either accept the conclusion of the argument or reject one of the starting principles. This chapter explains what makes an argument succeed, what you can do with a successful argument, and what it means to commit a *fallacy* in reasoning.

Logic

You can't put forth a successful argument in philosophy without using *logic*. Logic is what gives a line of thought a rigorous structure, allowing you to "connect the dots" and, as discussed in Chapter 1, argue from certain principles to other ones. *Logic* and *logical* are technical terms in philosophy, referring to the specific workings of logic itself. Thus, to "argue logically" in philosophy does not simply mean to make plausible statements that seem to be connected to one another. In everyday speech, you may say things like "That sounds logical," which just means "That makes sense" and doesn't necessarily refer to any actual use of logic per se. Within philosophy, however, the term *logic* refers specifically to the formal process of logical reasoning itself. This is a separate issue from the plausibility or meaning of any given statement. As you'll see, the truth of particular statements informs the results that logic gives, but logic is first and foremost about structures of valid reasoning that tell you what would *have to* be true *if* certain other things are true.

Conditionals

Of course, you want to know whether certain things are true or false. The only reason to bother asking questions and making arguments in philosophy is to get at the truth of something. But logic, in and of itself, can't tell you whether a declarative statement is true or false. You can't simply take a statement of fact and feed it into a "logic machine" that tells you whether it is true or false or whether it is logical (that is, makes sense) in the informal sense of the word. What logic does do is tell you how to make connections between the truth of one thing and the truth of another—that is, how to reason validly using a conditional statement (or *conditional*, for short), a statement that begins with the word *if*. You cannot make an argument without using logic, because all arguments are of a conditional form: they say that if statements A, B, and C are true, then statement D must also be true.

A true conditional doesn't tell you whether any of the statements within it are actually true or not. A conditional tells you that *if* something is true, *then* something else must be true. It has an "if" part and a "then" part. A conditional is true whenever, because of the meanings of the statements within it, the statement that comes after *if* (the *antecedent*) entails the truth of the statement that comes after *then* (the *consequent*). That is, if the antecedent is true, then the consequent has to be true. Stated in negative terms, if a conditional is true, then it cannot be that the antecedent is true and the consequent is false. For example, take the conditional "If I buy a new car, it will have a sunroof." If this conditional is true, then it may or may not be that I do buy a new car, but *if* I do, it *will* have a sunroof. If I buy a new car without a sunroof, this would show that the conditional is false.

Formal Relations of Consequence

As just mentioned, conditionals have a certain logical form: there is a certain logical relationship between its antecedent and consequent. *Form* means the way the meanings of statements relate to one another, rather than the specific meanings of the statements. The overall logical *form* expressed by a conditional, with its *if* and *then* clauses, is one of *consequence*. When a statement or argument is analyzed in terms of its logical form, you'll see letters used in place of statements. This is done for the same reason that letters are used in algebra: the language of algebra is about the mathematical forms that express mathematical relations. Whatever numbers you plug into an equation, the mathematical relations are the same. Analogously, the language of logic expresses the forms of consequence that govern how the truth or falsity of a statement affects the truth or falsity of other statements. A certain set of statements might be logically related to each other in exactly the same way as a different set of statements are logically related to each other. This structure that can be had in common between one set of statements and another is the subject matter of logic.

For example, in algebra, $2x = y$ tells you that the relation between x and y is such that y will be twice whatever x is. This is the same relation whether you plug in 2 and 4, 78 and 156, or 1,000,000 and 2,000,000. In the same way, any conditional of the form "If x is an A, and all As are Bs, then x is a B" is true purely by virtue of logic; it expresses the relations of meaning between the statements within the conditional. Thus, the following conditionals are both true simply because they are both instances of the previously stated formalized conditional: "If Ed is a horse, and all horses are mammals, then Ed is a mammal," and "If Ted is a boat owner, and all boat owners are rich, then Ted is rich."

A true conditional is said to be logically *valid*. In ordinary speech, you may say that a point or perspective is valid if it makes sense or is worth considering. But in logic, *valid* is a technical term: a conditional is valid only if its antecedent really does entail its consequent. (Likewise, an argument is valid only if its premises really entail the argument's conclusion. We'll examine arguments in the next section.)

Truth Is Not Enough: In Search of Necessary Connections

It is worth emphasizing that a conditional can be true whether or not its constituent statements are actually true. For example, the following is a true conditional: "If oatmeal is a vegetable, and all vegetables are beverages, then oatmeal is a beverage." Its logic is just as valid as that of the previous examples (for which the constituent statements also happened to be true), because *if* oatmeal actually were a vegetable, and *if* all vegetables were beverages, it would have to be true that oatmeal is a beverage. Of course, in actual practice, you care whether the statements you are dealing with are true or not. Philosophers certainly care about this too. But philosophy's primary task is to deal with valid connections between statements. So you have to tease apart the logical structure of statements from the question of whether any given statement is true or not, which is actually a separate issue.

Likewise, any two given statements might be true, but that's not enough to tell you that there's a necessary connection between them. A conditional might have an antecedent and a consequent that are both true, but that doesn't necessarily mean that the conditional is true. Many times, people talk as though just pointing out two facts suggests that there's a connection between them; for example, "Government spending is increasing, and the economy is sluggish." But any two statements can both be true, even if one does not entail the other. If you can't show that one entails the other, you haven't demonstrated a necessary connection between them. To show these logical connections, you have to put the statements in the form of a conditional and see whether the conditional is true. So when using logic in philosophy, you first have to determine whether the purported logical connections are valid and then go on to assess the truth or falsity of particular statements to see what the result would be.

As we have seen, a true conditional (that is, one whose logic is valid) can tell you that if the antecedent is true, you can be assured that the consequent is also true. A conditional can be true even if its constituent statements are actually false. What about a true conditional in which the consequent is obviously false, like the one given earlier about oatmeal and vegetables? Its consequent stated that oatmeal is a beverage. Is this consequent false because there is something wrong with the logic of the conditional? No, because the conditional is true—its logic is valid. Since the conditional itself is valid, the consequent is false simply because the antecedent happens to be false: oatmeal is not a vegetable, and not all vegetables are beverages. (Even if only one part of the antecedent is false, that makes the whole antecedent false.) So a true conditional can also tell you that if its consequent is false, you can thereby validly conclude that the antecedent is false—that it is either entirely or just slightly wrong. If the consequent of a valid conditional is false, you know that its antecedent must be false; if the consequent were false but the antecedent were true, the conditional couldn't be valid. A valid conditional can't have a true antecedent and a false consequent.

On the other hand, if the whole conditional is false (not valid), then the antecedent might be true but the consequent false. This is called a *counterexample* to the conditional. Even if it's not actually the case that the antecedent is true and the consequent false, the possibility of there being a counterexample is enough to disprove the conditional. A true conditional is one for which a counterexample is not possible, and a false conditional is one for which a counterexample is possible. For example, "If the streets are wet, then it must have rained" is false, because it is possible that the streets are wet because the street cleaners went over them this morning; in that case, it is possible that the streets are wet even if it did not rain. Even if the streets are wet because it rained, the conditional is false because rain is not the only possible explanation for their being wet.

Figure 2.1 summarizes the important parts of a conditional and what it can tell you. As you can see, for a conditional to be true, it's not enough for its antecedent and conditional to actually be true. A valid conditional has to have a real connection of entailment between its constituents such that it is not possible

FIGURE 2.1   The "workhorse" of logic is the conditional statement. A true conditional statement expresses a necessary connection between two facts such that it is not possible for the antecedent to be true but the consequent false.

for the antecedent to be true but the consequent false. If a counterexample is possible, the conditional is invalid, and you can't do any logic with it.

 Still Struggling

Philosophers try to figure out what has to follow from what. This is why logic is so important to philosophy; logic expresses necessary connections between statements.

Arguments in Philosophy

As we discussed in Chapter 1, an *argument* in philosophy is not a mere disagreement but a rigorous way of demonstrating that when we are committed to certain principles, we are thereby committed to other principles or to particular judgments of fact. (Thus, when we say that someone "argues that *x*," it doesn't mean "argues against *x*." It is possible to argue either for or against something.) Logic, as discussed in the previous section, is the manner in which necessary connections are made between the truth of one statement and another. When we discern the logical form of a statement or set of statements, we point out exactly what these connections are. The formal connections expressed in arguments provide a scaffolding that makes possible a systematic discussion of principles and what it means to be committed to them.

From Premises to Conclusion

In philosophy, an argument is basically a conditional, having an antecedent and a consequent. The consequent of an argument is usually called its *conclusion*. The antecedent, however, usually consists of more than one distinct statement; such statements are called *premises*. A valid argument is one in which all the premises together entail the conclusion. So given a valid argument, if all the premises are true, then the conclusion must be true.

In the discussion about conditionals, you saw that the first thing to check in an argument is whether it is logically valid. This is what philosophers do when they propose an argument for something: they first ascertain that the truth of its premises will guarantee the truth of the conclusion. Then they go on to examine the premises to see whether they are true or not. If they have a valid argument for which the premises are true, bingo! The argument is *sound*—that is, it is valid and its premises are true, so its conclusion is true. Figure 2.2 shows a flowchart that represents the overall process of constructing a successful argument.

To have successfully argued for the truth of a conclusion means that specific reasons have been given for that conclusion. An argument is sound only when

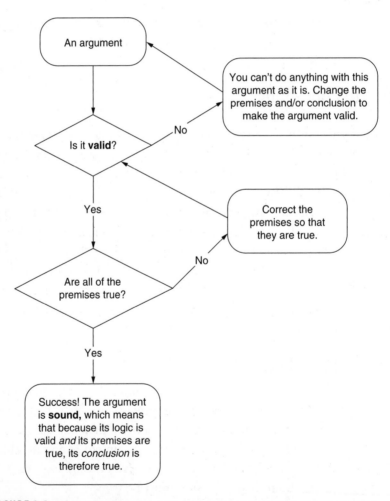

FIGURE 2.2 For an argument to be successful, it must first be valid: all the premises together must lead to the conclusion. If the argument is valid and the premises are true, the argument is sound; the conclusion is proven true by the truth of the premises.

it is valid and its premises are true; its conclusion is proven true because of the truth of the premises. On the other hand, if an argument is valid but its conclusion just happens to be true, it is not sound. If an argument's premises are false but its conclusion is true, that truth is due to some other reason than the truth of the premises. For example, consider this argument: "All ravens are birds, and all birds are black; therefore, all ravens are black." It is valid, because if the premises were true, the conclusion would be guaranteed to be true. As it turns out, the conclusion is true. But it's obviously not true that all birds are black, which indicates that it is not just because ravens are birds that they are black. This example is to emphasize what a sound argument is: the meaning of the premises must be closely related to that of the conclusion, such that their truth would ensure the truth of the conclusion as a consequence. A sound argument has a true conclusion, and this is the whole point, but not all arguments with true conclusions are sound. Rather, the premises of an argument are supposed to be such that, if true, they would explain *why* the conclusion is true.

What Arguments Look Like and How They Are Used

When philosophers write, they don't always state their arguments explicitly and spell out every step (although they are often quite explicit about the conclusion). You might have to do some close reading of the text to discern exactly what the philosopher thinks are the premises of a proposed argument. Any argument can be laid out in an explicit form, and when it is, you can see exactly how it works—or doesn't work, as the case may be. Following are some examples of ethical arguments (which are discussed in detail later in this book) in explicit form.

1. Fetuses are innocent human beings.
2. It is immoral to kill innocent human beings.

_____

Therefore, it is immoral to kill fetuses.

   This is a simple, classic ethical argument. You have probably already heard it in some form or other, even if not in these exact words. Notice first that the premises (1 and 2) are listed separately because they are independent of each other. Neither entails the other, so the truth or falsity of either one stands on its own. Therefore, they must be considered separately. Also note that although the premises are numbered, it does not really matter in what order they are listed. It is not as though 1 leads to 2, 2 leads to 3, and so on. Since an argument is a conditional, there are just two main parts to it: its antecedent and its consequent. The antecedent is composed of all the premises together. They are supposed to entail the conclusion jointly. For purposes of clarity, it may often make sense to list the premises of an argument in a certain order. (In the case cited here, it makes the logic as clear as possible.) But nothing about how an argument logically works hangs on the order in which you list the premises.

Chapter 1 emphasized that the doing of philosophy pivots on principles. Every argument uses one, so another important thing to notice about a philosophical argument is that at least one of the premises is a general principle. (Bear this in mind when trying to unpack the premises of an argument from a text.) Premise 2 in the argument given in our example is the general principle. The major principle is what really "does the work" in an argument. Without it, you can't make the logical connections that an argument is supposed to make.

The logical form of any given premise, whether it is a fact or a principle, has to be stated in terms of a generality; that's how connections are drawn from one subject to another. An argument may consist entirely of principles, with the premises brought together to argue that commitment to these principles should entail a commitment to a further, different principle. This sort of argument is common in ethical theory, which primarily deals with general principles rather than particular cases. In applied ethics, on the other hand, philosophers want to find the right answer to a question about a particular issue. Our example is one of these arguments, addressing the particular issue of abortion. It cites a general fact about what kind of thing fetuses are and a general principle about circumstances in which killing is wrong. Its logical form can be stated as follows:

1. All As are B.
2. All Bs are C.

Therefore, all As are C.

In other words, "All fetuses are innocent human beings. All innocent human beings are such that it is wrong to kill them. Therefore, all fetuses are such that it is wrong to kill them." The logical form makes it crystal clear that it is a valid argument. Using this form for an ethical argument says, "Here's this moral principle that most everyone is already committed to (premise 1). And here's a pertinent fact about this kind of case (premise 2). To hold consistently with this stated principle (that is, to not be a hypocrite and only apply it when you feel like it), you must apply it to this particular case by judging about it accordingly."

When philosophers propose an argument, after establishing that it is valid, they go on to try to convince their audience of the truth of each of the premises in order to establish the argument's soundness. To do this, they may offer another argument for the truth of one of the premises. Alternatively, they may simply appeal to commonsense intuition to establish that, in many ordinary cases, the audience is already committed to a certain principle. In our abortion example, it shouldn't take too much convincing to persuade the audience that they are already committed to the principle expressed in premise 2 or something very much like it. If you cite a very intuitive and plausible principle that does the major work, you have the makings for a powerful argument. All that's left to do is plug and play: "All As are B, so you have to judge A cases the same way as you already would B cases."

As already noted, once you have a valid argument, you have the resources to advance the discussion beyond mere disagreement. That's because a valid argument forces you to either accept the conclusion or deny at least one of the premises. The premises are stated in such a way as to make the argument valid. The proponent of the argument is going to defend its premises exactly as they are stated, so as to defend the argument's soundness and thus its conclusion. On the other hand, someone who wants to resist the argument's conclusion, if he or she grants that the argument is valid, has to deny one of the premises. This may take some ingenuity if the premises of the argument already seem plausible. A philosopher who wants to deny one or more plausible-seeming premises may do so by making a case that what the proponent is really committed to is not the premise exactly as stated, but a slightly different version of that premise which, if true, would invalidate the argument. In the present example, we may suggest that we are not actually committed to premise 2 but to something a bit different. And if that different version of the premise is plugged into the argument, the argument may no longer be valid:

1. Fetuses are innocent human beings.
2. It is immoral to kill innocent human persons.

Therefore, it is immoral to kill fetuses.

This version of the argument is not valid: with a new premise substituted for the original premise 2, this revision leaves open the possibility that, if fetuses are not persons, it may not be immoral to kill fetuses. To make the argument valid, you would need the further premise that fetuses are not only (biologically) human beings, but also human persons, which may be more debatable.

On the other hand, if you want to defend the revised version of the argument (thus allowing for the possibility that it is not immoral to kill fetuses), then you would have to defend the choice of the new premise 2 over the original as the principle to which you are really committed in all cases: that you are committed to the immorality of killing innocent human persons but not necessarily the immorality of killing innocent human beings.

Philosophers have to use ingenuity in defending the premises of an argument—so as to establish a sound argument with a true conclusion—or in criticizing the particular way in which a premise is stated—so as to change the wording to a form that invalidates the argument. You'll find that the bulk of the text in philosophical essays is spent in one or the other of these tasks, defending or critiquing the premises of an argument.

Validity of an Argument and the Truth of Its Premises

As we have seen, a valid argument may have premises that can be tweaked to a slightly different form to allow for a counterexample. An argument also may have plausible premises but not be quite valid as stated. Informally, many people make arguments with plausible premises that suggest some kind of connection but do not add up to a valid argument. Here's another example of an argument that will be considered in more detail in Chapter 9. This argument, in favor of the permissibility of torture, was critically considered by philosopher Henry Shue (Shue 1978).

1. Combat killing in wartime is morally acceptable because the combatants are not defenseless.
2. Subjects of interrogational torture are not defenseless.

Therefore, interrogational torture is morally acceptable.

Premise 1 is plausible to many people simply because they are not pacifists; most people believe that wartime killing (provided the war is just) is permissible because the combatants are not defenseless. Premise 2 can be considered true because potential subjects of interrogational torture presumably can, at any time, divulge the information the torturer is after and thereby stop or prevent torture from occurring. The argument is plausible, because we may naturally tend to think that the conclusion, if true, may be explained by the truth of the premises. So what's wrong with the argument? Even if we grant the truth of the premises, the conclusion may not be true: the fact that battlefield combatants are not defenseless, even if that makes combat killing permissible, may not be what makes torture permissible (if anything does). The argument, therefore, is not actually valid. To make it formally valid, we have to add another premise. The revised (formally valid) argument can be stated as follows:

1. What makes combat killing in wartime morally acceptable is that the combatants are not defenseless.

2. Subjects of interrogational torture are not defenseless.

3. Whatever makes combat killing in wartime morally acceptable is sufficient to make interrogational torture morally acceptable.

Therefore, interrogational torture is morally acceptable.

With this version, we have a valid argument and may next examine the truth of the premises. As it happens, our added premise 3, needed for the validity of the argument, is questionable; it is not obvious that whatever makes combat killing morally acceptable would also apply to interrogational torture.

This case illustrates why you must start with a valid argument. To make a valid argument is to show how its premises, if true, must make the conclusion true. An argument may rely on plausible premises yet not be valid. In that case, you can spell out what premises would make the argument valid and see whether they are true. In this way, by making it very clear what would make the argument valid, you can also clearly point to how it is unsound. If the argument is shown not to be sound, the conclusion remains unproven.

The possibility of a sound argument is the possibility of proving a conclusion true instead of having to settle for "Yes, it is!" and "No, it isn't!" (And maybe seeing who can yell the loudest.) To pursue the possibility of proving the conclusion that a sound argument promises, you have to go through the process of trying to construct an argument that not only is valid but also has plausible and defensible premises. This goal leads to a back-and-forth between proponent and critic: the proponent wants to make a valid argument and defend the truth of its premises; and the critic tries to invalidate the argument by suggesting that different premises are true. The process is potentially never-ending, and logic provides the rules of the game that both sides must follow.

There is a kind of argument that, even if it is valid and sound, philosophers are careful to avoid making—an argument that "begs the question." This phrase sounds like it means "raises a question," and many people actually misuse it this way. The expression really means to "assume in advance what it is that is to be proven." In effect, such an argument subtly invites the listener to accept the conclusion in order to accept the truth of one of the premises. This kind of argument defeats the whole purpose of argumentation, which is to draw a connection from starting principles to a conclusion that the listener may not already accept. If accepting the truth of one or more of the premises of an argument requires accepting the conclusion—or some significant part of it—in advance, then you may as well give up the pretense of trying to make an argument in the first place; you may as well just say, "This conclusion just makes sense, and you should see it the way I do." Philosophers rarely fall into this trap, but those who are not professional reasoners are often not so careful when trying to make an argument. You must remember the point of a philosophical argument: to think through the consequences of what you already accept in order to determine what it would require for you to also accept what you don't already.

Inductive Arguments

It is worthwhile now to mention a different type of argument. The kind of argument discussed thus far is known as a *deductive argument*. Such arguments are meant to "deduce" what the conclusion must be, given the truth of its premises. A valid deductive argument is such that you cannot affirm the premises but deny the conclusion, at least not without being inconsistent (contradicting yourself). A different kind of argument is an *inductive argument*. Like a deductive argument, it has premises and a conclusion. But instead of trying to prove that a certain conclusion must be true (as a deductive argument does), an inductive argument shows that given the truth of its premises, the conclusion is probably true. In an inductive argument, it would not be flat-out contradictory to suppose the premises to be true and the conclusion false, although doing so might raise eyebrows.

For example, a simple and straightforward inductive argument is as follows: "The sun has risen every day for more than five billion years. Therefore, the sun will rise tomorrow." It is a case of induction from past experience to say that a certain pattern will continue, unless there's an excellent reason for it not to. It is not logically inconsistent to suppose that, even though the earth has unfailingly spun on its axis continuously for the last five billion-plus years, it will stop doing so tomorrow. But anyone who wanted to suggest that it might would have an enormous burden of proof: he or she would have to have an extremely good reason to overturn the overwhelming presumptive weight of billions of years of unfailing regularity.

One common way in which inductive arguments are applied (at least implicitly) is in the natural sciences. Science discovers laws and regularities that have always held true whenever they apply. But by definition, it cannot be proven logically that they will continue to hold at all times in the future. Even so, an inductive argument that states that an exceptionless regularity will continue to hold in the future is as powerful an argument as you can make for that conclusion. In general, inductive arguments are made in cases where if you could make a deductive argument, you would, but the nature of the subject matter necessitates an inductive argument instead. Foretelling what will happen in the future is one of these cases; although it is impossible to deduce an outcome logically, inductive reasoning can be a powerful resource.

Still Struggling

Logical validity is important to arguments in philosophy because a valid argument has the potential to prove its conclusion true. As was discussed in Chapter 1, the entire goal of philosophy can be considered as the systematic avoidance of hypocrisy. Taking a valid argument seriously is the most important rule of this game: given a valid argument, you must either accept its conclusion or deny at least one of its premises in order to avoid hypocrisy.

It Ain't Necessarily So: Logical Fallacies

As you have learned, the significance of logic to philosophical arguments is that it shows what necessary connections you can make between statements. In this way, it shows how if you affirm the truth of one statement (an antecedent of a conditional), you also have to affirm the truth of another (the consequent of a conditional).

Just because a conditional is true, however, doesn't mean you can use it to make any connection you like. The reason is that the "if-then" structure has an inherent direction to it. Conditionals are often formally stated by using an arrow: "If A, then B" can be expressed as "A → B." It's not for nothing that the arrow goes in only one direction: the direction indicates the pattern of inference you can make from the truth of one statement to another. A logical *fallacy* involves misusing this direction of inference and affirming a conclusion that, while it may well be true, isn't necessarily true based solely on the truth of the conditional; as we say in philosophy, the conclusion "doesn't follow."

In addition to logical fallacies, there are other informal fallacies of argumentation that still involve affirming conclusions that don't necessarily follow from the starting material. Discussions and examples of the various kinds of informal fallacies can be found in any number of critical thinking texts. But in light of this chapter's overall focus on the formal, logical validity of conditionals, we will focus exclusively on logical fallacies.

Valid Patterns of Inference

One of the valid patterns of inference you can make from a true conditional is the straightforward one that was just discussed. Given a true conditional, if the antecedent is true, this satisfies the conditional, which spits out a value of "true" for the consequent; that is, if the antecedent is true, then the consequent must be true. This valid way of using a conditional is referred to by the Latin name *modus ponens*, which means, "way of affirming": you affirm the truth of the antecedent, and the conditional tells you that the consequent must therefore also be true.

The other valid way of using a conditional can be illustrated by our earlier oatmeal example: "If oatmeal is a vegetable, and all vegetables are beverages, then oatmeal is a beverage." Even though this is a true conditional, its consequent is false. This alone is sufficient information to validly infer that the antecedent must be false, even if you didn't already know that oatmeal is not a vegetable and not all vegetables are beverages. Thus, from just a true conditional with a false consequent, you can validly infer that the antecedent must be false. This valid pattern of inference using a conditional is referred to as *modus tollens*, or "way of denial." It is valid because if the consequent were false but the antecedent were true, the conditional would be false. Note that this is the same reason that instances of modus ponens are valid inferences: if the antecedent were true but the consequent were false, the conditional would be false.

As stated earlier, a valid argument is such that you must either affirm the conclusion or deny one of the premises. If you deny the conclusion, the only valid inference you can make from it is a modus tollens—in other words, you must then deny the antecedent (at least one of the premises). The logical form of the conditional makes it such that you can only reason with the conditional by means of modus ponens or modus tollens: other attempted forms of reasoning will not work.

Invalid Patterns of Inferenc

As counterpoint to the valid patterns of inference, there is such a thing as an invalid inference. An invalid inference tries to use a conditional to demonstrate a necessary connection for a conclusion that does not necessarily follow from the starting information and the truth of the conditional. As discussed earlier, people unintentionally fall into logical fallacies, in general, when they affirm the truth of a certain conditional (perhaps implicitly) but treat that conditional as though it is a necessary connection that runs both ways. In other words, it is treated as the equivalent to "B if and only if A." This is logically distinct from a conditional that only says, "If A, then B" (or, equivalently, "B if A"). "B if and only if A" would be true if the directional "arrow" in the conditional went both ways. But as already emphasized, the arrow in an ordinary conditional goes only one way. Now, it could be that "B if and only if A" (a conditional that goes both directions) is true, but that fact would be beyond what an ordinary conditional could tell you. So if all you have to go on is an ordinary conditional, you have to be careful not to draw conclusions that go beyond the valid conclusions allowed by that conditional.

Invalid patterns of inference are the inverse of the valid patterns of inference, modus ponens and modus tollens. To recognize an invalid inference, you must determine the direction of inference, because the crucial thing about a conditional is the direction in which you proceed from the antecedent to the consequent. Consider an instance of modus ponens: it is valid because it proceeds from the truth of the antecedent to the truth of the consequent. This goes in the right direction, the one inherent in the conditional. The easiest logical fallacy to commit with a conditional is assuming that it also allows you to proceed from the falsity of the antecedent to the falsity of the consequent. But this is a mistake: a conditional allows you to proceed from the truth of the antecedent to the truth of the consequent. Modus ponens is valid because, given a true conditional, supposing the antecedent to be true but the consequent false would be contradictory. The only alternative is to proceed from the truth of the antecedent to the truth of the consequent.

On the other hand, starting with the falsity of the antecedent doesn't force an analogous conclusion: if the antecedent is false but the consequent is true, this does not contradict the truth of the conditional. The only thing that would contradict a conditional is if the antecedent were true but the consequent were false. If the antecedent is false, it doesn't force you to conclude that the consequent is false, but rather just that the conditional doesn't apply; you can't tell anything one way or another about whether the consequent is true. This fallacy of invalidly trying to infer the falsity of the consequent from the falsity of the antecedent is called "denying the antecedent."

Here's an example: "If it rains, the streets will be wet." An invalid use of this (true) conditional is to conclude that "it's not raining, so the streets won't be wet." The conclusion is not necessarily so, because the streets might be wet for some other reason. You may well suppose that it didn't rain but that the streets are wet because the street cleaners went over them this morning; this would not contradict the conditional. In terms discussed earlier in this chapter, it would fail to be a counterexample to the conditional.

The other invalid way to use a conditional is to suppose the truth of the consequent and to use it to infer in the wrong direction. That is, to start with the conditional and the truth of its consequent and then to affirm the truth of the antecedent. This fallacy is called "affirming the consequent." As with the wet street example, the conclusion doesn't necessarily follow, because the alternative fails to be a counterexample: it could be that the consequent is true but the antecedent is false, and this would not contradict the conditional. Again, take the example "If it rains, the streets will be wet." Committing the fallacy of affirming the consequent would be to say, "The streets are wet, therefore it's been raining." For all the conditional tells you, the streets may still be wet for some other reason, such as street cleaning, and that would not contradict the conditional. Affirming the consequent is a fallacy for the same reason that denying the antecedent is: to suppose that a conditional's antecedent is false but its consequent is true does not constitute a counterexample to the conditional. The only thing that contradicts a conditional is to suppose the antecedent to be true but the consequent to be false—*this* would be a counterexample. Table 2.1 summarizes the principles by which you can recognize valid and invalid reasoning with a conditional. Above all, take careful note of the direction involved in the inferences noted, as expressed by the "from-to" pattern dictated by the if–then structure of the conditional.

In general, to understand what a logical fallacy is, keep in mind its contrast to logical validity. Logical validity tells you what necessarily follows from what. Logical fallacies are attempts at logical validity that fall short. A conclusion drawn by means of a logical fallacy does not necessarily follow from the starting material. If someone commits a logical fallacy, it does not necessarily mean that the conclusion is false; it just means that it is unproven. The contrast is whether

TABLE 2.1 Valid and Invalid Ways of Using True Conditionals			
If you reason from	**to**	**this inference is**	**because**
a true antecedent	a true consequent	valid	if the antecedent were true and the consequent false, the conditional wouldn't be true.
a false consequent	a false antecedent	valid	if the antecedent were true and the consequent false, the conditional wouldn't be true.
a false antecedent	a false consequent	invalid (fallacy of denying the antecedent)	the antecedent could be false and the consequent true, and the conditional could still be true.
a true consequent	a true antecedent	invalid (fallacy of affirming the consequent)	the antecedent could be false and the consequent true, and the conditional could still be true.

something is proven (by means of logical validity) or unproven (because of logical invalidity). If you diagnose a logical fallacy, you would commit a further fallacy by inferring that the fallacy's conclusion is thereby proven false! "Not proven" or "unproven" does not mean "proven false." Logical validity means that a conclusion necessarily follows, and a logical fallacy (failure of validity) simply means that a purported conclusion does not necessarily follow.

Chapter Summary

Philosophy seeks to show, given a commitment to certain principles, what other principles you have to be committed to in order to remain consistent. This is done by using arguments, which demonstrate necessary connections between statements to show what follows from what. The formal patterns of reasoning by which you make these connections is the subject matter of logic.

Arguments take the form of conditional statements. A true conditional is such that if the antecedent (premises of an argument) is true, the consequent (conclusion of an argument) must also be true. This means that a logically valid argument can demonstrate what conclusion must follow, given the truth of certain starting statements.

Inferences that do not conform to the rules of how conditionals work are said to be invalid. An invalid inference is one for which, even if the conditional statement is true, the conclusion does not necessarily follow from the premises.

QUIZ

1. The logic of an argument is what dictates whether the argument _____.
   a. is plausible
   b. has true premises
   c. has a conclusion that you are willing to accept
   d. has a conclusion that follows from its premises

2. A true conditional statement is one for which _____.
   a. the consequent follows from the antecedent
   b. the antecedent and consequent are both true
   c. anyone would be convinced of the consequent
   d. the antecedent is plausible

3. A counterexample to a conditional _____.
   a. disproves the consequent of the conditional
   b. says that the conditional's antecedent is false
   c. says that its consequent may be false while the antecedent is true
   d. says that its consequent may be true while its antecedent is false

4. The premises of an argument correspond to _____.
   a. a conditional
   b. the antecedent of a conditional
   c. the conclusion of a conditional
   d. the direction of the inference in a conditional

5. Every argument contains _____.
   a. a true conclusion
   b. at least three premises
   c. at least one true premise
   d. at least one premise that is a general principle

6. An inductive argument is one in which _____.
   a. the conclusion is not logical
   b. the premises are scientific in nature
   c. the truth of the conclusion is shown to be probable
   d. the premises logically entail the conclusion

7. **An invalid argument is one for which** _____.
    a. the premises are false
    b. the conclusion is false
    c. the premises might be false but the conclusion true
    d. the premises might be true but the conclusion false

8. **To commit a logical fallacy is to** _____.
    a. make an argument with false premises
    b. make an invalid inference
    c. reject the premises of a valid argument
    d. reject the conclusion of an argument

9. **Given a true conditional statement, which of the following is a valid form of inference?**
    a. From a false antecedent to a false consequent
    b. From a false antecedent to a true consequent
    c. From a false consequent to a false antecedent
    d. From a true consequent to a true antecedent

10. **Which of the following would be involved in an invalid inference?**
    a. Claiming something that isn't really a counterexample to be a counterexample
    b. Claiming that a conditional statement is false when it is actually true
    c. Trying to make an inference from the falsity of a conditional's consequent
    d. Disagreeing with the conclusion of a valid argument

Part Two

Ethical Theory

chapter 3

Value Theory: What Really Matters?

In this chapter, you will learn the following:

- How philosophers think about questions of ultimate value
- What kind of values may properly be considered "ultimate"
- What philosophers mean by *happiness*

One of the most basic kinds of questions to think about in ethics is to consider what should be valued most fundamentally and pursued in life overall. You may have heard it said that "the unexamined life is not worth living." One of the things this sentiment expresses is high praise for the value of philosophy itself in thinking about what we value in life. This arena is really a prime example of what philosophy is *for*: clear thinking about fundamental principles. The purpose of such thinking in this arena is also valuable: namely, the thought that our ultimate values in life guide, or should guide, our overall pursuits. The application of philosophy's principled approach to questions in this area is known as *value theory*; a philosopher who works in this area may be called a value theorist.

Studying philosophy is a matter of learning not nearly so much *what* to think but *how* to think. This chapter gives an overview of how ethicists think about questions of value. Learning how best to think about certain issues is a valuable ability in its own right; moreover, assuming there is a right answer of what to think, a careful pursuit of value theory may be the best way to arrive at that answer, whatever it may be.

The Value of Value Theory

Every philosophical subdiscipline is in search of some theory or other, and in philosophy, the term *theory* means just what it does in science—not a guess or speculation, but rather an explanation that makes sense of available data. In value theory, the data is basically the things that we want, and the theory is the attempt to explain why we want them. Simpler theories are better, just as they are in science, because they can potentially explain more data using less conceptual resources. So a value theorist drives at the ground level of fundamentality in what we value. The goal is ideally to find out that there is one value that is the foundation on which all the other values we may have are built. The benefit of this inquiry is that finding the bedrock value on which other values are based helps to explain what those subsidiary values really *are*. When the theory connects right up to the level of particulars, to the choices we make in daily life, we then have the benefit of knowing what the nature of *those* choices are and what they are really about. Figure 3.1 gives a schematic picture of how a system of value theory would work to connect our everyday decisions and actions with the most general kinds of values we can have.

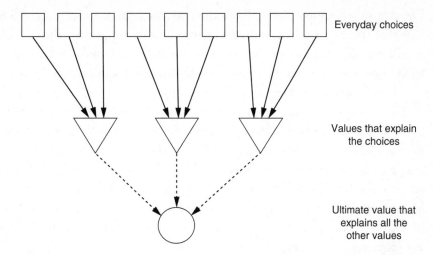

FIGURE 3.1   Value theory seeks to "drill down" to the most fundamental level of values that motivate us so as to make sense of our less-fundamental goals as well as our everyday actions.

For example, at the level of everyday experience, you may have a variety of choices of what to do with your time. What determines the choices you make comes from a larger picture or overall plan that you have also chosen. If you're in school, then you put a high priority on going to class and studying, because that's what you're there for. And what you're there for is determined by whatever overall life trajectory you've planned for yourself and includes going to school. Maybe you're in school to get a college degree so you can get a better job than you'd be able to get without one, and you don't want just any old job, but something you'd be interested in. With a view to this goal, you chose a major and a plan of study that is a path toward fulfilling that major. Thinking things through at this level, you will have arrived at this point: the reason you get out of bed in the morning while you're in school is because you want to eventually get a good job doing something you like. Putting it together like this is one step toward living an examined life in which you understand why you do what you do with yourself every day.

You can go even further and think, "Why do I want a good job, and what do I think makes a job 'good'? Do I just want to earn as much money as possible, or is there something else I value and want to do with my life? If so, whatever else I want besides money might compete with the goal of making money. How do

I fit that other value together with the material goal of making a comfortable living? If these two values compete with each other, does that mean they have nothing to do with each other, or can they be harmonized in terms of some more fundamental value that would make sense of them both and tell me how to get the optimal mixture of both?"

Even at its most basic, value theory is inherently big-picture thinking—as big as it gets. It's not only thinking about the most basic kinds of values, but it has the goal of connecting all the way up to the level of what we do every day and, ultimately, why. As you may have already guessed, you might ask questions about not only how to choose what to do with yourself each day in order to align yourself with your values, but also about how to choose among a variety of ultimate life values you may have. This question arises naturally from the very structure of the inquiry into values itself.

Look at Figure 3.1 again: the goal is to arrive at a theory that has as few fundamental values in it as possible (ideally, just one); that way, more things can be explained with fewer resources. The goal is not just to have a list of some values that you happen to have. Rather, a value theorist wants to know why you have *those* values and, in particular, if they can *all* be explained by some more fundamental value. This is why you must end up with a choice between the possible fundamental values you may have: if you could adopt all of them, then different life choices would fall under different ultimate values, and then there would be no explanation as to what those values have to do with each other and why you chose them.

Questions about choosing your ultimate values, however, have to come after you have already laid some groundwork. None of us begins life choosing our ultimate value and then choosing everything that will align with the pursuit of that one value. Rather, when we first begin thinking about such things, some values are already implicitly in place, whether or not they can be harmonized together or not. The first task, then, is to figure out what those existing values *are* by making sense of what we already think and believe and determining how it all fits together. Once we have distilled our choices down to the most fundamental values that motivate us, we are in a position to understand what, if any, ultimate value(s) we already have. Only then are we in a position to understand the significance of the possibility of adopting a *different* ultimate value. The significance of this momentous choice has to be assessed in terms of how it stacks up against other possible ultimate values, as well as its ramifications for aligning our life choices so as to pursue and be consistent with that ultimate value (as in other contexts in philosophy, you can think of the motivation here as avoiding hypocrisy).

Intrinsic Values: Things That Are Good for Their Own Sake

As has already been discussed, we choose certain pursuits because they help to further our overarching goals. This is a case of one thing (everyday actions) being pursued for the sake of something else (values). The more particular thing is being pursued for the sake of the more general thing: if particular actions are chosen for a principled reason, they are not based simply on whatever they get us but, more importantly, on whatever value the goal of those actions represents. Value theorists refer to things that are pursued, not for their own sake, but only to further some other goal as *instrumental goods*: they are good only because whatever they bring about is valued for some other reason than the value of the action itself.

The possibility of instrumental goods also points to the possibility of valuing more general things that can be considered good for their own sake: in other words, the idea of an instrumental good points to the idea of something that is not merely instrumentally good but that is valued for itself and is the very reason the instrumental good is pursued. Value theorists call such things *intrinsic goods*. *Intrinsic* is a term that you'll find popping up everywhere in philosophy, and it requires some clarification. As you may realize, its natural opposite is the term *extrinsic*. In philosophy, we talk about properties or attributes that are either intrinsic or extrinsic. If something has an extrinsic property or attribute, you must bring in something other than that thing, something outside it, for the thing to have that extrinsic property. For example, the value of paper money is almost exclusively extrinsic; it is only valuable to us because of the conventional arrangements of a financial system in which we use it as currency—it *represents* monetary value. In contrast, if something has an intrinsic property, then even if the rest of the universe were to disappear, the thing would still have that property. Thus, it has the property purely by virtue of itself, as opposed to having a property by virtue of some other thing. The application of this distinction to value theory with respect to instrumental versus intrinsic goods should now be fairly clear: value theory tries to find out what intrinsic values—things valued for their own sake and not just for what else they can bring—may be pursued.

For example, consider the good of eating. Most of us consider eating to be "good" at some level. But what do we think it is good *for*? Eating is enjoyable in and of itself, but it is not the fundamental reason why we eat: the natural function of eating, at least, is to keep us alive. (Staying alive may be the fundamental value, or it may only be instrumental to something else.) The enjoyment of eating, then, can be considered as serving the more fundamental value of staying alive (for reasons other than to keep on eating). If we have to eat to stay alive, then why shouldn't this activity have the built-in positive reinforcement of bringing pleasure as opposed to merely avoiding hunger pangs? If we see the good in eating as instrumental to the greater good of sustaining life, then we can view the pleasure of eating as serving that greater good, instead of seeing eating and the pleasure thereof as good for its own sake.

In contrast, consider a view that places the pleasure of eating among the intrinsic goods in life. If eating were intrinsically good, we could disassociate it from everything else in life, including the need to stay alive, and it would have the same value as it has in actual fact. In the movie *Defending Your Life*, the protagonist, after having died, finds herself in a sort of intermediate afterlife state. It's not quite heaven—but rather a "holding area"—in which everything about it is constructed to make existence as pleasant as possible for those who are in it. At the "restaurant" in this place, the protagonist is pleasantly surprised to find that she can eat pie after pie after pie without ever getting full. The good that she gets from eating is thus portrayed as having no intrinsic connection with bodily sustenance. That is, being able to eat and eat with no definite limit implies that eating is not, in that state, needed to exist; moreover, the fact that it is portrayed as an intrinsically good thing to be able to eat unlimited amounts of food implies that she would thereby enjoy more of the intrinsic value of eating that way than she would have ordinarily when her stomach filled. Altogether, this implies a commitment to the evaluation that the intrinsic value of eating per se, whether on earth or on some other plane of existence, is just the gustatory pleasure of it. This same intrinsic value was placed on eating in the "vomitoriums" of the ancient Romans, who were said to indulge in all-you-can-eat spreads indefinitely by periodically vomiting out what they had already eaten so as to have an empty stomach to fill again.

If placing intrinsic value on the pleasure of eating seems crass and misplaced to you, it is likely because you consider eating to be an instrumental good whose value is only found in its function of providing physical sustenance.

More generally, you'll understand what it means to distinguish intrinsic goods from instrumental goods and the importance of the distinction.

From Intrinsic Value to Ultimate Value

Once we have determined that a pursuit is chosen purely as an instrumental good, we can then look at the ultimate goals for which that pursuit is instrumental: they may be completely intrinsic in their value, but it is likely that they have some instrumental value mixed in as well. If the latter is true, then they will point to some more fundamental good whose value should be more intrinsic to itself, and so on. The more intrinsic a value's good is, the more fundamental it is, because the more possible instrumental goods may exist whose value is subsidiary to that more intrinsically good value.

Refer again to Figure 3.1. The very nature of systematizing our pursuits and values into a hierarchy determined by whether a goal is more or less fundamental is such that as we think about pursuits and choices being instrumental or intrinsic in their value, we should be distilling a system of value down to fewer and fewer fundamental values. That is, the drill-down direction in Figure 3.1 reflects the search for intrinsicality in value that must also push toward a single value that explains all the others. Aristotle, in his far-reaching and hugely influential *Nichomachean Ethics*, argued that a consistent pursuit of intrinsicality in value would, by itself, be sufficient to arrive at a single fundamental value such as that represented in Figure 3.1. In other words, if we take seriously the drive to systematize our values into a theory that shows what we are pursuing for the sake of what, these efforts must end in finding a single, fundamental, ultimate value for the sake of which we pursue everything else in life.

Here is Aristotle's argument that there must be some intrinsic goods in life that we pursue (as discussed by Julia Annas [Annas 1993: 31–34]):

1. If *everything* we want is pursued simply for the sake of another thing, then it would lead to an infinite regress, and all our desires would be in vain.

2. Our desires are not all in vain.

Therefore, our lives must be oriented toward intrinsic goods—things valued and pursued for their own sake.

Recall from Chapter 2 what we do when presented with an argument: we check that it is valid. The argument as presented is a valid instance of reasoning by modus tollens: Premise 1 is a conditional, premise 2 negates the consequent of the conditional, and the conclusion of the argument is supposed to be equivalent to the negation of the antecedent of the conditional in premise 1. That is, goods are either instrumental or intrinsic. If they're not all instrumental, then some of them must be intrinsic.

It is hard to argue with premise 1. But why think premise 2 is true? What lends premise 2 support seems to be the fact that most of us have a palpable sense of value about whatever we pursue, whether the goods being pursued are instrumental or not. If we didn't, we wouldn't bother to get out of bed in the morning. And we tend to think that we actually *do* have legitimate reasons for getting out of bed, which implies that in doing so, we are pursuing something worthwhile. The argument concludes that if there is something worthwhile to be pursued, it must lead to something intrinsically valuable. To reject premise 2 would make us swallow a bitter pill indeed and come close to a commitment to *nihilism*—the belief that nothing is intrinsically worth pursuing for its own sake, nothing is inherently to be valued. Absent a strong reason for believing in nihilism about value, hardly anyone would want to go that route.

But Aristotle goes further, claiming that we do not just pursue intrinsically valuable goods, but that we each have (or should have) one fully intrinsic good that is our ultimate value. The alternative is to have several different ultimate goals that are unrelated to each other. No one can live in a rational way guided by several different *ultimate* values; how would we choose between them? If we spent an equal amount of time pursuing each ultimate goal, that would be to treat them each equally. But on what basis would we treat multiple ultimate

Still Struggling

At first it may seem as though it is possible to value a number of different things for their own sake. But if you are able to structure your life in such a way as to make it possible to partake in all those values, that implies that they are not all disconnected from one another. This in turn implies that all of those values fit together in some way, which would mean that they all "feed into" some one intrinsic good, for which they are instrumental goods. This is why Aristotle thought that each person must have one ultimate intrinsic value.

values equally or unequally, or indeed have all of them as ultimate values in the first place? Wouldn't it be simpler to pick just one and go with it? On the other hand, if we do sustain commitment to multiple pursuits, that in itself implies that they all *do* relate to each other in some way and are all instrumental toward the pursuit of some single ultimate value.

Aristotle takes it for granted that anyone who is motivated to look at his or her life ethically will also want to look at it as a whole, which means harmonizing the various parts of life into something that makes sense together. It seems that this can't be done without a unifying principle that makes sense of all the parts of life as aspects of *one thing*. This, then, constitutes his argument for thinking that once we start thinking in terms of intrinsically good values, we have to end up thinking in terms of a single ultimate value based on which everything else we do can be explained.

Happiness in the Ethical Sense

We have looked at value theory first to get the "lay of the land" and to make clear what shape any particular value theory must take. Now we are in a position to examine various contenders for the role of ultimate value, how they would work as regulatory principles for life overall, and reasons for choosing one over another. The word value ethicists have for the ultimate value, whatever it may look like in particular, is *happiness*. For the purposes of this discussion, we can think of happiness in the schematic sense given by value theory as "whatever it is that is the ultimate value." It is a role determined by what is represented at the bottom of Figure 3.1, to be filled in by any of a number of competing contenders as to what the nature of that ultimate value should be.

American society is often said to be based on the pursuit of happiness. Whatever else *happiness* may mean, it can thus be seen to have a fundamental role in considerations of value theory as a name for whatever people have as their ultimate pursuit in life. What is it, then, that constitutes an ultimate pursuit in life; an ultimate value? The subtleties of this issue may be clouded by the fact that in contemporary English usage, the meaning of the word *happiness* is significantly tinged with the subjective. In other words, the state of being happy is defined only in terms of certain positive feelings experienced by the subject of happiness. This could be what philosophers mean by *happiness* in the more systematic context of value theory, but not necessarily. Happiness can also be thought of as some objectively defined state in which a person may not be experiencing positive feelings.

Hedonism

The subjectively defined approach to happiness is referred to by value theorists as *hedonism*. In the informal context of philosophies of life, *hedonism* means the single-minded pursuit of the most physical, intense, and immediately gratifying kinds of pleasure available. But value theorists mean something a bit different. Hedonism *is* the pursuit of pleasure, but it needn't mean just the most commonly available, sensate, physical kinds. Most noteworthy value theorists throughout history who were themselves hedonists didn't, in fact, refer to those kinds of pleasures, but that is only because they thought that "higher," more "refined" kinds of pleasures were actually more pleasurable. For example, the ancient Greek philosopher Epicurus's name is now commonly associated with the philosophy of life of Epicureanism—the pursuit of sensory pleasures in food, drink, and other finer things in life—even though Epicurus himself was actually not this sort of hedonist at all. Epicurus was a hedonist who encouraged moderation in all things, as well as mental and emotional tranquillity. He advocated these things because he thought they brought the most pleasure. He also thought the best way to obtain tranquillity of mind was in the application of careful philosophical thought—hardly what we would call a hedonist in the ordinary sense of the word! Yet he was a hedonist in that he felt that philosophical contemplation was the best way to dispel mental anxieties about worries like death. What all hedonists ultimately value is the subjective sense of well-being as the intrinsically valued good. Where hedonists may disagree is on the best means to that end. Epicurus was a hedonist because he thought subjective feelings of well-being were the supreme intrinsic good; he valued moderation and philosophical contemplation, not as ends in themselves, but as instrumental goods that he thought best furthered the supreme good.

Alternatives to Hedonism

The other approach to defining happiness is to think of it objectively rather than subjectively. You can think of it, not as attaining the highest sorts of pleasures, but as attaining a state of being or quality of life that is objectively the best, independent of how it may make you feel. Ancient Greek ethicists such as Aristotle had a term for this: *eudaimonia*, which is often translated as "happiness," but this again can be misleading, since the ordinary English sense of the word strongly connotes subjective experience. It might be better translated as "well-being." An example of the kind of thing that might be pursued as a supreme intrinsic good, regardless of how it makes you feel, is virtue. The ancient Greek school of thought known as Stoicism exemplifies the single-minded valuing of virtue as the supreme intrinsic good. For the Stoic, it is possible to be supremely happy in being tortured to death if the cause is virtue and a result of the tenacious pursuit of principle regardless of the cost. (This is why we consider someone "stoic" if he or she presses dutifully forward with life heedless of personal suffering.) If this seems extreme, consider the flipside: for the complete hedonist, whatever brings the most overall pleasure—no matter what that is—should be pursued. The hedonist can only value virtue, if it is valued at all, as a mere contingent means to an end: so if vice would bring more overall pleasure for everyone, then to be consistent with the hedonist's commitments, vice must be pursued.

These extremes function mainly to bring out the contrast with how the supreme good is defined by the hedonist on one hand and the stoic, or other virtue-pursuer, on the other. The difference is in which direction the definition is based. For the stoic, the good is defined objectively, not subjectively: in that case, it *could* turn out that living in accordance with eudaimonia brings pleasure, but if so, it is only because of the goodness of eudaimonia itself, which is where the ultimate value is. For the stoic, eudaimonia must by definition be good and is pursued for that reason alone. Conversely, hedonists can claim that they can value things like virtue, but only if they tend to lead to more pleasure. The monumentally influential nineteenth-century political philosopher John Stuart Mill (especially in his *Utilitarianism*) claimed that we value *being* good only because it normally makes us *feel* good; if it didn't, we wouldn't value it at all.

The main challenge to hedonism is the idea that we can be harmed by something even if we're not subjectively saddened by it—indeed, even if we don't know that we're harmed by it. This idea is brought out by the following argument by Russ Shafer-Landau (Shafer-Landau 2010a: 36), another nice, neat example of modus tollens:

1. If hedonism is true, then you can only be harmed by something if it saddens you.
2. You can be harmed in ways other than by being saddened by something.

Therefore, hedonism is false.

This idea of being harmed by something even if it doesn't sadden you can be illustrated by fairly extreme cases of people who are "happy" being immoral. Most of us feel intuitively that although such people may experience subjective well-being, they do not live a "good life" in accordance with what is truly intrinsically valuable. In that case, by being immoral, they are harming themselves even if they don't know it (for a concerted argument on the harm of immorality, see Bloomfield 2008).

This idea can also be brought out by less-extreme examples involving people who are subjectively "happy" and not so much immoral as deprived of some other good that thoroughgoing hedonism cannot seem to take into account. For example, consider the populace of the meticulously engineered society depicted in Aldous Huxley's *Brave New World*: everything about people's lives is engineered to keep tension and dissatisfaction to an absolute minimum and to maximize sensual pleasures and subjective experiences of well-being. Yet we tend to pity such people, as they are deprived of things we tend to think are intrinsically good, such as autonomy, self-determination, and the opportunity for moral betterment through struggle. Although these goods might be subsumed under an ultimate good of virtue or something else, they cannot be given any intrinsic value if the ultimate good is simply pleasure and avoidance of pain.

Likewise, consider the thought experiment proposed by philosopher Robert Nozick (1974) called the "experience machine"—a machine to which you could hook yourself up and that would give you any subjective experience you wanted, an experience that was *just as if* you were doing any of a number of things that you would consider worthwhile. The hedonist would say that getting all the experiences one wants in the experience machine would be just as valuable as the real thing, even though you would actually only be lying unconscious with electrodes stimulating your brain. Someone who rejects hedonism can offer an account of what is wrong with this scenario: the experience machine disconnects you from reality. The nonhedonist says that living in accordance with reality is part of the supreme intrinsic good, but the hedonist can give no principled reason for turning down the chance to surrender his or her whole life to the experience machine. The character in the movie *The Matrix* who turns against his fellows to accept a life of pleasurable experiences lived out in a digital simulation and says "I know none of this is real, but *I don't care*" is evidently a thoroughgoing hedonist. Those who prefer to find value in their struggles in the bleakness of "the real world," on the other hand, are the committed nonhedonists.

Similarly, we can bring out the idea of wanting to be rooted in reality in terms of a desire to live in accordance with our real abilities and potential. It could be that we would be "happier" if we could turn into a cat or a bird, but then we would lose all the unique and irreplaceable talents and potential we have. (When I was in junior high school, I recall times that I actually wished I was a cat, with no responsibilities and nothing to worry about! Nowadays, I have many more responsibilities and things to worry about than I did then, but I evidently also have an increased ethical maturity.) Remember, the hedonist has to say that you should pursue whatever increases your sense of well-being, but you can do this in any number of ways that also directly violate the reality of the kind of being you are. On that note, consider the following anecdote by leading ethicist Philippa Foot:

> I recall a talk by a doctor who described a patient of his (who had perhaps had a prefrontal lobotomy) as "perfectly happy all day long picking up leaves." This impressed me, because I thought, "Well, most of us are not happy all day long doing the things we do," [but then I] realized how strange it would be to think that the very kindest of fathers would arrange such an operation for his (perfectly normal) child (Foot 2001: 85).

In conclusion, to figure out if you think that hedonism is true or not, ask yourself these questions:

- Are there values that are truly *objectively* good—that is, should you pursue them regardless of how doing so may make you feel?
- On the other hand, if you were able to choose a path that resulted in the greatest overall pleasure in your life, would you pursue it regardless of what else might befall yourself and others?

Most everyone, hedonist or not, will agree that we value pleasure and virtue in some way or another. The difference is in which good is said to be *fundamental*; it's a chicken-and-egg, cart-and-horse question. Either way latches on to a single ultimate intrinsic good in accordance with the goal of value theory. The cost of doing so, as in other areas of philosophy, is that if you commit yourself to a single, all-governing principle like that, you have to bite the bullet and remain consistent with it no matter what. Otherwise, you can forget about the pretense of living an examined life and instead just go where the wind blows you. The pursuit of value theory offers an alternative to that.

Still Struggling

The two main approaches to ultimate value define it *objectively* (without need-ing to refer to human feelings or perceptions), or *subjectively* (with reference to human feelings or perceptions). The objective point of view does not necessarily *devalue* pleasure, but rather makes it *subordinate* to objective values such as virtues, which are regarded as the ultimate good. The *subjective* point of view, on the other hand, takes it the other way around and values things like virtue only insofar as they may lead to *subjective* well-being such as pleasure, which is regarded as the ultimate good.

Chapter Summary

Value theory is a basic ethic of life that seeks to sort out why we do what we do, what ultimate goal is served by our everyday choices. The fact that there has to be an (that is, *one*) ultimate good can be seen when we think in terms of intrinsic value as opposed to merely instrumental value. An intrinsic value is where explanations stop; it is something that is pursued for its own sake. If we had more than one ultimate intrinsic value in life, it would be like living more than one life; there would be no principled way to choose between dif-ferent intrinsic, incommensurable goals. If values *are* commensurable with one another, on the other hand, it is because they can be understood in terms of one ultimate value that makes sense of them all.

Ultimately, we want to "live a good life." What determines whether a life should be considered "good" is another question. Hedonism, the view that the ultimate good is a subjective sense of well-being, is a perennial contender for the theory of a good life. However, hedonism runs into some serious challenges due to its failure to take into account ultimate goods that can only be defined objectively—that is, rooted in some aspect of reality without ultimate refer-ence to the quality of our subjective experiences. While value theory focuses on the ethical dimensions of "the good life," the next chapter will look at ethical theories that seek to tell what it means to "do the right thing" to at least avoid immorality.

QUIZ

1. Value theory is primarily about _____.
   a. doing the right thing
   b. things that are pursued for their own sake
   c. the nature of moral responsibility
   d. the value of morality

2. When we first give thought to the overall set of values that explains our life choices, we _____.
   a. choose an ultimate value and then align all of our actions to it
   b. recognize that everything we do has intrinsic value
   c. think about what is pursued for the sake of what
   d. likely find that nothing we do is worthwhile until we know what intrinsic values they promote

3. An instrumental good is pursued _____.
   a. for the sake of other goods
   b. for its own sake
   c. because it is the ultimate value
   d. because it brings pleasure

4. A thing that is intrinsically valued is valued _____.
   a. for the sake of other goods
   b. for its own sake
   c. because it brings pleasure
   d. because it is virtuous

5. On what basis did Aristotle argue that we must have intrinsically valued goods that we pursue?
   a. If all our pursuits had only instrumental value, they would all be meaningless.
   b. It would be immoral to have no intrinsically valued goods to pursue.
   c. Everyone who lives an examined life will pursue things of intrinsic value.
   d. Things of only instrumental value are not worth our time.

6. Aristotle thought that we must have *one* ultimate, intrinsic value in life, because he thought that if we had more than one ultimate value, _____.
   a. our values would conflict with one another
   b. there could not be enough instrumental goals to serve all our values
   c. we would never have time to pursue them all
   d. we could not make sense of them all together

7. A hedonist, in philosophical usage, is one who values _____ above all else.
   a. sensory pleasure
   b. morality
   c. experiences of well-being
   d. virtue

8. A hedonist will be committed to which of the following claims?
   a. Objective states of well-being are to be valued the most.
   b. Objective goods like virtue are not worth pursuing.
   c. Objective goods like virtue can only be given instrumental value.
   d. Subjective states of well-being can be given instrumental value.

9. One alternative to hedonism is a view that _____ is valuable above all else.
   a. contemplation
   b. virtue
   c. pleasure
   d. happiness

10. The main challenge to hedonism is the idea that _____.
    a. not all pleasure leads to happiness
    b. hedonism requires immorality
    c. the pursuit of virtue does not always lead to pleasure
    d. we may be harmed by something even if it does not diminish our pleasure

Normative Ethics: What Makes Actions Right or Wrong?

CHAPTER OBJECTIVES

In this chapter, you will learn the following:

- The two main competing approaches to the moral evaluation of actions
- The various theories that attempt to explain what makes an action, in and of itself, right or wrong

Part Three of this book examines various approaches and arguments that aim to establish the best moral choice regarding a particular ethical issue such as poverty, capital punishment, and animal rights. One way of looking at particular ethical issues is simply to figure out what seems to be the best principle as it applies to that particular situation. Another approach is to take a step back from the particulars of a situation, think about what principles we are committed to as to what would make an action morally right in any situation, and then think about how such principles may apply to the present situation. The latter approach is potentially powerful in establishing a conclusion and persuading others to agree with it.

Ethicists draw support for the principles they advocate, not only based on their contention that such principles yield the best answers to moral problems, but also based on the generalizability of such principles. That is to say, it is inherent to the search for ethical principles that such principles should apply to as many particular situations as possible. In contrast, if you need to cite a different principle as governing each particular issue, then you may be making up "principles" on the fly just because they give you the answer you want on a specific occasion!

So general principles that determine what makes an action right or wrong are important in their application to particular ethical issues. Keep in mind that ethicists not only try to discover what normative principles people are already committed to, but they also often try to determine what normative principles one *should* be committed to, objectively speaking. In this chapter, you will learn about ethical principles themselves, independent of how they may be applied to some specific ethical problem. Then, when you get to Part Three, you will be able to recognize some of these theories and thus better understand the arguments that apply to individual issues. The ethical subdiscipline that examines such general theories of right conduct is called *normative ethics*. As already discussed in Chapter 1, norms are ethical principles that you can look to, to tell you whether an action is morally right or wrong. These standards are supposed to pull objective weight and apply generally to anyone in any situation. The theoretical benefit of identifying proper norms is that you can then give a principled basis for morality itself. Thus, if you get someone to agree with you on what the right normative theory is, you may be able to use that agreement to argue successfully as to what the right action is in a particular case, even if that someone did not already agree with you on the issue at hand. The cost, on the other hand, is that once you appeal to norms to explain the basis for ethical choices, you have to hold consistently to those avowed norms wherever they may apply; if you don't, you fall into hypocrisy, which in philosophy means you're out of the game.

Should the Morality of Actions Be Judged Solely in Terms of Their Effects?

All of the normative ethical theories can be classified into one of two groups. One of these approaches to normativity says that an action is right only if its consequences are good and wrong only if its consequences are bad. Naturally enough, this view is known as *consequentialism*. A theory of normativity that is true would presumably explain a lot of commonsensical ethical judgments that we would tend to make anyway. And, as it turns out, consequentialism has some of these benefits. As examples, you could point to plenty of actions that almost anyone would consider morally good, such as generosity, kindness, and forgiveness; you could cite them all as having good consequences. According to consequentialism, their having good consequences would be exactly what makes them right. Likewise, think of morally bad actions such as murder, theft, and abuse—one thing they seem to have in common is their ill effects, and consequentialism says that those ill effects are precisely what makes such things wrong.

But, you may well wonder, what about other things that might make an action good or bad, such as the intention with which it was done? In particular, the consequences of an action might be unforeseen, such that we wouldn't necessarily condemn someone who acted with good intentions but achieved bad results. Can't we take into account both consequences and intentions? Bear in mind what consequentialism sets out to do as a normative theory: it tries to give a perfectly general answer as to what makes actions right or wrong. That means you can't simply add stipulations to it to make the theory justify the kinds of actions you already accept. If you do, you will have two unrelated theories, each of which you choose to apply based on what you already want the outcome of the judgment to be in a specific case. That isn't a theory at all; rather, it defeats the whole purpose of principled explanation that a theory is supposed to give you.

Suppose we try to accommodate the idea of intentions into consequentialism. Once you take the step of having normative criteria hinge on someone's knowledge or something else that goes on purely in a person's head, then whether the action is good or not is going to have to hinge on something other than the action's consequences. And this puts the whole program of consequentialism in jeopardy. The only way to include other kinds of standards into the theory is if you can make sense of it all together as a whole; that is, show either that accommodating considerations of intention is required by consequentialism itself or that the need to take both consequences and intentions into account can be explained in terms of some more general theory. As it turns out, it is difficult to see how you might do this. This just goes to show that to take a normative theory seriously, you have to think carefully about whether you're really willing to take it as the most general theory that gives principled (that is, not ad hoc and arbitrarily chosen) reasons for judging actions to be morally right or wrong and then apply it with perfect consistency.

One of consequentialism's main attractions (if not *the* main attraction) is that it offers a relatively clear criterion for figuring out whether an action is to be considered good or not: simply look at the results. But once this becomes the single final arbiter of moral rightness or wrongness of an action, you have to look at the idea of rules in a distinctive way. The most extreme, thoroughgoing kind of consequentialist has to say that we have certain moral rules—such as those against lying, cheating, and killing—merely because in practice, we usually get better results when we follow these rules than when we do not. But these rules are to be taken as no more than mere rules of thumb. Even if, all other things being equal, it's generally best to follow these rules, a better outcome might result in some cases if we break those rules. To follow a rule without exception simply because it's a rule is seen by an extreme consequentialist as mere "rule-worshipping" (Smart 1956). A consequentialist views the matter this way: "In most cases, it's more beneficial not to steal than to steal, but in some cases, one may need to steal in order to bring about the best results. And if, in a certain case, following a rule doesn't bring out the best outcome, then one should ditch the rule and do whatever in fact brings about the best outcome. What's the point of following a rule in a case in which it doesn't bring about the best outcome?" This is the thinking, in effect, behind a consequentialist's view of rules as mere rules of thumb.

Whatever other form it takes, a consequentialist normative theory has to place the goodness of the action completely on the goodness of its results. So once, as a consequentialist, you have placed all your eggs in the basket of consequences in assessing the morality of actions, you need a way to measure these all-important consequences. To begin with, you could ask, "Consequences for whom?" You might want to focus on whatever actions will have the best consequences for others, the best consequences for yourself, or some combination of the two that will yield the best outcome for everyone. This last option certainly sounds the best, since *everyone* includes both yourself and others—that includes every being for which there is a greatest good, so any consequentialist theory should certainly aim for this. There are two main approaches to consequentialism, which, although they both aim toward achieving the most good for everyone, involve very different ideas as to how this should be accomplished.

Ethical Egoism

Some philosophers have maintained that to bring about the most good for everyone, the best results will be obtained if each person looks primarily after his or her own self-interest. This view, known as *ethical egoism*, has been defended by people such as the novelist Ayn Rand (although she is not really considered a philosopher by most philosophers) and Friedrich Nietzsche (see especially his *Beyond Good and Evil*), although it finds few adherents among current professional philosophers and can certainly seem counterintuitive. But here is an argument for it:

1. The supreme good for each person is whatever is best for that person.
2. For each person, the person who is best at looking after that person's interests is that person.

Therefore, to maximize the greatest good for everyone, each person should primarily look after his or her own interests.

A slight variant on this argument would be to say that since the best possible world will be one in which each person's good is maximized, and each person is best at looking after his or her own good, then it follows that the only way to bring about that best possible world is for each person to primarily look after his or her own interests.

One of the linchpins of this type of argument is premise 2. Why should we think that premise 2 is true? Simply because any alternative would take the form of "meddling" in others' affairs, in paternalism that seeks to tell others what's best for them, as though they can't figure it out for themselves. The basic argument for ethical egoism says that the best kind of life may be basically the same kind of thing for each person or different for each person, but the bottom line has to be that people have to figure it out for themselves, simply because they're in the best possible position to know themselves and therefore know what's good for them. The position needn't commit one to the claim that everyone *does* know what's best for themselves, only that, all other things being equal, it's generally safe to assume that if anyone knows or can figure out what's best for any given person, it is that person. This means that if you act solely in another person's interest—through charitable donations, for instance—you are actually not helping that person, because you are preventing that person from doing what he or she alone can do best—look after his or her own interests. As with so many premises of arguments, it's debatable, but it is not without substantial weight.

Now, what about premise 1? It may well be that the greatest good for each person is whatever is best for that person, but there is a way to understand this premise that makes it into a mere tautology (a statement that is automatically true by virtue of its meaning). An example of a tautology would be "If I am wearing blue jeans, then I am wearing blue jeans." Indubitably true, but uninformative and without content, as in this case: "The supreme good for each person is the supreme good for each person." So what lends premise 1 its initial plausibility may simply be the fact that it is automatically true, without saying anything substantive.

Would this understanding of premise 1 even be sufficient to make the conclusion of the argument follow from it? Not exactly. The conclusion of the argument says that the stated aim is to maximize the greatest good for everyone. Does it follow that the supreme good for each person, added up collectively among all the individuals in the world, is going to add up to a maximized good for everyone? In fact, it doesn't. The easiest way to see why would be to consider what "the greatest good" would look like for each individual. Would the sum total of all those greatest goods even be compatible with each other? Probably not. It may be that my greatest good can only be accomplished at the expense of your greatest good. What are we to do, in that case, but fight it out to the death, as it were? For the argument to be valid, then, we would have to change its conclusion to refer simply to "the greatest good" as defined from each individual's standpoint. And that in no way guarantees that if every individual in the world single-mindedly pursued only his or her own self-interest, this would result in the greatest good for every individual.

In the end, a consistent and thoroughgoing ethical egoism has to simply maintain that the morally best thing to do is always whatever happens to be best for ourselves. It says that the morally best actions are determined purely by self-interest. Most of us wouldn't be satisfied with this as a system of morality. Nietzsche, however, was ready and willing to bite that bullet and go with it. In *Beyond Good and Evil*, he wrote,

> Mutually refraining from injury, violence, and exploitation, placing your will on par with the other's: in a certain, crude sense, these practices can become good manners between individuals when the right conditions are present. . . . But as soon as this principle is taken any further, and maybe even held to be the fundamental principle of society, it immediately shows itself for what it is: the will to negate life, the principle of disintegration and decay. Here we must think things through thoroughly and ward off any sentimental weakness: life itself is essentially a process of appropriating, injuring, overpowering the alien and the weaker, oppressing, being harsh, imposing your own form, incorporating, and at least, the very least, exploiting—but what is the point of always using words that have been stamped with slanderous intentions from time immemorial (Nietzsche 2002)?

Books could be (and have been) written on the implications of a passage like this, but for our purposes, it is sufficient to understand that Nietzsche wholeheartedly embraced the conclusion that the best thing each person can do is whatever happens to be best for him or her and "to hell with everyone else."

Another way to make the "greatest good" argument valid would be to have premise 1 state, "Each person's own ultimate good is the ultimate good (period)." This points to the deeper problem with ethical egoism, which is that all it can ultimately take into account is the greatest good as individually defined for each person. From a consequentialist standpoint, it would make more sense to maximize the good results for everyone, but ethical egoism can only tell you what the greatest good might be for each individual, as defined by that person, as though an island.

Ethical egoism can work perfectly if we are convinced that the ultimate good (period) is only our own ultimate good and self-interest. But why on earth would anyone think that? What we want from a consequentialist normative theory is an objective answer of what criterion works for everyone to tell us whether an action is morally good or not. But all ethical egoism can give is an answer that's essentially different for each person; it's about what the best overall consequences would be for you alone (and even that's assuming that stepping on other people to get what's best for you doesn't harm you). In other words, in adhering to ethical egoism, you're going to find that the ultimate good is just—"me"! But why you: just because you're you? That would make sense if you were the only conscious being in the universe, but if you don't think that's the case, you may want to look elsewhere for a normative theory that gives you the right results.

Utilitarianism

Another consequentialist theory of normativity is available. In finding what makes actions right, ethical egoism focuses exclusively on the good of each individual taken in isolation. In sharp contrast to this, the theory of *utilitarianism* offers objectivity and impartiality in spades. Utilitarianism, the most historically significant form of consequentialism, more or less came of age in the nineteenth century with the British political and ethical philosophers Jeremy Bentham and John Stuart Mill. (Utilitarianism is really the first form of consequentialism to have found a voice in philosophy at large; it was only later on that philosophers realized it is an instance of consequentialism.)

Utilitarianism is a normative theory that states that actions are right when they maximize the overall utility, or "happiness," among the population at large.

Now recall what was said about happiness in Chapter 3: the general philosophical sense of happiness is "whatever the ultimate good is." When a utilitarian uses the word *happiness*, though, he or she specifically means pleasure, the subjective sense of well-being, as the ultimate good to be maximized. So it is important to realize that utilitarians are inherently committed to hedonism in value theory (again, see Chapter 3). And practically all hedonists are probably going to be utilitarians.

The cardinal virtue of utilitarianism is its objectivity, or impartiality. This may especially be a virtue in light of the fact that many of us think selfishness—which precludes impartiality—does not usually lead to morally good actions. The impartiality of utilitarianism stems from its view that maximizing well-being (in the hedonistic sense) is the final good. So in the drive to maximize the overall good, any being capable of experiencing well-being is considered, without partiality for any other criterion. In fact, insofar as most of us think nonhuman animals are capable of experiencing well-being, we must consider them too.

Drawbacks to Consequentialism

As already mentioned, there are realms of morally significant aspects to our actions that consequentialism, by definition, cannot seem to take into account. These shortcomings amount to a number of important drawbacks that are serious enough to warrant discussion.

Lack of Account for Expected and Actual Consequences

One of those morally significant aspects that consequentialism by its nature must neglect is the intention with which an action was taken. We often speak of something being done with good intentions, which means that a person performed the action fully believing that good would result from it. But if the results are bad for reasons that the person could not have reasonably foreseen, consequentialism says that we should view the person's actions as morally bad and the person as guilty of moral wrong. Most of us see this as the wrong result and will not want to accept it as a consequence of the theory or else reject the theory.

So how can consequentialism take account of people's intentions? If the sole criterion for judging acts morally right or wrong is their results, it's hard to see how we could find principled room for letting mere intention make a difference. We may want to say that, all things considered, it's best to have good intentions, simply because good intentions tend to bring about good results. But recall what was said earlier about a consequentialist's view of rules: in cases where following a rule does not bring about the best effects, there's no point in following it. Likewise, to be consistent, the consequentialist apparently must say that in cases where the best intentions go awry in their effects, what's the good of having good intentions? A consequentialist cannot, it seems, give any moral credit to the intention of a good outcome in and of itself. To be consistent, the proof has to be all and only in the pudding—the results of the action in question.

Neglect of Moral Agents as Such

The fact that expected outcomes per se do not seem to figure in the consequentialist theory of normativity points to a more general issue: in focusing exclusively on the outcomes of given actions, this theory apparently leaves the moral agent out of the picture. A *moral agent* is a person who has virtues or vices, who deliberates and decides, and who can be praiseworthy or blameworthy—in short, who is held morally responsible for the goodness or badness of whatever acts he or she commits. Consequentialism says that a person is morally responsible only for the outcome of an action—something that has no essential connection to the moral agent—as described in the earlier case of good intentions and bad results. This should seem strange indeed for a theory of normativity. Before the "modern" age of the last few centuries, no philosopher, going all the way back to the famous Greeks such as Aristotle, ever thought of separating the consequences of an action from the motivations from which it sprang: for them, it was all one. Consequentialism is only a modern invention, and if it is correct, then every theory of normativity that came before it was completely offtrack.

A consequentialist theory such as utilitarianism may, in fact, be understood from a historical perspective in terms of the Industrial Revolution of the nineteenth century. Once the production of outcomes began to be engineered on a large scale, it began to seem more natural to handle ethics this way too—in terms of what can be called a "hedonic calculus," maximizing utility in terms of "happiness" for the greatest number of people. But a large-scale, engineered machine is hardly one in which a moral agent has any part to play.

Neglect of Justice

Another consideration that consequentialism conspicuously leaves out of the picture is that of justice. We tend to think that, whatever else may be the case about a situation, justice being served is always inherently a good thing, and injustice is always inherently bad. But consequentialism can't pay any attention to justice per se. Here's an example that illustrates why. Suppose that, for some reason, to save the lives of ten people, a random innocent person would have to be killed. A consequentialist theory like utilitarianism makes this decision easy: kill the one person to save the ten, because ten people have more overall utility, or "happiness capacity," than one person does. But, we want to object, what about the innocent person's rights? Utilitarianism can't seem to consider anyone's rights; it has to say that whatever injustice there is in sacrificing an innocent person, it's overridden by and irrelevant to the dictates of maximizing utility, which according to the theory on offer is the only thing that makes an action right or wrong.

We could just conclude that common sense is wrong and that the conclusions utilitarianism yields should be embraced along with the overall theory of consequentialism. But most of us hold existing intuitive commitments strongly enough that we tend to conclude it is the theory that is radically off target.

Strange Results with Regard to the Obligatory and Supererogatory

Another thing to notice about the case for sacrificing one person for ten is that utilitarianism does not just yield the conclusion that killing an innocent person may in some circumstances be permissible; the theory actually says it may be obligatory. If the criterion of moral goodness or badness is that of maximizing utility, then any case in which we fail to maximize utility would be a moral failing. So not only would it be permissible to kill the innocent person to save the other ten; it would be morally bad not to do so. Someone who sympathizes with consequentialism and wants to side with whatever happens to be the best outcome for the most people might just say that killing an innocent person to maximize utility may be permissible but not necessarily obligatory. But, on utilitarian grounds, maximizing utility is always obligatory; utilitarianism doesn't seem to leave room for anything being morally good but not obligatory.

The reason for this basically stems from the fact that utilitarianism simply identifies moral goodness with increasing utility and moral badness with lack of utility. If increasing utility is the greatest good there is, and maximizing utility is always obligatory no matter what, then utilitarianism obliges us to the utmost good at all times. This aspect of utilitarianism—not allowing for anything to be morally good but not obligatory—is part and parcel of, and ultimately comes from, consequentialism as a whole. In ethical egoism, for example, take pursuing your own self-interest as the ultimate good. Ethical egoism has to say that whatever furthers your own self-interest is always not only permissible but obligatory. Nietzsche and Rand thought that failing to pursue your own interests and considering others' interests at the expense of your own was a moral failing.

The overall point is that beyond the impermissible, permissible, and obligatory, there is another moral category that we tend to think should be taken into account: the realm of the *supererogatory*, or "praiseworthy but not obligatory." Actions that are supererogatory are morally good, but they are considered so good that we would not hold somebody to be morally wrong if he or she did not do them. A problem with consequentialism is that it does not seem able to assess any actions as supererogatory. Instead, it makes all good actions obligatory. Figure 4.1 illustrates the gap in consequentialism with respect to commonsense ideas about normativity.

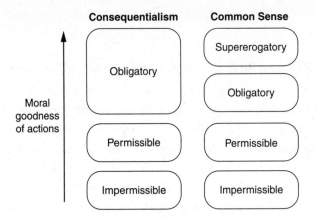

FIGURE 4.1   Any consequentialist normative theory has to say that all morally good (that is, neither morally bad nor morally neutral) actions are obligatory. However, this fails to leave room for any actions being characterized as supererogatory, or "good, but not obligatory."

Intrinsic Goods Being Assigned Only Instrumental Value

Finally, recall the discussion of means and ends in the previous chapter on value theory. What is held to have intrinsic value is that which is an end unto itself. Any normative theory also places intrinsic value on certain things as ends, whereas other things are assigned instrumental value; they are valued only as means to intrinsically valued ends. Perhaps the most counterintuitive thing about consequentialism can be stated in terms of this means-and-ends relation. Because the theory places ultimate, intrinsic value only on results, consequentialism is committed to the following claim:

> C. Any action (no matter what it is) that brings about the best results will be judged as (only) instrumentally good.

Two components of claim C point to different (although related) problems with consequentialism. The first is the "no matter what it is" phrase: any action will be judged morally good if its consequences happen to be good, even if the action sprang from a moral agency that is somehow bad (this is the flipside to the earlier problem of good intentions and bad results). The second component is the word *only*: moral goodness in the moral agent is assigned only instrumental value at best (and that's just as long as its consequences are good). But intuitively, this puts things backward. Most of us tend to think that intrinsic aspects of the moral agent—things like virtue, honor, sobriety, wisdom, and courage—are themselves intrinsically good rather than merely instrumentally good. But consequentialism says that such things can only be instrumental goods; they are good only insofar as they bring about good effects and are considered of no value if they do not.

In the most general terms, this problem with consequentialism is rooted in the fact that instead of placing intrinsic value in characteristics of the moral agent per se, it places intrinsic value only on consequences "downstream" of the moral agent and his or her actions. Thus, anything "upstream" of an action's consequences can be given only instrumental value; even bad moral motivations can be valued (instrumentally) if they have good consequences, and good moral motivations can be valued only instrumentally (never intrinsically). This is what leads to the possibility of moral praise for a bad moral agent whose actions happen to have good consequences and moral blame for a good moral agent whose actions happen to have bad consequences.

Still Struggling

Consequentialism does *not* say that the best intentions, or the most virtuous dispositions, are those that result in the best actions. It is not even interested in intentions, dispositions, or virtues as such. Therefore, it does not assess different virtues or qualities in a moral agent. Rather, pure consequentialism is only interested in whatever may produce the best outcome (in whatever way that may be assessed).

Some Alternatives to Consequentialism

Let's step back and take a breath. This chapter has covered a lot of ground already, and it is only halfway done (if that). To the modern thinker in search of a theory of normativity, the first and most basic choice is whether to go with consequentialism or not. Consequentialism at least provides a unified and clear-cut standard by which to define morally right and wrong actions. The alternative is to find a theory that defines the morally good in some other way, which may be more difficult.

From that jumping-off point, the next selection is basically among a list of "isms." In covering a number of these, the objective is not to bewilder you with a laundry list of theories or to be thorough and exhaustive; it is rather to provide a taste of specific principled ideas in normative theory, some of which have had adherents since almost the beginning of recorded philosophical history. For introductory purposes, it is sufficient simply to gain a basic appreciation for what motivates various alternatives to consequentialism—that is, reasons for embracing each theory based on the kinds of explanations and results it gives.

To this end, the rest of the chapter gives an overview of three normative theories that are not consequentialist. The basic requisite for understanding each theory is to realize what makes it not consequentialist—that is, where the theory places the focus of moral goodness in and around the moral agent as opposed to following consequentialism's placement at the outcome of the action downstream from the moral agent. Each of these theories tells a different story about where the moral goodness is found.

Divine Command Theory

For many people, the idea of morality is closely associated with the idea of God. This tends to take shape in the thought that morality overall comes in the form of proscribed laws that we are to follow—this is morality's normative force. These laws seem to be objective, such that they are not mere feelings or sentiments and that we did not make up and cannot change them at will. As for where these laws came from, the natural conclusion for the believer in God is that the normative force behind such moral laws comes from God. The thought can basically be put in the form of the following conditional:

> D. If God exists, then whatever objective normative force is behind moral laws comes from God.

Recall what was said in Chapter 2 about valid inferences based on conditionals. Suppose that we accept the truth (and logical validity) of D. If we supposed that God did not exist, it would not follow that there can be no objective moral laws (this would be the fallacy of denying the antecedent). Based on what D says, if God did not exist, there might be some other basis for objective moral law. It would also be a fallacy to conclude, from the assumption that there are objective moral laws, that God must exist (this would be the fallacy of affirming the consequent). So nothing about what D says allows us to validly conclude that God exists or that if God doesn't exist, there cannot be an objective basis for morality. What it does say is that *if* we believe in God (on whatever basis) and also believe in objective morality, we will want to make a connection between the two, such that whatever objective normative force there is in morality comes from God. In other words, if there are laws and an authoritative lawgiver, the lawgiver must have given the laws. Attempts to spell out the nature of that basic connection, as expressed by D, fall within the realm of *divine command theory.*

As a normative theory, divine command theory at its most basic sets out to answer the question "What makes an action morally good or bad?" in terms of whether God commands or forbids an action. Unlike consequentialism, this places the moral goodness or badness of an action squarely in the lap of the agent—in this case, whether he or she is obedient or disobedient to God's commands. Various questions and complications can be raised at this point—for example, how do these laws come to us? Is it a simple matter of reading them in a book? If it were, this would make things pretty straightforward. Some adherents to divine command theory hold that at least some of God's moral commands are found in the Bible or Koran or some other holy book and are applicable to people at all times and in all places. But even most such adherents to divine command theory do not think of *all* of God's moral commands as explicitly written down. And for even those commands that are written in a holy book, our following them is not thought of as simply a matter of consulting a book about things that we would otherwise have no idea about. Rather, a believer in divine command theory would tend to think that the normative force that comes from the divine lawgiver meshes together with the normative force that we already tend to associate with accepted moral codes that people hold largely in common with each other regardless of religion. In other words, most divine command theorists would say that whatever moral codes we already accept, it is on the basis of D that we can be assured that they have an objective normative force—that is, are not simply things we feel and believe strongly.

But this leads to a dilemma. We posit divine command theory to explain whence objective normative force comes, other than the simple fact that we think the moral codes to which we subscribe should be followed. But if that explanation is closely identified with the normative force we already feel the moral codes have, it becomes less of an explanation and more a sort of window dressing. On the other hand, if we say that objective normativity comes from divine command independent of what we may think is true, then how do we even know we have the right moral code? Supposing divine command theory to be true, what we think is moral could actually be immoral and vice versa.

And without an explicitly written, divinely given moral code, how can we ever know if that might be the case?

The Euthyphro Dilemma

This basic problem is known as the Euthyphro dilemma, and it was first eluci-dated in Plato's dialogue *Euthyphro*. Here, Euthyphro is going up to the tem-ple to pay homage to the gods, and Socrates (all of Plato's dialogues feature Socrates as the questioner, who stumps people with his probing queries) asks him why he is doing this. Euthyphro replies that piety is something the gods demand. "So then," Socrates answers, "piety is good because the gods require it. But then, what if the gods required you not to exercise piety? Would *not* being pious then be what is good?" Euthyphro retracts his initial position, saying that the gods always command whatever is good. Socrates comes back, "But if the gods must only command what is good, then the reason for doing a good thing is just because it is good—for if this is the gods' reason for commanding it in the first place, there can be no higher reason for doing good than for good itself! And if this is the case, whence the need to bring in the idea of a divine lawgiver as the reason that one does what is good?"

The basic dilemma is represented in Figure 4.2. The point of divine com-mand theory is to give an independent explanation for what makes morally good actions good. But to appeal merely to divine command as the source of this normative force, as the left horn of the dilemma in Figure 4.2 shows, is to separate the morality from the "commandedness" to such an extent that anything God commanded—even an immoral action—would have to be con-sidered moral on the basis of its being commanded. With this basis for morality, any intuitively good action that happened to be commanded by God would be judged objectively moral—either way, it's commanded, so it's morally obliga-tory. (In any event, even if we supposed that God, in fact, only commands what is good, we would still have to explain why we can apparently come to know this goodness for ourselves without being explicitly commanded to behave in such-and-such a way.) On the other hand, if we bring the moral goodness back closer to its status as a "commanded" thing, thus ensuring that God will only command what is good, then to be consistent, we would have to conclude that it is just goodness that makes things good; in which case, it's not an action's commandedness that makes it good but its goodness. This apparently under-mines the point of the theory, which is to explain the normative force behind moral goodness on the basis of something else.

The Euthyphro Dilemma for Divine Command Theory

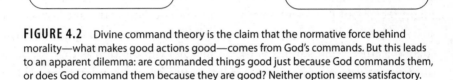

Are actions good because God commands them?

No — No

Does God command actions because they are good?

Yes

Yes

Then any action would be good just because God commanded it, even actions we would consider immoral.

Then God is subject to morality, and then morality itself must be the lawgiver, rather than God.

FIGURE 4.2 Divine command theory is the claim that the normative force behind morality—what makes good actions good—comes from God's commands. But this leads to an apparent dilemma: are commanded things good just because God commands them, or does God command them because they are good? Neither option seems satisfactory.

Sophisticated divine command theorists have subtle and interesting ways out of this dilemma, and they mainly involve rejecting the idea that there's a dilemma—in other words, saying that it's not an either-or situation, but rather a both-and situation. For the purposes of present discussion, we can say that, the Euthyphro dilemma shows that if we are looking for a serious normative theory, we probably won't be satisfied with saying, "Moral actions are obligatory simply because God commands them." Rather, we need to say exactly what this purported close relationship between divine command and moral obligation is (if it's not simply one of the two horns of the dilemma as shown in Figure 4.2) and how it's supposed to work (if it has the explanatory power it is supposed to have in giving a basis for normativity).

Duty-Based Ethics

Another theory that seeks to place the morality of an action squarely in the lap of the moral agent rather than the action's consequences is the duty-based approach to normativity discussed by the eighteenth-century philosopher Immanuel Kant, especially in his *Groundwork for the Metaphysics of Morals*

(Kant 1949). To zero in on whatever it is that makes actions morally good, Kant focused on aspects that are about as intrinsic as they can be to the moral agent. He thought the very epicenter of morality, whence the highest moral good comes, is in the good will. As this theory has it, anything that flows from a good will is to be considered morally good, and without the operation of a good will, there can be no morality. In fact, Kant thought that the most moral actions are those done purely out of a good will, with no motivation from anywhere else, even from an interest in an action's consequences. Some people are bothered by this suggestion because it may sound like it means that morally good actions *have* to be all and only those that we grit our teeth to do. But this isn't what Kant is committed to, but rather that whatever palpable goodness flows out of morally good actions is not to be the primary thing desired. The thing that morally good actions have to have in order to be *morally* motivated is by desire to do what is right regardless of how one might feel about it. Absent any motivation to do one's ethical duty, one might still feel inclined for other reasons to do good, and this is no point against the theory. Rather, Kant's point is that a morally right action is that for which a dutiful motivation to do what is right would be sufficient by itself (Herman 1993). If people always did only the right things but only because they never had any inclinations to do otherwise, then they would have no need for any concept of morality. Kant said that our feelings about morally right actions, even while they may be "subjective restrictions and hindrances, . . . far from concealing [duty] or rendering it unrecognizable, rather bring it out by contrast and make it shine forth so much the brighter" (Kant 1949:14). So it is not that the only good actions are those done from duty and without any other inclination. Rather, such cases are those in which the result of a good will can be most clearly *perceived*.

Kant did not say that duty *is* a good will, but that the good will is a *kind* of duty. So although having a good will does not necessarily capture all of one's duties, if one does all of one's duties, this will include having a good will (Kant 1949: 14). Specifically Kant thought that the good will involved (1) knowing your duty to do what is right and (2) doing that duty for its own sake—which would be acting purely out of good will. But we still need to know what kind of duty is involved in a good will, and to find that out without presupposing the very goodness that is to be explained. This is where Kant's main innovation comes in. His overall theory attempted to explain the basis of morality in terms of rationality. The duty involved in a good will is what rationality demands of you, and failing to do that duty is immoral because it is irrational. More exactly, Kant thought that one could *not* act immorally so long as one is acting fully in accordance with rationality. One motivation behind Kant's focus on rationality is that he thought that this was the only way to transcend individual and cultural variations in psychology and inclination, which he thought should have no place in determining objective moral rightness. Kant has been standardly understood to have put forth his view of morality in terms of rationality as a way to show what the most fundamental normative principles are.

Here's how it works. The whole idea of rational action is based on a means-and-ends structure. That is, if your goal is to accomplish x, it is rational to do y as a means to that end (and irrational not to, given your goal). This is known as a hypothetical imperative. The "if" part is the hypothetical, which states your goal, while the what-you-must-do-to-accomplish-your-stated-goal part is the imperative. So rationality can basically be defined as doing what is appropriate to further whatever your goal is. But as applied to morality, there's a big obstacle: you may do what is rational to serve the goal of morality, but why be moral in the first place? (Not to mention, how do you figure out what is moral?) Could it be shown that it is irrational to be moral? Not, at the very least, without knowing what morality is in the first place. And even then, how can you prove that rationality itself requires you to be moral? Couldn't you rationally choose to be immoral?

The solution is to change the hypothetical imperative into a *categorical imperative*: what you must do in all circumstances. Where the hypothetical imperative has an "if" that makes the imperative contingent on what the goal of an action happens to be, the categorical imperative is meant to give conditions that determine whether any action is rational at all. The important part of the categorical imperative states that the only rational goals are those in which the reason for action is such that if everyone acted that way, the goal of the action could still be fulfilled. In Kant's jargon, a categorical imperative contains a goal and an action that pursues that goal, such that the maxim of the action (the reason for which it was done) can be universalized (i.e., if everyone acted by that maxim, the goal of the action could be accomplished).

Although it may seem somewhat technical, Kant's theory gets at some fairly straightforward, commonsense ideas about normative standards. For example, think of sentiments like "What if everyone did that?" or "How would you like it if I did that to you?" These point to immoral actions being those that if everyone acted the same way, disaster would occur. It is not just that especially bad things would result, but that the goal of the action could not be accomplished if everyone acted in the same manner; this is where the crucial role of irrationality plays out in analyzing what makes immoral actions immoral. As a real-life example, lying is wrong, because if everyone did it all the time, no one would ever believe anyone and the fundamental goal of communication itself would be undermined. That is to say, the maxim of the action—lying but wanting to be believed—cannot be universalized. Likewise, robbing banks to get rich cannot be universalized, because if everyone did it, banks wouldn't have any money left—or they might become impregnable fortresses that theoretically could not be robbed—and then no one could get rich that way.

Here's the basic method of applying Kant's theory to tell whether an action is moral or not. First, what is the maxim of the action (the action plus the goal toward which it is oriented)? Suppose everyone acted according to that maxim—that is, did what you are doing and for the same reasons (the maxim is universalized). Would the goal of the maxim be achieved for people generally? If so, you are acting rationally and according to your duty and therefore morally. If not, you are acting irrationally and contrary to your duty and therefore immorally.

To assess Kant's theory, we have to think through some cases and see how, or whether, the theory works. We would want to see that, for cases of clear immorality, we would plug the facts into Kant's decision procedure described in the previous paragraph and get the result that such a case is immoral (and vice versa for clear cases of morally right action). As the earlier lying and robbery examples show, Kant's theory seems to work in many instances. We could explore many complications and permutations in his normative theory, but there is no room here to go into these matters in depth. Perhaps the biggest weakness in Kant's theory is its apparent inability to account for goals that are themselves irrational or immoral. Specifically, if the goal of an action is malicious, then we could plug it into the decision procedure and get the result that its maxim can be universalized: that if everyone acted maliciously in this way, the goal of the action (say, wanton destruction for no apparent reason) would still be achieved (indeed, perhaps even better than if just one person acted thus).

Kant's theory seems suited for application to actions that have at least some practical rationality to them, that have at least self-interested goals in terms of which the actions can be assessed. If nothing else, Kant's duty-based theory is a highly ingenious and valiant attempt to tie together some commonsense intuitions about normativity into a coherent, self-contained, explanatory theory.

Still Struggling

Kant's duty-based theory has several layers to it, which can make it seem confusing. The point of it is to analyze what makes for a good will. Kant thought that a good will meant doing your duty for its own sake—that is, regardless of anything else—and that duty is given by whatever anyone should do if he or she were in the same circumstances you are (this is the whole point of the categorical imperative).

Virtue-Based Ethics

One of the oldest approaches to normative ethics is to analyze good actions in terms of the virtues from which they spring. Again, in sharp contrast to consequentialism, this places the moral focus on inherent features of the moral agent, not on things downstream of that agent. A virtue ethicist would say that morally good actions with morally good consequences only happen on anything like a regular basis (that is, not by accident) because they come from a moral agent who has cultivated virtue in her or his life. This cultivation of virtue is learned over a long period of time and results in a habitual disposition to do the right thing. Aristotle, as expressed in his *Nicomachean Ethics*, was the primary virtue ethicist of Western culture. He made much of the idea that cultivating and manifesting virtue is habitual—that we learn by doing, so the best way to become good is to do good. The experience and seasoning we gain by this cultivation gives us an ever-increasing sensitivity to the salient aspects of our choices. Interestingly enough, Confucius, a near-contemporary of Aristotle, albeit half a world away, was also a kind of virtue ethicist, and his ideas had many affinities with those of Aristotle. In his teachings, Confucius put the same sort of premium on careful cultivation and experience in learning virtue by a gradual process.

Aristotle also felt strongly that the single thing all good choices have in common—the thread that holds them all together—is their manifestation of a mean between extremes. For example, being neither indiscriminately generous nor stingy, but somewhere in the middle; eating neither too much nor too little. Aristotle thought an important result of the process of seasoning ourselves as part of learning virtue is a sharpened ability to choose the mean between extremes.

Choosing an extreme is easy and requires minimal subtlety or sensitivity. But since the good, as Aristotle thought, is a mean between extremes, finding the "just-right" measure of all things does require subtlety and sensitivity. Hence, Aristotle held that the careful, attentive seasoning process needed to acquire virtue fits in exactly with what is required to choose the good in all situations.

Earlier in this chapter, it was pointed out that a utilitarian is inherently committed to hedonism as a value theory (see also Chapter 3): the two go together like a hand in a glove. In virtue ethics, we have another example of a normative theory that carries with it an ipso facto commitment to a certain value theory. In this case, that commitment is to eudaimonia, a happiness that is understood in terms of an objective state of well-being (as opposed to a mere subjective sense of well-being). Virtue ethics is committed to this stance in that what it most values are virtues, which are objective features of the moral agent. Often, eudaimonia has the connotation of "living in accordance with virtue." Whereas utilitarianism seeks to maximize happiness in the hedonistic sense, which is based purely on outcomes for which there is no need to consider features specific to moral agents, a virtue ethicist holds that the best world is one with the greatest amount of virtue among the moral agents in that world. What is to be valued, in that case, is an objective well-being like that included in the concept of eudaimonia and not simply pleasure for its own sake.

Virtue ethics has a lot to be said for it, especially in its emphasis on what is good about moral actions. In contrast, divine command theory puts it all in terms of obedience to laws and rules; yet it seems intuitively right to think that the virtuous person is more moral than someone who does all the same things only because he or she is following certain rules. In aspects that are intrinsic to the moral agent, the virtuous person can be said to be intrinsically good in his or her sensitivity to all the morally salient aspects of a situation, which may not be adequately captured by some rule or other. This ethical sensitivity, acquired through long practice and experience, has the advantage of potential application to any situation that might arise, as a function of the intuitive sense that a virtuous person has developed for locating the mean between extremes and thus choosing the best courses of action.

But keep in mind that, as a normative theory, virtue ethics has to tell us what makes both agents and actions morally good, and it has to say that they are each good for the same reason. But in assessing the morality of actions, virtue theory gives answers that sometimes seem counterintuitive. Whereas consequentialism can at least say that what makes an action such as rape wrong is that it harms someone, virtue ethics says that rape is wrong simply because a virtuous person would not do it. This may seem backward; most of us would want to say instead that a virtuous person would not rape because it is wrong to do so. This is known as the priority problem for virtue ethics and is perhaps the biggest drawback to the theory (analogous to the Euthyphro dilemma for the divine command theorist).

Another drawback is that being virtuous may look different to different people, such that two people who may be considered equally virtuous end up disagreeing on some moral issue. The virtue ethicist could respond that this result may well be expected if there are no single right answers to some ethical issues; in that case, the goodness of being virtuous may include the possibility of contradictory answers (at least from different people, with different perspectives). As with every normative theory, there may be bullets to bite and revisions to make, and further work to be done in hammering out the explanatory power of a given theory and its merits relative to other available theories. This is what normative ethicists do all day.

Chapter Summary

Normative ethics is the part of ethical theory that tries to determine what, in general, makes an action morally right or wrong. To come up with a normative theory, we have to sort out our existing commitments to see what principles we may already be committed to and then see how and whether those may fit together systematically into a single theory. Consequentialism may be the easiest normative theory to apply, because it is based on visible, measurable results of actions. But it has several drawbacks, which other, nonconsequentialist, normative theories do not have. However, other normative theories have weaknesses and drawbacks of their own, some of which consequentialism does not have.

A normative theory attempts to fill in the blanks in the following statement: "An action is morally right only when it is _____ and morally wrong if it is _____." A theory that gives a unified explanation for what makes actions right or wrong must eventually settle on a single explanation that points to the source of the force of normativity. The advantage to this is that we have a principled and consistent basis from which to determine the right ethical judgments in particular cases. However, a unified theory may give results that, in some cases, are counterintuitive or just plain unacceptable, so we have to weigh the explanatory benefits of the theory with the cost of accepting or rejecting its results.

QUIZ

1. **Which of the following questions can be addressed most directly from within normative ethics?**
   a. Are moral judgments based on matters of fact or opinion?
   b. Under what circumstances, if any, should abortion be permitted?
   c. How important is wisdom to making good moral decisions?
   d. Could something be morally right in one culture but not in another?

2. **Utilitarianism is a normative theory that is committed to maximizing _____.**
   a. virtue
   b. pleasure
   c. rationality
   d. usefulness

3. **Ethical egoism states that it is immoral to _____.**
   a. neglect looking after your own interests
   b. let other people have what they want
   c. take what you need at the expense of others
   d. only consider your own supreme good

4. **Which of the following is not a weakness of consequentialism?**
   a. It leaves the moral agent out of the picture.
   b. It cannot take considerations of justice into account.
   c. It can only consider actual, not expected, results.
   d. It cannot take other people's needs into account.

5. **Utilitarianism can assign only instrumental value to _____.**
   a. utility
   b. happiness
   c. good intentions
   d. eudaimonia

6. **Utilitarianism cannot seem to consider supererogatory acts because it _____.**
   a. cannot take a sense of duty into account
   b. is interested only in the consequences of actions
   c. intrinsically values only pleasure
   d. makes everything that is morally good obligatory

7. **Divine command theory says that** _____.
   a. God only commands actions that are morally good
   b. whatever God commands is morally good
   c. we can know God exists because of the force of moral laws
   d. if God did not exist, everything would be permitted

8. **"I am going to the store to buy a gallon of milk." In terms of Kant's theory of the categorical imperative, which of the following is the maxim of this action?**
   a. The objective of buying a gallon of milk
   b. The process of spending money
   c. The desire to go to the store
   d. The knowledge of one's duty

9. **Aristotle thought cultivating virtue was well-suited to making good choices because** _____.
   a. good is well-suited to virtue
   b. good is a mean somewhere between two extremes
   c. choosing good requires a great amount of effort
   d. virtue tends to lead to good results

10. **Which of the following is a common weakness between divine command theory and virtue ethics?**
    a. It can be difficult to learn what actions are morally good.
    b. If true, the theory may still give contradictory answers to ethical questions.
    c. Moral goodness is defined in terms of an entity rather than an action.
    d. They focus on moral goodness in something other than the moral agent.

Metaethics: What Kinds of Things Are Moral Judgments?

CHAPTER OBJECTIVES

In this chapter, you will learn the following:

- The apparent need for moral objectivity and the various kinds of challenges that can be raised to it
- Theories of morality and their consequences for thinking about the nature of moral judgments

Most of us have a moral philosophy. Since *philosophy* is just the subject matter having to do with general principles, moral philosophy has to do with the principles that apply to various situations, principles to which we point when we need to explain why we think certain things are morally praiseworthy and other things repugnant. The particular principles involved in a moral philosophy that point to various criteria by which we may decide whether to consider actions right or wrong were the subject of the previous chapter on normativity. People use their moral philosophy and normative principles to back up their moral judgments.

The nature of moral judgments is yet another issue in ethical theory. It arises when we take a step back and think about what it means for something to be right or wrong in the first place. When we make any moral judgment, we are not just applying a principle in a calculating or abstract manner. When we say that a certain action or kind of action is wrong, we ascribe some kind of property or attribute to that action. On the face of it, we seem to be citing a fact of some kind, simply pointing to it as we would any other kind of fact: "The earth spins on its axis once every twenty-four hours"; "My car has a flat tire"; "It's immoral to cheat."

The mere fact that we make moral judgments—regardless of what normative principles we try to uphold when doing so—raises a plethora of philosophical questions. This is mainly because moral judgments tend to sound just like ordinary judgments of fact, yet the subject matter of morality seems radically different from ordinary, fact-based realms of knowledge. If we think there *are* such things as moral facts, we may then ask, "Where and what are these moral facts?" and "How do we come to know about them?" If we think there *aren't* any such things as moral facts, on the other hand, we need to ask, "What are moral judgments about?" and "What sorts of things are moral disagreements?" As briefly introduced in Chapter 1, these metaphysical questions about the nature of morality itself (having to do with the basic features of reality and our place in it) are the province of *metaethics*.

The Need for and Problem of Objective Moral Facts

Any person of sound mind goes through life making moral judgments about situations that he or she encounters or thinks about. When we think about moral judgments, we soon discover that they are a unique sort of thing. The moral judgments we make have two salient features that jointly make morality a unique sphere of discourse. The first is that when we give voice to moral judgments, they come in a straightforward declarative form: "That's wrong," or "That's the right thing to do." Moral judgments are, well, *judgments*, which are the kind of thing that seem to be about objective facts, rather than merely our feelings—bottom line, a moral judgment, unlike an expression of taste, seems to be the kind of thing that can either get things *right* or *wrong*. It has this in common with judgments about things that have nothing to do with morality, such as historical facts or mathematics.

The second salient factor about moral judgments is quite different from the first: that is, the fact we are invariably emotionally invested in our moral judgments. No one, when making a moral judgment such as "That's wrong!" does so in a cool and calculating manner. Rather, we *care* that a thing is adjudged morally wrong or right, and if someone disagrees with us, we often strongly want to (if we don't in fact) go to bat on behalf of our convictions in an attempt to get that person to agree with us. Furthermore, if we see someone doing something we think is wrong, we want him or her to stop. Each of these two salient aspects is pervasively true of moral judgments as they actually happen in everyday circumstances.

Each of us seems to make moral judgments in such a way that we believe them to be correct. The first cardinal question in metaethics is, not "Which moral judgments are correct?" but a step removed from that, asking "What does it *mean* for a moral judgment to be correct?" This is a pressing issue because, as already mentioned, morality is such a different arena from others in which we make judgments. It is unlike science or economics, say, where we can point to certain facts that make a certain judgment correct or incorrect—or at least back up the judgment in terms that everyone will accept; in morality, we are hard-pressed to point to any moral facts as such. For example, if someone is harmed by an action, perhaps it is an indisputable fact about the action that it harms someone; but it is a further judgment *beyond* that to say that it is *immoral* to harm someone. What *this* kind of judgment is about, in the world or in ourselves, is the fundamental question in metaethics.

Given our convictions about the moral judgments to which we are each committed, the most straightforward account of what moral judgments are about would include there being such things as moral facts. Moral facts would be what make moral judgments correct—correct judgments get the facts right; incorrect judgments get the facts wrong. Thus, the existence of moral facts would also help us understand what it means for a moral judgment to be incorrect, so that we would know what is at stake when we morally disagree with someone. We want to be able to say that our moral judgments are correct, particularly as opposed to a competing moral judgment that we want to say is incorrect.

So, on the one hand, we want to be able to say that our own moral judgments are just plain *correct*—not only so we can be right about things, but because we feel as strongly about our moral convictions as we do about pretty much anything else. On the other hand, in a purely philosophical sense, we need to be able to make sense of the realm of moral judgments as a whole so we can know what they are about. We would want to know this anyway, but the fact of diversity and disagreement in moral judgments makes the issue acute: if there were real moral facts "out there" about which we can make reliable judgments, we would expect most people to be able to come to a consensus on them. But since this doesn't usually happen (at least not easily), the issue is naturally raised as to what moral judgments are actually *about*: if there are such things as moral facts, where are they, and why can't we agree on them? And if there are no moral facts, then what are moral judgments *really* about?

Just as the main tension in normative theory is between consequentialism and its alternatives (see Chapter 4), the main tension in metaethics is between the need to point to objective moral facts and the need to have a consistent and philosophically plausible theory about morality. The reason for this tension is simply that it is challenging to explain of what moral facts might consist; it is relatively easier to tell a story about the nature of morality that does not include moral facts as we might like to have them.

Moral Realism

To start with, let's characterize the metaethical position that says, "Yes, there are moral facts such that our moral judgments can be correct or incorrect about them." These moral facts are supposed to exist objectively; that is, they stand alone, independent of our thoughts about them. As this view has it, we don't decide what those facts are going to be—rather, we somehow perceive them the way they are, and if our judgments about them are right, it is because we are right about the way *they* are, not because of anything to do with the way *we* are. A philosophical theory that holds that we perceive certain kinds of things truly or falsely based on the way they are, independent of how we think about them, is known as *realism*. For example, *scientific realism* says that the entities postulated by our confirmed scientific theories really exist, that they are objectively just how our science says they are, and that they would have been the same even if we had never discovered them. (Scientific antirealism, on the other hand, holds that theoretical entities like electrons only "exist" insofar as they figure in the context of scientific theory.) Likewise, *moral realism* says that there are moral facts that hold true regardless of what anyone thinks about them.

To understand realism, keep in mind that it is a *metaphysical* view, one that attempts to get at the nature of reality as it is, independent of what anyone may think or say about it. It says, first, that there *is* a reality that is the way it is on its own; whatever we may believe about it has no bearing on what it is really like. Realism also says that our thoughts and beliefs about reality can be true or false *about* reality: the question of whether what we say is true or false is settled by facts about reality, not facts about ourselves. Realism is *not* the view that people *think* morality is objective (this would be a psychological, or perhaps sociological, perspective). It's that morality itself *is* objective. And if there is an objective moral reality, it is objective whether anyone thinks it is or not. Indeed, realism says that the moral facts themselves "are what they are," even if everyone is mistaken about them. It is perfectly compatible with realism to suppose that most people, or even everyone, is wrong about all or most of the moral facts. Other metaethical views, on the other hand, would have it that moral judgments are so rooted in our feelings about things, that it would not be sensible to think of people as morally wrong about most things. (Some of these antirealist views will be discussed later in this chapter.)

For many philosophers, there is an intrinsic motivation for being a moral realist: like most of us, they want to be able to say there are moral facts that would make it true (if it *is* true, as we think it is) that immoral actions are immoral. One philosopher has even argued that realism about morality ought to be embraced for *moral* reasons—that in order to uphold morality itself as we find it, it is imperative that we maintain a foundation for it (Dworkin 1996). It was certainly Immanuel Kant's view (see Chapter 4) that whatever that realm of morality might be, above all it must be objective and *not* based on individual sentiment (Kant 1949). But there are also intrinsic difficulties with establishing realism in ethics, since the realm of morality is so different from most other areas in which we tend to go about making declarative, purportedly factual statements. So, contemporary realist theories in metaethics tend to be particularly ingenious, intricate, and subtle—to the extent that none of them can really be discussed in any detail within the scope of this book. To give you a taste, though, here is a brief mention of some of these theories.

One example is the view that moral facts are abstract but really determined hypothetically by whatever the wisest person, in ideal conditions of rational reflection, would want, all things considered (Smith 1994). This is a realist view, since it holds that the moral facts are what they are regardless of what anyone actually thinks about them. Another view makes an analogy between morality and health; it tries to explain a theory of morality in which immorality is unhealthy and is as real a deficiency as lack of health is (this view dates back at least to Socrates and is explored in more contemporary works such as Bloomfield 2001). Yet another realist view, closely associated with the natural-law tradition in normative ethics, says that moral goodness in humans is a special case of "natural goodness," the same sort of standard by which we can tell that any living thing is flourishing and doing well according to the natural means of life proper to its species (e.g., Foot 2001).

The Challenge of Moral Antirealism

Metaethical theories that oppose realism primarily make their living on the fact that it is hard to see what kinds of things moral facts could be. These "antirealist" theories tend to be grounded on the problems with moral realism. Such theories point up how difficult it is for realism to account for certain things and then explain how much easier it would be to account for them if we were to drop our commitment to the idea of the existence of objective moral facts and look for other kinds of explanations instead.

For example, here's a realist view in metaethics: since we *seem* to be able to reliably perceive moral facts (as evidenced by the fact that we tend to believe strongly that we do), we must have a certain unique intuitive ability to perceive and grasp them directly. A philosophical criticism of this view is easy: "What is this ability, and how does it work? What, precisely, does it detect in the real world?" The antirealist critic is then in a strong position to go on to say, "Isn't it much more likely that, instead of having a special ability to grasp peculiar sorts of facts that cannot be grasped in any other way, our moral judgments are really just expressions of our preferences, similar to matters of taste?" The antirealist ethicist may thus have the advantage of being able to paint a more philosophically plausible picture of what is going on when we make moral judgments. However, it is at the cost of not being able to maintain that *any* moral judgments are objectively correct, even the most obvious moral truisms that anyone would agree with, such as "It is heinous to eat babies." To remain consistent, the antirealist who makes a criticism like the one stated here has to bite the bullet in the end and say that even a judgment such as "It is heinous to eat babies" is simply an expression of preference—no different from those pertaining to matters of taste.

The rest of this chapter looks at some specific approaches to metaethics that, instead of championing realism about moral facts, opt instead for the philosophical appeal of a theory that seems to explain more easily what all the salient features of morality itself are really about.

Still Struggling

Within metaethics, the questions are all about the most general aspects of morality itself. Remember this when trying to keep track of what all the isms are about. Metaethics is not primarily about what people *think* morality is (this would be psychology, sociology, or anthropology) but about what morality *really* is. For example, the metaethical position of realism does *not* mean lack of naïveté with regard to how people behave. It is also not about applying moral principles in such a way as to take into account as many "facts on the ground" as possible. Rather, it is about the very making of moral judgments and answering the question "What are we making judgments *about, really*?" by maintaining that there are objective moral facts such that our moral judgments about those facts can be either right or wrong, just like judgments about any other facts.

Some Alternatives to Moral Realism

Recall the two salient features of morality discussed at the beginning of this chapter. There is the fact-stating form that moral judgments take and our emotional investment in our moral judgments (and perhaps the further fact that these two features are so closely intertwined). Whereas realism focuses on the apparent fact-stating role of moral judgment and thereby also tries to do justice to our actual convictions, the various forms of antirealism focus on the essential role of our emotional investment in our moral judgments and tries to explain what morality is really all about in *those* terms. As already mentioned, such theories tell us some things about morality that may be counterintuitive, requiring us to give up the idea that morality is objective. All in all, the strongest reason for believing in ethical antirealism is that it may be the best route to a theory of morality that we can understand philosophically. The strongest motivation for rejecting antirealism is the thought that antirealist theories of morality do not get the target subject matter right, that they cannot be reconciled with our prior commitments as to what morality has to be (Dworkin 1996).

When reading about these theories, don't look at them as merely a list of isms, but rather as together representing a spectrum of different possible positions in metaethics. Whatever makes each position distinctive from the others points to a particular metaethical issue and one possible way to come down on the issue. Understanding the possible positions to be taken on these issues is simply the best way to become familiar with the territory itself and the philosophical questions that come up in it.

Ethical Relativism

It is common for young adults going off to college to begin to (1) encounter a plurality of different ethical views, including many that are different from those with which they were raised, and (2) think philosophically about universal issues such as ethics. When you're first trying to make objective sense of the fact of moral diversity and moral disagreement (thinking about what morality would really have to be like in order to explain diversity and disagreement), moral realism often begins to take a backseat to some form of antirealism. In this setting, you often hear things like "Morality is subjective." The thought behind this kind of statement is that our strong feelings about our moral judgments indicate that the perceptions involved in moral judgments are about our own feelings toward an issue rather than perceptions of objective facts about the matter. You may also note that in sharp contrast to other realms of knowledge, such as science, in which you may point to specific facts that would confirm the truth of a system of knowledge about a certain area, there does not seem to be anything observable in the world that would confirm or deny any particular moral view (Harman 1977).

For someone who is impressed by the diversity of ethical views and by the persistence of moral disagreement, ethical relativism can have immediate appeal. *Relativism* means that facts about a matter are not simply true or false; rather, they are only true or false with respect to a certain context. When people say things like, "That may be true for you, but it's not true for me," they are expressing a commitment to relativism about the facts of the matter. The relativist maintains that although people make moral judgments of the form "That's wrong" or "That's right," what makes those judgments correct or incorrect is a set of facts that applies only in a limited range—a range that perhaps only includes the person making the moral judgment in question.

Moral relativism holds that moral facts of some sort or another exist, but the scope and applicability of these facts are limited. Thus, moral judgments such as "That's wrong" or "That's right" are incomplete as stated and cannot be literally true or false in that form. Strictly speaking, for moral judgments to be correct or incorrect, they have to be spelled out fully in a form in which they make sense: "That's wrong for x," where x is whatever range the moral judgment in question is relative *to*. Different forms of relativism thus each specify a different range within which it makes sense to make moral judgments (the range of "for x").

Individual Relativism

The most basic form of ethical relativism is individual relativism, for which the set of moral facts that can make moral judgments true or false is specific to each individual. Different individuals may, and often do, have different sets of ethical norms, such that when an individual makes a moral judgment, he or she implicitly references the facts of his or her own ethical norms. This is the underlying thought expressed by "That's true for you but not for me." The ethical relativist—who may also be an individual relativist—says this, thinking of moral facts as specific only to the individual.

Individual relativism would make sense of the diversity of moral views that we find: if relativism were true, we would expect there to be many different and conflicting moral judgments among people at large. We would also expect that when people do disagree morally, these disagreements usually don't get settled—at least, not simply by one person pointing to some facts that the other person may have missed—if the relevant moral facts were specific to each person. That is, if there were general moral facts, we might expect to be able to point them out in an effort to convince someone with a different moral view that our judgment is correct. But since we can't, we may conclude that the best way to account for this is that the moral facts that figure in moral judgments are specific to each person.

Drawbacks to Individual Relativism
Although it has explanatory benefits when looking at the phenomena surrounding moral judgments from an objective standpoint, relativism seems to be revisionary of our actual practices in making moral judgments; if true, it would force us to revise what we tend to think our own moral judgments are really about. In spontaneously making a moral judgment, we typically do not simply note our own opinion or state what the dictates of our private morality are. Rather, the process seems to inherently involve a prescriptive element in which we also state what *other* people should believe. So, from an objective standpoint, the diversity of moral views may make them look as though they are based entirely on subjective individual beliefs rather

than on objective moral facts. However, from the subjective viewpoint, we do *not* tend to think of our moral judgments as subjective. Rather, in making moral judgments, we normally believe that we are reporting the straightforward *facts* of the matter and that others should also appreciate those facts and reach the same judgment we have. Accepting relativism about morality would thus require us to say about others' moral views, "That may be true for you but not for me"; however, with regard to our own moral views, we would have to accept the statement "That may be true for *me* but not for *you*." (The alternative, applying the theory so as to deflect others' moral views as relative to themselves while considering our own moral views as prescriptive to everyone, would be inconsistent, not to mention blatantly self-centered.)

Ethical relativism may be especially hard to swallow when the rubber really meets the road and someone else's moral views include the acceptability of harming *you*. In that case, if the moral facts relative to a person allow him or her to make a judgment that it is morally acceptable to harm you, then it will be futile for you to object on the basis of your own set of moral facts that indicate being harmed is wrong! It is perfectly consistent with—indeed, required by—relativism for the other person in such a circumstance to say, "That may be wrong from your perspective but not from mine." In such a circumstance, you could either acquiesce to what is dictated by the other person's moral facts, even if it harms you, or both of you could act according to your moral judgments and fight it out to the death. Individual relativism does *not* allow you to point to a generally applicable moral standard (because, according to individual relativism, there is no such thing) by which a third party could rightly judge that it is wrong for the other person to harm you.

Cultural Relativism

One possible improvement on individual relativism is to broaden the base of facts to which moral judgments must answer, so as to allow a common set of norms to be shared among people. This way, different people may be judged by moral standards that are shared by the population of which they are a part. This is one motivation for adopting cultural relativism, the view that the set of moral facts on which moral judgments are based is shared within a culture. As with individual relativism, one of the motivations for cultural relativism itself is the observation that moral norms can differ among cultures. A commonly cited example is that given by the Greek historian Herodotus, who reported that among the ancient Persians, some cultures buried their dead, while others always cremated the deceased. Given that each culture thought the practices of the other culture to be morally depraved, the best explanation may be that each culture was right from its own perspective, and there is no way to decide objectively between them who was "really" correct.

In summary, realism and both forms of relativism affirm the existence of moral facts—they differ in their view of the scope of these facts with respect to moral judgments. Figure 5.1 shows a diagram that illustrates the difference between these positions.

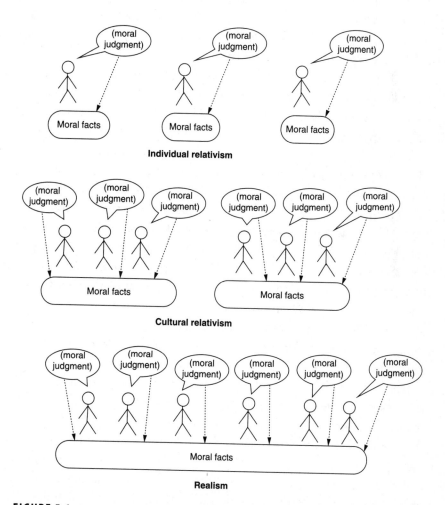

FIGURE 5.1 Moral relativism holds that different sets of moral facts pertain to each individual or culture, so any given moral judgment can only be considered correct or incorrect *relative to* the moral facts that apply to that individual or culture. In contrast, realism says there is one set of general, objective moral facts that is applicable to everyone, everywhere, at any time; thus, our moral judgments can be either correct or incorrect *period*, not just for a person or culture.

Drawbacks to Cultural Relativism The same kinds of explanatory benefits that apply to individual relativism apply in an analogous manner to cultural relativism. Yet the same kinds of drawbacks apply as well. Although cultural relativism can provide a basis by which moral disagreements between individuals may be adjudicated, it has the same problem as individual relativism in judging between different moral norms; the norms are simply those of cultures instead of individuals. In the earlier example of Persians who either buried or cremated their dead, cultural relativism may provide the best way to view the difference, at least for those of us who do not see anything unethical about burial or cremation. But again, as in individual relativism, what about moral norms that are held strongly within our own culture?

Accepted practices in other societies may be morally repugnant to those steeped in Western culture. In these cases, we don't really want to say that such things are acceptable for that culture and should only be considered unacceptable if they are practiced in our culture. For example, among the medieval Japanese, it was considered lawful and acceptable for a samurai to test the sharpness of a new sword by cutting a random, wayfaring stranger at the crossroads in half with a single stroke. There was even a word for this practice, *tsujigiri*, literally "crossroads cut" (Midgley 1981). As another example, in some cultures in west Africa, it is standard practice to amputate the clitoris of young girls, without anesthesia, before they reach puberty, in an effort to prevent them from becoming sexually promiscuous. (This is sometimes euphemistically referred to as "female circumcision," although it is more analogous to castration.) Such practices seem clearly immoral and arouse our indignation to the extent that it seems difficult to accept that our outrage could only properly apply if such things were done in our own culture and is not applicable to others. Yet we must accept it if we embrace cultural relativist metaethics.

Another problem that cultural relativism has in common with individual relativism is in morally assessing other cultures whose ethics threaten our existence. For example, the ethics adopted by Nazi Germany held that the rest of the world must be conquered and nonwhite races exterminated. The philosopher and novelist Jean-Paul Sartre is a real-life example of a cultural relativist and one who participated in the Resistance during the Nazi occupation of France in the early 1940s. As a cultural relativist, he had to maintain that what the Nazis were doing was right *for them*, even though it was not right for others. Since Sartre himself was one of the "others," he conscientiously acted in accordance with the moral norms of his culture in resisting the Germans. To be consistent as a cultural relativist, he had to acknowledge that if the Nazis won the war, that would make the Resistance movement immoral, since the French culture (along with all others) would be superseded by the Nazi culture, which would then be in a position to establish the moral norms that would apply to everyone. In a strange way, Sartre was motivated as a Resistance partisan, not merely by the rightness of his cause, but by the desire that his cause could continue to be considered right, at least from his own cultural perspective.

From Relativism to Subjectivism

Another major drawback with ethical relativism in general is that however the moral facts are determined, they seem to be true automatically for whatever range to which they apply. For example, if moral facts are only applicable with respect to each individual, it would seem that each of us gets to decide what moral facts apply to ourselves. Consequently, no one could ever be morally wrong about anything! The same applies to cultural relativism: if moral facts are determined by the culture itself, then any particular culture is morally infallible with respect to itself. Conversely, if anyone's moral norms differ from those of his or her culture, he or she is automatically wrong on that count alone.

Again, one of the drawing points for relativism is the fact of widespread disagreement and diversity in moral views. The relativist can say, "If relativism were true, we should expect a diversity of moral views with no objective way to decide between them." But the relativist has a special problem telling what is even going on in moral disagreements. The realist needs an answer to the question, "What are moral facts?" The relativist also needs an answer to it, but relativism itself does not really provide an answer. But whereas the realist can at least say that an ethical disagreement is a situation in which one person is right and the other wrong about the generally applicable moral facts (even if it is hard to say what those facts might be), since relativism says there are no generally applicable moral facts, the relativist needs an account of what an ethical disagreement *is*. But since the relativist is committed to moral facts of a limited scope, the only answer he or she can give is a bit awkward. The relativist has to say that in spite of the fact that moral facts only apply to an individual or a culture, people who differ and disagree with one another are still going to try to convince each other of the correctness of their own moral views, because no one realizes that the moral facts are only relative to the individual or culture.

All of this means the relativist still wants to take account of moral facts in some sense or another by making them "objective" yet limited in scope. That is, a moral relativist can think not only that moral facts may conflict between one person or culture to the next, but that it is objectively true that they do. But if we're making the facts specific to a given point of view, why think of them as objective at all? Rather, if we take the phenomena of diversity and disagreement seriously, then instead of being content with relativism about facts whose truth is still objective in some way, it might make more sense to base our theory of morality purely on the *subjective* aspect of moral judgment. In that case, if the crucial fact about morality is its subjectivity, then instead of the moral facts being the same as those the realist accepts (although limited in scope), why not make our account of moral facts match up as closely as possible with their subjectivity? That way, we might have an easier time accounting for moral facts.

A purely subjective theory would prevent automatic infallibility about objective facts (since the facts would be inherently subjective, in which case there would be no problem about infallibility with regard to those facts) and give more credence to the idea that intractable moral disagreements are not so different from matters of taste. The remainder of the views to be discussed in this chapter do just that—they go further than relativism by fully embracing antirealism in basing morality on wholly subjective features. These theories also appeal to those who want to say that morality is subjective but are a bit more thoroughgoing in their approach.

Sentimentalism

The eighteenth-century Scottish philosopher David Hume (who has been called the greatest philosopher to have written in English) may well have taken the subjective aspect of ethics more seriously than anyone before him and was enormously influential in doing so. In his *Treatise of Human Nature*, Hume proposed a systematic way of viewing human perception and knowledge that divided all human thought as falling under the faculty of either rationality or the "passions." Our rationality is used to discriminate and judge things quantitatively, and it does not, in itself, motivate us. Our passions, on the other hand, do motivate us. So given that morality motivates us by means of its associated passions, Hume thought it followed straightforwardly that we use our passions rather than our rationality to make moral distinctions of right and wrong. *Rationality* is defined as "the discovery of truth and falsehood," so since rationality is not a part of making moral judgments, moral judgments do not discern the truth or falsehood of some external fact.

Hume began an entire tradition in metaethics, part of which is carried on today in the form of a perspective that has come to be known as *sentimentalism*. Sentimentalism says that the motivations behind our moral judgments cannot be understood except with reference to the sentiments we have with regard to what happens (D'Arms and Jacobson 2000). This is a departure from the realist view of moral facts, because instead of saying that moral reality is what it is independent of what we may think and feel about it, sentimentalism says that moral facts—if there are any—would have to match up somehow with our sentiments.

The crucial thing about sentimentalism is that it places human-centered constraints about what possible moral judgments may exist that could be correct (this is what sets it apart from realism, which is compatible with everyone being wrong about their moral judgments). A consequence of this is that there are very few ways, if any, in which a moral judgment could be wrong, provided it was motivated by a fitting sentiment. Sentimentalism does not seem to depend on any particular conception of moral facts, but it is compatible with the view that there are moral facts. It would just have to maintain that such facts are rooted in our sentiments and that their possible range is constrained by those sentiments. Therefore, sentimentalism has to reject the idea of *objective* moral facts.

Still, our moral judgments *seem* to be about objective moral facts, and sentimentalism has a distinctive way of accounting for that, which was a crucial part of Hume's own theory. It says that although moral facts reside in us and not in the world, we *project* our sentiments onto the world around us, just as if they were features of the world itself. So even if moral judgments *seem* to refer to objective reality, if they are about any moral facts at all, they are simply facts about the way we feel. In Hume's vivid terms, we "paint" our sentiments about things onto the world just as if they were features of the objective world, which explains why our moral judgments *seem* to report facts about the world. Just like a film projector, there is something about which facts can be stated, but it is not really happening "out there," in the world, but on the film in the projector (i.e., in us).

As far as moral correctness goes, sentimentalism says that any moral sentiments are appropriate and correct as long as they are "fitting." Whereas some people would say that if it is morally correct to have a certain sentiment, then that sentiment is fitting, sentimentalism says the reverse: if a sentiment is fitting, then it is morally correct to have it (D'Arms and Jacobson 2000). Again, the constraint that determines what is morally correct is human-centric, not rooted in facts about objective reality. We may then ask, "What is it about sentiments that makes them 'fitting'?" If it's aspects of the humans who have them, then what if we happened to think that, say, cruelty is good? Would that be a fitting sentiment to have, just because we happened to have it? The sentimentalist would have to reply that since sentiments are rooted in human values, whatever is valued is such that it is fitting to have positive sentiments toward it. Therefore, if we did value cruelty, it would not be immoral. But a sentimentalist would probably also say that due to how deeply our values are embedded in our human nature, it is not possible that we could value cruelty. In any case, sentimentalism says that anything to be judged as morally bad, such as cruelty, is immoral simply because it conflicts with actual human values.

Moral Nihilism

We can also take the emphasis on the subjective in morality far enough that we explicitly deny the existence of moral facts. That is, we could go so far as to say that morality is all about emotions, pure and simple. The approach to metaethics that denies the existence of moral facts is known as moral *nihilism*. Recall from Chapter 3 that nihilism about value denies that there are any values worth valuing. In metaethics, however, nihilism need not involve denying the existence of any moral values; what it does deny is the existence of moral facts. As with all metaethical views, it is primarily a metaphysical view about the nature of reality rather than moral practice itself.

To explain what morality is while denying outright the existence of any kind of moral facts, the nihilist has to endeavor to explain away what moral judgments are supposed to be, since they at least *seem* to be about moral facts. There are two very different ways to approach this.

Error Theory

One way to do without moral facts is to deny that they exist while also maintaining that, as the moral realist says, moral judgments are really supposed to be about moral facts. This differs sharply from subjectively oriented, antirealist views that try to maintain that moral judgments are, contrary to appearance, not really about moral facts. So the view that moral judgments are about moral facts, combined with the view that there are no moral facts, entails the view that all moral judgments are wrong. This view is known as *error theory*.

Error theory states, as has already been suggested elsewhere, that if moral facts existed, they would have to be strange kinds of facts. As mentioned earlier, Hume pressed the point that facts are objective sorts of things that can be discerned purely by the use of reason and cannot motivate us in themselves; on the other hand, moral evaluations are done by exercising the passions. The error theorist takes this line too and says that if there were moral facts, they would be peculiar sorts of facts indeed, completely unlike any other kinds of facts in that they would have intrinsic motivational power. In other words, they have "to-be-pursuedness" built into them, whereas no other kinds of facts have anything like this property. The following argument, from J. L. Mackie, perhaps the most well-known error theorist, is based on this supposition.

1. If moral judgments are to be correct, they must correctly refer to moral facts.

2. If moral judgments correctly refer to moral facts, moral facts must exist.

3. If moral facts existed, they would have to be utterly unlike any other kind of fact in having "to-be-pursuedness" built into them.

4. But there are no facts that have "to-be-pursuedness" built into them.

Therefore, moral facts do not exist, and moral judgments are all incorrect (Mackie 1977).

The conclusion that all moral judgments are incorrect and that the very idea of morality is in error is a harsh one indeed. To accept something like error theory, the reasons for it have to be overwhelmingly powerful. But the error theorist is convinced of it on the strength of premises 3 and 4 of the preceding argument. This is a prime example of following a chain of reasoning wherever it leads and biting the bullet to accept its consequences, whatever they are. Few people will find it palatable to say that all moral judgments, even those everyone agrees with (like "It is heinous to eat babies"), are just incorrect. Even if one grants the strength of the error theorist's argument, it is possible to step back and assess the morality of a metaethical position and conclude that, all things considered, it is more likely that error theory is somehow wrong than that it is not heinous to eat babies. In the final analysis, this would be a perfectly acceptable and nonhypocritical moral position to take, even if it does leave metaethical questions unanswered.

Expressivism

The other main branch of metaethical nihilism also denies the existence of moral facts, but unlike error theory, it denies that moral judgments even purport to be about moral facts at all. Rather, although our moral judgments may seem to report moral facts, they actually report how we feel. Unlike sentimentalism, this view states that moral judgments don't actually even report facts about how we feel; rather, they *express* how we feel. Naturally enough, this view is known as *expressivism*. Since moral judgments are simply expressions of moral sentiment, in this view, they function essentially the same way as do utterances such as "Yuck," "Hooray," "I like that," or "Stop it." In other words, when we say, for example, "Genocide is immoral," we are really saying something like, "Genocide—*boo*!" And when we say, "Generosity is morally good," we are really saying, "Generosity—*hooray*!" And since, unlike declarative sentences, such expressions simply cannot be either true or false, moral judgments themselves cannot be correct or incorrect. So although there are no such things as moral facts, moral judgments are not incorrect, but neither are they correct.

Expressivism takes on the part of Hume's metaethics that emphasizes how moral judgments reveal and express tastes and sentiments, and it maintains that moral judgments are really just a way of expressing our tastes. Unlike sentimentalism, though, it doesn't need the story about projection to explain where the moral facts are that we seem to refer to in moral judgments. This is because expressivism doesn't even try to account for moral facts. Rather, it says that, regardless of the semantics used to express moral judgments, there isn't any projection or, indeed, any judgment; rather, there's just expression. Table 5.1 shows how all of the metaethical theories discussed in this chapter stack up against one another and what is distinctive about each.

The main challenge for expressivism, then, is giving a plausible analysis of moral language that explains how it can be only about expression of taste (even though it seems to be reporting facts) and why, in making moral judgments, we simply express our feelings (even though none of us thinks we are). One of the main reasons for thinking that moral judgments at least purport to be stating fact is that there is such a thing as moral reasoning. Moral reasoning uses arguments, and arguments use premises. Premises have to be things that are true or false; otherwise, an argument that contains them could not be valid (or invalid!), let alone sound. Moral reasoning is how we apply a given ethical principle to a certain situation to make a moral judgment about that situation. Straightforward examples of moral reasoning are not hard to come by. For instance, "Killing humans is wrong, abortion is killing a human, therefore abortion is wrong." One of the premises of this argument might be false, but it's certainly a valid argument (see Chapter 2). You support the argument by arguing that its premises are true or oppose it by arguing that at least one of its premises are false.

The expressivist certainly has some explaining to do to maintain, against the realist, that there are no moral facts that are true or false, and against the

TABLE 5.1	A Summary of Representative Metaethical Positions		
Position	**Are there such things as moral facts?**	**What are moral judgments really about?**	**What makes moral judgments correct or incorrect?**
Realism	Yes	Generally applicable moral facts	Whether they are true to the moral facts
Relativism	Yes	Individual- or culture-specific moral facts	Whether they are true to the moral facts as they pertain to the individual or culture
Sentimentalism	Yes	How we feel about things (although we project our sentiments onto the world as though they were features of the world itself)	Whether they are true to how we feel about things
Error theory	No	Objective moral facts	Since there are no objective moral facts, no moral judgments are ever correct; rather, they are all incorrect.
Expressivism	No	How we feel about things	No moral judgments are ever correct or incorrect, because they are simply expressions of how we feel.

error theorist, that moral judgments don't even claim to be correct or incorrect. What's worse for the expressivist, people seem to have genuine moral disagreements. This would make sense if moral judgments at least purport to be about moral facts, but if they don't, we have to translate a moral disagreement as one side saying, "Hooray," and the other side saying, "Boo," which isn't so much a disagreement as a sharp divergence in taste. (On the other hand, framing a moral disagreement in this light *would* help make sense of why moral disagreements are hardly ever resolved to the satisfaction of either party.)

To succeed in painting a plausible picture, the expressivist has to employ a tremendous amount of ingenuity, as Allan Gibbard does in his *Wise Choices, Apt Feelings* (1990). It takes a master theorist like Gibbard, on the slender basis provided by expressivism, to try to take into account all of the salient features of morality and how we make ethical judgments and decisions. In place of requiring commitment to moral reasoning that requires purported moral facts, Gibbard gives a theory of morality based on what it "makes sense to feel," given acceptance of a certain "system of norms." He sensitively brings in a rich range of considerations and observations of how we actually go about making ethically loaded decisions to draw a complete and relatively plausible picture. The details of how such a theory works cannot be explored within the scope of this book, but suffice it to say that it is about as daunting a task to formulate a complete expressivist metaethical theory as it is to come up with a good realist one.

Still Struggling

To understand the various metaethical views discussed in this chapter, you have to realize the primary reasons why philosophers believe in them. Theories in metaethics try to take into account some major aspect of morality and make a case that the whole realm of morality should be understood in terms of that—whether "that" is truth, sentiments, subjectivity, or something else.

Chapter Summary

Metaethics is the discipline within ethical theory that seeks to answer questions about the most general aspects of morality, to find out where it fits in with everything else, as well as what place it has in objective reality. The primary question in metaethics is the nature of moral judgments, which is particularly difficult to sort out because of their objectively and subjectively defined aspects. Moral judgments seem to be about some kind of moral facts, but if there are moral facts, then we need to know what such things *are* so moral judgments can make reference to them. On the other hand, we may reject the idea of the existence of moral facts in favor of a theory of morality based on its subjective aspects.

It is difficult to come up with a metaethical theory that makes intuitive sense of all the commonsense realist ideas about moral judgments and relatively easier to paint an antirealist picture of morality; however, it is difficult in practice to accept all of what antirealism says about the nature of moral judgments as we actually practice them. As in other areas of ethical theory, we have to weigh the explanatory benefits of a metaethical theory with the consequences of accepting its principles across the board.

QUIZ

1. **Which of the following questions could be addressed most directly within metaethics?**
   a. What theory of morality can best account for the fact of moral diversity?
   b. Could it ever be moral to ignore the consequences of your actions?
   c. Under what circumstances could you violate your duty?
   d. Should euthanasia ever be allowed?

2. **Moral realism is committed to the view that _____.**
   a. people think their moral judgments apply generally to everyone
   b. we should find out as many facts as possible before making moral judgments
   c. there are moral facts that are what they are regardless of anyone's beliefs about them
   d. emotions do not play any role in moral judgment

3. **Ethical relativism is the view that _____.**
   a. the right thing to do varies with the situation
   b. moral facts are specific only to certain people or groups of people
   c. there are no such things as moral facts
   d. we should never make moral judgments

4. **The primary motivation for ethical relativism is the need _____.**
   a. for objectivity
   b. to account for diversity in moral judgments
   c. to account for subjectivity in moral judgments
   d. to reduce conflict

5. **A cultural relativist must say that _____.**
   a. any culture's moral norms could be wrong
   b. individuals cannot be morally wrong
   c. anything a culture accepts is right for that culture
   d. morality is ultimately a matter of taste

6. **The most counterintuitive thing about subjectively based theories of morality is that they _____.**
   a. cannot take into account moral disagreement
   b. say moral judgments are neither true nor false
   c. say morality is dictated by the passions
   d. say our moral judgments are not about objective moral facts

7. A projection theory of moral judgment says that _____.
    a. our moral judgments are really about facts pertaining to our sentiments
    b. we intend to refer to our sentiments when making moral judgments
    c. reason and the passions are both used in making moral judgments
    d. moral facts in the world would have to have their own motivational power

8. Nihilism in metaethics is the view that _____.
    a. there is no such thing as morality
    b. there are no values worth pursuing
    c. everyone is morally wrong
    d. there are no moral facts

9. Error theory is primarily motivated by the idea that _____.
    a. moral facts, if they existed, would have to be facts with built-in motivational power
    b. there is so much moral diversity that there is no way to know who is right
    c. moral motivations are inherently subjective
    d. people are mostly wrong about morality

10. Expressivism in metaethics says that _____.
    a. all moral judgments are correct
    b. all moral judgments are incorrect
    c. moral judgments are neither correct nor incorrect
    d. moral judgments refer to facts about the individual

PARTS ONE AND TWO TEST

1. **Which of the following is a philosophical question?**
   a. Why does anything exist at all?
   b. What are the fundamental laws of the universe?
   c. Do most people believe that there are moral facts?
   d. How much do moral judgments vary between cultures?

2. **What is meant by *consistency* in philosophy?**
   a. Having plausible arguments
   b. Not contradicting yourself
   c. Making commitments to principles
   d. Never changing your mind

3. **Which of the following is an ethical question?**
   a. How many abortions are performed in the world each year?
   b. What is the crime rate in countries that do not practice capital punishment?
   c. What rights do women have now as compared to a century ago?
   d. Is it ever permissible to take someone's life against his or her will?

4. **Which of the following is an epistemological question?**
   a. What sorts of people believe in an afterlife?
   b. Why do people forget most of the things they learn?
   c. What does it take for a true belief to qualify as knowledge?
   d. How much philosophy does the average person know?

5. **Which of the following is a metaphysical question?**
   a. What does it take for several things to compose one thing?
   b. How many solar systems in our galaxy have planets in them?
   c. How long ago did the universe begin to exist?
   d. What happens to all the energy in the universe?

6. **Which of the following questions is best addressed by value theory?**
   a. What investments will pay off the most ten years from now?
   b. Have I chosen a suitable career?
   c. How can I make the most money?
   d. When is it permissible to break the law?

7. **Which of the following questions is best addressed by normative ethics?**
   a. Why are some people immoral?
   b. Is it ever wrong to break a promise?
   c. Do most people think their ethical judgments are fact-based?
   d. How does a child learn the difference between right and wrong?

8. **Which of the following questions is best addressed by metaethics?**
   a. How do most people go about making difficult decisions?
   b. How much moral reasoning can a child engage in?
   c. Is torture ever morally permissible?
   d. What is the nature of moral disagreement?

9. **Which of the following questions is a concern of applied ethics?**
   a. What do most people mean by *happiness*?
   b. What would be the consequences of legalizing drugs?
   c. Could terrorism ever be morally justified?
   d. How do dictatorships stay in power?

10. **Consider the following argument:**
    1. **Horses have hooves.**
    2. **Some dogs are brown.**
    Therefore, some horses are brown.
    This argument is _____.
    a. invalid
    b. valid and sound
    c. sound but invalid
    d. valid but unsound

11. **Consider the following argument:**
    1. **All beverages are carbonated.**
    2. **Orange juice is a beverage.**
    Therefore, all orange juice is carbonated.
    This argument is _____.
    a. invalid
    b. valid and sound
    c. sound but invalid
    d. valid but unsound

12. Consider the following piece of reasoning: "If I get sick tomorrow, then I will lose my job. I won't lose my job. Therefore, I won't get sick tomorrow." This inference is _____.
    a. a valid use of modus ponens
    b. a valid use of modus tollens
    c. an instance of the fallacy of denying the antecedent
    d. an instance of the fallacy of affirming the consequent

13. Consider the following piece of reasoning: "If my DVD player works, then we'll watch a movie. My DVD player doesn't work. Therefore, we won't watch a movie." This inference is _____.
    a. a valid use of modus ponens
    b. a valid use of modus tollens
    c. an instance of the fallacy of denying the antecedent
    d. an instance of the fallacy of affirming the consequent

14. Consider the following piece of reasoning: "If you drove your car here, then its engine will be warm. Its engine is warm. Therefore, you drove your car here." This inference is _____.
    a. a valid use of modus ponens
    b. a valid use of modus tollens
    c. an instance of the fallacy of denying the antecedent
    d. an instance of the fallacy of affirming the consequent

15. Consider the following piece of reasoning: "If birds fly, then I can speak French. Birds do fly. Therefore, I can speak French." This inference is _____.
    a. a valid use of modus ponens
    b. a valid use of modus tollens
    c. an instance of the fallacy of denying the antecedent
    d. an instance of the fallacy of affirming the consequent

16. One pursues value theory with the goal of _____.
    a. figuring out what is most important in life
    b. determining what morality is
    c. appreciating life more fully
    d. determining which activities are worthwhile

17. **An instrumental good is one that** _____.
    a. leads to some other good
    b. is only good when it is experienced
    c. is important for its own sake
    d. has value independently of anything else

18. **Whatever ultimate value we have in life, it must be** _____.
    a. necessary to sustain life
    b. unrelated to anything else
    c. the basis of an explanation for everything we do
    d. something that brings an experience of well-being

19. **According to ethical egoism,** _____.
    a. whatever you want will also benefit other people
    b. you should never consider the desires of other people
    c. it is always ethical to do whatever is in your own interests
    d. you should think of yourself as always doing whatever is ethical

20. **A weakness of consequentialism is that it** _____.
    a. requires too many rules
    b. does not take into account the intention with which an action is done
    c. cannot assign moral responsibility to those who act
    d. cannot explain why many actions that we would consider wrong are wrong

21. **The Euthyphro dilemma is a dilemma between** _____.
    a. objective moral facts and subjective judgments
    b. God's commands being arbitrary and God having to answer to a higher authority
    c. God's commands being unknowable and God's commands being too difficult
    d. God's existence and God's nonexistence

22. **Kant's duty-based normative theory maintains that morality can be explained in terms of** _____.
    a. virtue
    b. consequences
    c. sentiments
    d. rationality

23. **A weakness of cultural relativism is that** _____.
    a. it cannot explain why moral codes vary between cultures
    b. it cannot adjudicate moral disagreements between individuals
    c. nothing that a culture accepts can be condemned by another culture
    d. an individual is always right within his or her culture

24. **According to David Hume's view of human nature,** _____.
    a. matters of fact have no motivating power
    b. any sentiment that a person has is fitting
    c. human passions are unreliable
    d. moral judgments are all in error

25. **A weakness of expressivism is that it** _____.
    a. does not account for the role of emotions in moral judgments
    b. cannot explain why moral disagreements are hard to resolve
    c. concludes that all moral judgments are incorrect
    d. has difficulty accounting for moral reasoning

Part Three

Applied Ethics

chapter **6**

Civil Liberties

In this chapter, you will learn the following:

- The reasons for valuing liberty
- Possible reasons for restricting liberty
- How to think about questions of overall justice
- The difference between an action's morality and legality

This chapter begins Part Three of this book, where we will finally look at specific ethical issues and how various arguments have been applied to them. You will recognize things you learned in Parts One and Two; namely, how the logic of arguments works and specific normative or other value theory perspectives. What is left in this book is simply to learn by example how they bear on particular arguments. This chapter introduces how to think about applied ethics in one of the most basic ways—with regard to freedom, morality, and the law.

Classical Liberalism

Virtually all known societies in the world are governed in some way. The method of government shows what values are most esteemed in that society. Most major civilizations throughout history have been governed by a strong authority from above, such as a king or an emperor. This powerful ruler would often have a sort of "cult" attached to him or her, and the entire population would more or less live in servitude for the sake of this leader's glory. So the values of such societies as reflected in their governance would be those of service to an all-powerful leader. In such settings, each person's greatest good would be considered to be fulfilled in service to the nation's leader.

In modern times, absolute monarchies have gone by the wayside, although the twentieth century saw the rise (and fall, thankfully) of totalitarian states such as Nazi Germany and Soviet Russia with their all-powerful governments. The lives of people living under such governments were entirely oriented toward service to the state, and just as in an absolute monarchy, the wishes and well-being of individuals for their own sake were not valued at all. The Western intellectual tradition as it pertains to governments, however, takes it as a given that totalitarian and other absolutist forms of government are inherently wrong, because they devalue what should really be valued and prevent people from achieving well-being. The tradition in political and social philosophy that examines the value of liberty in society and investigates why it is valued is known as *liberalism*. This word is often used in a political setting to place a person in a certain "philosophical" camp with regard to what kinds of laws or policies he or she is likely to favor, but in political and social philosophy the term means something different. Here, it is used in a more high-level sense to mean valuing liberty as opposed to coercion or restraint. So almost everyone in our society and other Western or westernized societies is a liberal in this sense.

When most people praise the value of liberty, they treat it as though it were an intrinsic value (see Chapter 3 on intrinsic versus instrumental value). But when philosophers think of the value of liberty (accorded to it by liberalism), they typically think about its instrumental worth: they want to know what, specifically, liberty is good for. The instrumental value of liberty—what it is good for—is actually not far removed from the value of liberty itself. The range of possible answers to this question, in fact, can be put simply in terms of the question "What do we value such that it would *not* be possible without civil (that is, societal) liberty?"

What Would Not Be Possible Without Civil Liberty?

Liberal theories of value attempt to answer the question of what liberty is good for: What is it that we value in life such that civil liberty is required to uphold the possibility of attaining that value? Chapter 3 discussed that the main divide between theories of value were hedonism, which defines value in purely subjective terms (how things seem to individuals), and eudaimonism, which values an objective good that transcends any particular feeling of happiness and defines value in objective terms (without reference to how things may seem). Analogously, within liberal theories of value there is the opposite pull between subjectivist and objectivist views.

The main objectivist view of the value of liberty is that the point of liberty is for individuals to reach their full potential. Without liberty, this may not be possible, since people's lives may instead be forcibly oriented toward things that have nothing to do with their own inherent potential, and they may be treated as existing merely to serve the state. According to the objectivist view, liberty is valued so that everything possible may be done to secure the possibility of people maximizing their potential. Thus, the most excellent, or perfect, society (in terms of its individuals) is that for which liberty is maximized. This view is sometimes called *perfectionism*.

Perfectionism says that the value of liberty is basically the same thing for everyone: even though each person's potential is different, the single value of allowing the maximization of whatever that potential is, is the one value that liberty is good for. Another viewpoint is *subjectivism*, according to which each individual's ultimate value will simply be whatever seems good to them. Subjectivism doesn't just say that people *think* that what's best for them is best for them—that much is undeniable—but that whatever makes people feel happy really *is* what's best for them and what *should* be valued for that person. Subjectivism can allow that if all a certain person wants to do in life is collect marbles (even if fulfillment of the person's greatest potential would lie in doing something else), then whatever allows the person to collect marbles is to be valued. In other words, allowing each person to do whatever subjectively seems best to him or her is what makes liberty valuable. This also means that the fundamental reason that liberty is valued will be different for each individual, as each person's subjectively defined value differs from the value of others.

The reason subjectivism says that the value of liberty is different rather than essentially the same for each person is because, according to this view, the definition of value is to be given subjectively rather than objectively. In this connection, recall the discussion in Chapter 3: if you think about the idea of objective value, it makes sense that there would be just one intrinsic ultimate value rather than a plurality of them "out there," independent of each other. This is what perfectionism says: perfection is the single objective value (even if it's idealized, such that actual perfection can never really be reached). On the other hand, when you open the door to a subjectively defined value of liberty, you have to accept that whatever people *think* is the value of their liberty *is* the value of their liberty, period. And you'll inevitably get differing views from different people as to what that value is; hence, with subjectivism, there will inevitably be many answers as to value instead of only one.

Liberty: Negative and Positive Definitions

In addition to the question of how liberty is valued in particular, there are various approaches to defining exactly what liberty is. In contrast to asking *why* we value liberty and what it is worth to us, this takes a step back and instead asks what we are talking about when we talk about liberty. We ask this question so that we will recognize what it is when we see it, and this is sort of prerequisite to being able to ask what we value liberty for.

It seems as though it would be easy enough to define liberty, but there are two possible ways of doing so, and they pull in opposite directions. One of them is the *negative* conception of liberty: to define something negatively is essentially to define it in terms of the *lack* of something else rather than as a thing in itself. The negative definition of liberty is perhaps the most natural: the lack of coercion to do and lack of restraint from not doing any particular thing (Gaus and Courtland 2010: §1.2). We may be at perfect liberty, according to this definition, without doing much at all; the important thing is that we *could* do any number of things. The negative definition of liberty thus works without having to refer to any particular thing that we actually do. Rather, the fact that we are not restrained from doing so by outside forces is sufficient to say we have liberty.

The negative conception of liberty is easy to formulate, but many philosophers would prefer a *positive* conception—a definition in terms of something that *is* rather than in terms of the lack of something. To thinkers who hold that liberty itself is supposed to be closely related to an ultimate value to be pursued by society, it's easy to see why a positive definition of it would be more satisfying. Positively defined conceptions of liberty, of which there are a few closely related varieties, involve what a person actually does in life. According to this view, the exercise of our freedom thus defines it, particularly with regard to self-determination. A person who has used his or her ability to live reflectively and with his or her best long-term interests in mind—as opposed to simply having this liberty but living in easy conformity with others—is truly at liberty (Gaus and Courtland 2010: §1.2). Whereas the negative definition of liberty has it that anyone with the freedom to exercise self-determination is equally free, whether they actually exercise it or not, the positive definition has the advantage that it can give grounds for saying that the person who does exercise his or her liberty actually *has* more liberty. Thus, the positive definition in itself already points to an excellent candidate for what is supposed to be valuable about liberty: the opportunity to live out our own potential to the fullest.

 Still Struggling

To say that civil liberty has an objective value is not to say that it doesn't matter that liberty may lead to a subjective sense of happiness. Rather, it simply means that no particular subjective measure needs to be brought into play to define what the value of liberty is. The objective value would be just as it is, even if no one happened to think it was valuable.

Liberty in Society

Classical liberal thought places paramount importance on civil liberty as the best way to ensure the well-being of individuals in society. The principle to which the liberal is thereby committed is something that has been called the fundamental liberal principle: "Freedom is normatively basic, and so the onus of justification is on those who would limit freedom, especially through coercive means" (Gaus and Courtland 2010: §1.1). It is "fundamental" because all other principles that fall within the purview of liberalism will stem from it in some way and because of the prime value placed on liberty: if liberty is the ultimate value, or the only way to secure the ultimate value, then it should be pursued and secured for society. This is what it means for something to be normatively basic—that it should be pursued as the highest priority.

The second part of this principle, the "onus of justification," says that good reasons need to be given for any restriction placed on civil liberties. This is because, due to the prime value of liberty, we want to ensure that whatever ultimate value liberty is necessary to secure (whether according to perfectionism or subjectivism), restrictions on liberty do not hamper that value's attainment. Because of the importance of liberty as the only way to secure this ultimate value, wherever liberty is limited, there is always a possibility of its value not being reached. This is where the onus of justification comes from: whenever restrictions on liberty are proposed, they have to be justified specifically to make sure that they do not trample on whatever is valuable about liberty.

So given a presumption of liberty within a liberal civil society, the next question to be addressed is "What legal restrictions on individual behavior should there be, and why?" The "why" part is the justification that must be given, due to the onus, or burden of proof, placed on the person or group that would restrict liberty. What decides the answer to this question is the particular conception of liberty that is in play. A philosophy of liberty will include what positive value is placed on liberty, and upholding this value determines what restrictions on liberty will be acceptable.

Mill on Liberty

The most obviously desired restrictions would be those on individual behavior that hurts other people. This is perfectly consistent with, and even required by, the need to uphold the value of individual well-being. So most liberal philosophers agree that such restrictions are not only acceptable but required for a civil society founded on liberal principles. Next we must ask whether there ought to be restrictions to prevent people from hurting *themselves*, even if such actions do not hurt others. You could try to argue that because individuals won't be able to meet their potential if they make poor choices, preventing them from hurting themselves is required to uphold the possibility of individual well-being and self-determination (if this is thought to be the ultimate value of liberty).

But you could also make a case that it actually makes more sense for a liberal civil society not to place restrictions on the liberty of individuals to make poor choices for themselves. The case for this position was made powerfully and influentially by the nineteenth-century British philosopher John Stuart Mill in his *On Liberty* (1978). Mill's conclusion came from a positive conception of liberty, according to which the good of individual self-determination is only fully realized when the individual completely "owns" the entire course of action by which he or she takes advantage of liberty to fulfill his or her potential. That is, if someone does well only because he or she has been restrained from doing otherwise, then that person is not realizing his or her potential for self-determination to the fullest. The full potential of a free person, according to Mill, can only be realized if the individual chooses *against* engaging in self-destructive behavior in favor of taking full advantage of his or her liberty. According to this view, to reap the full benefits of liberty, the individual must not only be free to take advantage of liberty but choose to do so as well. A person must therefore be *free to choose*; if he or she is not free to choose, the full value of liberty is prevented from coming to fruition. Thus, as Mill wrote,

> The interference of society to overrule [the individual's] judgment and purposes in what only regards himself must be grounded on general presumptions; which may be altogether wrong, and even if right, are as likely as not to be misapplied to individual cases, by persons no better acquainted with the circumstances of such cases than those are who look at them merely from without. In this department, therefore, of humans affairs, Individuality has its proper field of action. (Mill 1978: Ch. 4)

Mill concluded that the ideal situation with regard to individual liberties is basically as represented in Figure 6.1: civil liberties should only be restricted if doing so enhances individual rights. This conclusion and the principle from

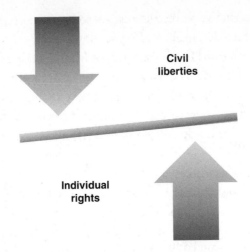

FIGURE 6.1 According to John Stuart Mill's model of civil liberty in society, liberties should be restrained *only* if doing so enhances individual rights. Thus, individual rights must be balanced with considerations that prevent the exercise of one's rights from hindering other people's exercise of their rights. This makes it acceptable to restrain people from hurting others but not to restrain them from hurting themselves.

which it stems leave quite a bit of leeway as to how it should be applied; people may vary in their views of what might count as an "individual right." Many drugs are illegal in most countries, presumably to prevent people from doing great harm to themselves. But someone who shared Mill's view on civil liberties may oppose the criminalization of certain drugs as restricting individual rights. But the criminalization of drugs could also be defended on the basis of preserving the individual rights of people to live in a society where there is not free and open abuse of drugs. Mill actually had a response to this line of thought—if people are free to make poor choices for themselves, the consequences of those choices will be more easily visible and serve as a lesson to others to help them make better choices for themselves.

Suffice it to say that Mill's principle provides one model for thinking about civil liberties. Even if people disagree on certain cases, the principle may still serve as common ground to enable them to dialogue meaningfully on the issue. Recall from Chapter 2 one of the basic benefits of making an argument that uses a general principle: if two people share a commitment to that principle but disagree on a particular issue, they at least have the potential of reaching an agreement on that issue based on how the principle applies.

The positive principle of self-determination that Mill made such important use of is quite similar to one that is emphasized in ethical egoism (see Chapter 4)—the individual is the one most interested in his or her own good and the most competent (if anyone is) to determine what that good is. Mill was apparently not an ethical egoist, however. Rather, he put that principle to use in determining what is best for everyone in society as a whole, not just for an individual. Yet similar to an ethical egoist, Mill's positive principle of liberty led him to conclude that it is worse to constrain individuals' liberty on matters pertaining only to them than for individuals to make poor choices and ruin their lives as a result. Thus, in terms of normative theory (see Chapter 4), Mill was evidently not a consequentialist.

Rawls on Justice

Another major concern in liberal social theory, besides that of liberty itself, is the issue of justice. Like the concept of liberty, justice falls within the purview of social and civil ethics, because it pertains in a basic way to a society as a whole, taking into account how an entire society functions. As in the case of liberty, certain general questions can be asked about justice, such as what it is, why we value it, and how to put it into practice. Answers are relatively easy with regard to the first two questions: we intuitively recognize when justice has been violated and have a basic moral commitment to the idea that injustice is morally bad and to be avoided. (More than this could be said, but in this context, we will be content with a little oversimplification.) The third question, which requires us to know what the basic features of justice are and what it looks like when implemented in a society, is the stuff of full-blown theories of social ethics.

John Rawls had just such a theory, which attempted to state the conditions to be met within a society to prevent any injustices from arising between groups. First of all, it needs to be stated that justice is an essentially relational idea about the distribution of goods between people or groups of people. The basic idea of distributive justice can be understood even by young children: if you give some children in a group more cookies than you give the others, those with fewer cookies will protest at the injustice of the inequality. The basic idea involved in justice thus seems to be "If people are treated differently without a good reason, this is unjust." Thus, what would be just to treat people differently only if there is a relevant difference in those who are treated in some exceptional way. Rawls spelled this out and assigned central importance to it. It is known as the *difference principle*, which basically says that there ought to be no difference in those people that justifies their differential treatment (Rawls 1971).

To apply the difference principle overall, according to Rawls, the default arrangement of opportunities and wealth must be equally distributed to all. For any inequalities to be just, they must be present to best further the interests of those who are least well-off economically. For example, lower-income individuals are taxed at a lower rate than those with higher incomes because it is the best way to ensure that the opportunities of the least well-off, who earn the lowest incomes, are maximized. Overall, Rawls's favored scheme is meant to ensure that no advantaged social group has those advantages at the cost of another group. If it did, the equilibrium would be upset and would have to be restored by application of the difference principle, which would mean that if the distribution of wealth should ever change in a direction away from less-advantaged groups, these groups would have to be recompensed.

Still Struggling

Justice is a different sort of concept from liberty, because unlike liberty, you may only be able to define it in negative terms. Justice is the lack of injustice, so conditions for the existence of justice have to specify what it would take to prevent inequality or at least say what other conditions would make inequality acceptable. This is what Rawls's difference principle is all about.

Legality and Morality

When thinking about ethics and laws overall, it is important to keep in mind that legality and morality are not the same thing. However, they are related in certain ways that constrain the possible relationships between what is considered immoral and what should be illegal. As this chapter stated at the outset, liberal social philosophy holds that it would be immoral to make so many things illegal that it would restricts people's liberties, as in the case of societies ruled by totalitarian governments. But a large part of the motivation anyone has for making a type of action illegal is almost always that the action is immoral. (From the other side of the coin, if something is ethically proper, it's presumably going to be legal as well.) Yet if something is deemed immoral, that usually isn't considered sufficient grounds for making it illegal in a liberal society; people are given the right to act immorally, especially in ways that only abuse themselves. Thus, there is a gap between legality and morality: things that are made illegal are considered immoral, but not all immoral actions are going to be illegal. A corollary of this is that if something is legal, it does not necessarily follow that it is ethical.

We have, then, a scheme that tells the relation of entailment between the moral and the legal; although something's being legal does not entail its being ethical, the converse does seem to hold. The scheme looks like this:

M. If something is moral, then it will also be legal.

Recall the rules of logical inference from Chapter 2. As applied to this situation, from the truth of M, you cannot infer that if something's legal, it is moral. That would be to commit the fallacy of affirming the consequent. Likewise, concluding from M that if something is immoral, it is also illegal would be fallacious, a case of denying the antecedent.

One of the valid inferences you can make with M is to apply modus tollens and turn it into a somewhat different conditional. This is called the *contrapositive* of the original conditional M, and it is obtained by starting with the negation of the consequent of M and proceeding validly to the negation of its antecedent, by which we obtain I:

I. If something is illegal, then it will also be immoral.

I states what is supposed to be the case. It does not mean that merely the fact of something's being illegal *makes* it immoral. Rather, it just gives the presumption that if something is made illegal, it is because that something is immoral. It is quite possible for the principle on which this presumption is based to be abused. For example, in the Nazi regime, it was illegal to hide Jews from SS death squads, but most of us agree that in spite of its being illegal in *that* setting, it was certainly moral to do so. This simply points to a case of a bad law. I is based on the presumption that laws are at least supposed to further everyone's good overall somehow, and this is the way good laws are expected to be set up.

So when people say things like, "You can't legislate morality," they certainly don't mean that laws aren't based on ethics. Rather, they're saying the whole of morality can't be encoded directly into the legal system, thereby making everyone as moral as possible. This reflects the basic principles of liberalism itself. One of these principles is that we should allow for people with somewhat different moral codes to coexist in the same society. To ensure this is possible, we don't want to make things illegal that some portion of society doesn't even consider immoral. Instead, the realm of the illegal will encompass more or less what everyone will agree is immoral. And we can see why this should be in a liberal society, whose laws will be ideally based on what almost everyone agrees should be the laws.

Another, more directly relevant principle that applies here is that of John Stuart Mill, which is that even if everyone agreed on all of morality (which is perfectly compatible with saying that some people are immoral and that everyone agrees they are immoral, even the immoral ones themselves), people should still be free to act immorally so long as they do not harm others. It may be moral for a civil society to permit certain actions, but the fact (if it is a fact) of their being immoral would still remain.

Chapter Summary

Liberalism is the name for the social philosophy on which all of contemporary Western society is based. It says that a presumption should be granted in favor of as much individual liberty as possible; if limits are placed on individuals' liberty to do as they please, those limits will need specific justification. Along with the guiding principle of liberty being maintained to ensure the greatest possibility for individuals to maximize their own potential, liberalism also gives great importance to justice—ensuring that no one's opportunities are maximized at the expense of others' opportunities. Liberal societies seek to enact laws that best uphold individual rights for the most people, with no particular preference to the moral code of any one group. Thus, even if a certain group of people think that certain actions should be illegal, maintaining civil liberties for society at large may require keeping such things legal.

QUIZ

1. Liberalism in social philosophy is the view that _____.
   a. there should be a presumption in favor of people's right to do as they please
   b. higher incomes should be taxed more than lower incomes
   c. all people should be treated equally
   d. abortion should be legal

2. Perfectionism in liberal theory is the distinctive view that _____.
   a. the value of liberty is for individuals to meet their greatest potential
   b. liberty is the most perfect value to be attained in life
   c. liberty is necessary to attain a more perfect society
   d. even imperfect societies will be made perfect by liberty

3. A negative definition of liberty _____.
   a. defines liberty in terms of something bad
   b. defines liberty in terms of a lack of something else
   c. states what will occur if liberty is not upheld
   d. states what liberty does not have to involve

4. A philosophy of liberty will always include _____.
   a. a set of laws that are to be recommended for a liberal society
   b. a recommendation for the best way to maintain liberty
   c. a reason for why liberty is valued
   d. a metaethics theory that explains what liberty means

5. According to the fundamental liberal principle, the onus of justification is placed on _____.
   a. the liberal philosopher to explain why liberty is valuable
   b. the individual to justify why his or her actions should be permitted
   c. the society that would treat all individuals as equal
   d. the society that would place restrictions on liberty

6. John Stuart Mill's liberalism holds that the only laws that should be made are those that _____.
   a. restrict the liberty of individuals
   b. uphold individual rights
   c. ensure equality for the most people
   d. keep people from hurting themselves

7. Mill's most fundamental reason for rejecting certain kinds of laws is
   that _____.
   a. laws should keep people from making poor choices in their lives
   b. everyone's liberty to do whatever he or she pleases should be upheld at all costs
   c. it is worse to have your own interests interfered with than to be kept from hurting
      yourself
   d. the purpose of having laws is to ensure that people attain their maximum potential

8. On the topic of justice, the primary question that social philosophers are concerned with is _____.
   a. what it is
   b. why it is important
   c. what conditions will ensure that it is obtained
   d. how to correct particular cases of injustice

9. Rawls's difference principle states that _____.
   a. each individual should make a difference in the society in which he or she lives
   b. there should be a difference in how people are treated based on their income
   c. it is unjust for some people to be richer than others
   d. if a group of people is treated differently, it should be because of some other difference
      in that group

10. Which of the following conditional statements should be considered true in a
    liberal society?
    a. If something is legal, it should be considered moral.
    b. If something is considered moral, it should be legal.
    c. If something is immoral, it should be illegal.
    d. If something is illegal, it thereby becomes immoral.

chapter 7

Abortion

CHAPTER OBJECTIVES

In this chapter, you will learn the following:

- The primary arguments for and against the morality of abortion, and how they potentially lead to a standoff

- Arguments for and against the morality of abortion that seek to transcend the standoff

Everyone agrees there ought to be laws that protect people from hurting other people. This is because everyone agrees that it is wrong to hurt other people. Not everyone agrees, however, on how far the morally protected status of "people" should be applied. Of course, people are humans, but are all humans "people" in that special, morally protected sense? Some say yes, and others say no; the area where this disagreement comes out most sharply is in the issue of abortion—the killing of an unborn embryo or fetus. In the United States, abortion has been legal since 1973. But as discussed in the previous chapter, the fact that something is legal does not mean it is moral. The fact that abortion is legal is due to the lack of unanimity as to its immorality. If there were a reasonable degree of unanimity, presumably it would become illegal again.

Those who argue for the immorality of abortion would presumably want it to become illegal again, and those who defend its moral acceptability are those who would have it stay legal. But questions of morality go deeper than questions of legality and have to be settled first. People can argue (and have argued) the moral status of abortion on various grounds. This chapter gives a survey of some of the major approaches and the various principles they call on to achieve resolution on the issue.

The Most Straightforward Argument For, and Against, Abortion

Remember that the aim of any philosophical argument is to get people who disagree with a certain conclusion to change their minds. A philosophical argument does this by bringing into play some principle that has the following characteristics: (1) it applies to the issue at hand, and (2) the person disagreeing with the conclusion might already accept the principle as it applies to issues other than the issue in question.

In the case of abortion, the principle most often used to argue against it is a pretty obvious one: whatever makes it wrong to kill innocent people would also be supposed to apply to abortion, making it wrong to kill unborn innocent people.

Fetuses Are Humans, and Humans Are Persons

The most straightforward argument against abortion is one that was given in Chapter 2 as an example of a logically valid argument. It is made often in a variety of forms, and it is based on a commonality that the arguer wants to establish between the immorality of killing in general and that of the case of abortion. A basic version of it runs thus:

1. Fetuses are innocent human beings.
2. It is immoral to kill innocent human beings.

Therefore, it is immoral to kill fetuses.

What makes the argument work—what makes it logically valid—is the implied involvement of a general moral principle. It says that whatever makes it wrong to kill innocent human beings also applies in the case of unborn human beings, making killing unborn human beings wrong in exactly the same way. It holds that it would be inconsistent to maintain that it is wrong to kill innocent humans but acceptable to kill unborn humans. The threat of inconsistency that would be involved in accepting the premises of the argument but denying its conclusion comes from the argument's validity. It forces someone to make a choice between denying one of the premises or accepting the conclusion.

So if we want to deny the conclusion, we have to deny at least one of the premises of the argument. But which one? Suppose we agree that it is wrong to kill innocent human beings—period. We may think that whatever is wrong with the argument is in how it applies specifically to abortion. In that case, we may wish to call premise 1 into question. Are fetuses innocent? It would be hard to deny that they are. Are they human beings? The criterion for deciding whether something is human is biological (this point has been emphasized by Noonan 1970), so it is here that the opponent of abortion would seem to find a particularly strong point on which to stand. All he or she needs to do is to point to the scientific, biological criterion of "specieshood," which is really not debatable.

Fetuses Are Humans, but Not All Humans Are Persons

If we want to deny the conclusion that abortion is as wrong as killing an adult human, we may well want to leave premise 1 of the stated argument alone. That leaves premise 2. But how on earth can we deny that it is always wrong to kill innocent human beings? We could try to preserve the sentiment behind the thought that it is wrong to kill innocent human beings by slightly rephrasing it. According to this line of thought, what makes it wrong to kill innocent human beings—in ordinary cases in which we would invoke that principle—is not that the beings being harmed are human (which merely needs a biological criterion to confirm) but that they are persons (or more informally, *people*). So we might say that premise 2 is true only if *human* means not merely the biological entity, but "a fully-fledged member of the moral community" (Warren 1973). The pertinent question, then, is not whether a fetus is a human being in the biological sense, but whether a fetus is a full-fledged member of the moral community.

Philosopher Mary Anne Warren explored this issue and gave some reasons for thinking that an embryo or a fetus should not be considered a person in this sense of a "fully-fledged member of the moral community." The traits she lists as some of the "most central to the concept of personhood" include consciousness, reasoning, self-motivated activity, the capacity to communicate, and having the concept of self. Not all of these are necessarily crucial, nor is having them all necessarily sufficient to attain personhood. We could revise this list in any number of ways or challenge whether any definitive list could even be made. However, Warren's point is simply that a "person" is someone for whom recognition of moral rights is due and that an embryo or a fetus clearly seems to lack some of the important characteristics with which we would naturally associate this sense of personhood. Therefore, so the point goes, there is reason to doubt whether an unborn human is the kind of being to whom moral rights are owed, even the right not to be killed, especially if the rights of unquestionable people might compete with them.

Warren says that defining a fetus as a human in the moral sense "begs the question" (that is, already assumes the argument's conclusion; see Chapter 2) about abortion by deciding that simply by being human, a fetus has the same moral rights as any other human. That is, the opponent to abortion needs the term *human*, as it appears in both premises of the argument, to mean just that for the argument to be valid. But Warren thinks that the most independently plausible (that is, most plausible without specific reference to abortion) version of premise 2 is actually as the one shown in the following revised argument:

1. Fetuses are innocent human beings.
2. It is immoral to kill innocent human *persons*.

Therefore, it is immoral to kill fetuses.

As mentioned in Chapter 2's discussion about valid and invalid arguments, this revised version of the argument is not valid: even if it is wrong to kill human *persons*, it could still be permissible to kill fetuses if they are not persons. Warren's position is clearly set out: the mere humanity of something is not sufficient to give it the right not to be killed. It has to be a person to have that right. As Warren vividly puts it,

> I think that a rational person must conclude that if the right to life of a fetus is to be based on its resemblance to a person, then it cannot be said to have any more right to life than, let us say, a newborn guppy (which also seems to be capable of feeling pain), and that a right of that magnitude could never override a woman's right to obtain an abortion, at any stage of her pregnancy. (Warren 1973: §3)

This is what someone in Warren's position is committed to, to be consistent with denying the original premise 2 in favor of upholding its revised version. But do we really want to say that a human may have no more right not to be killed than a fish if we adjudge the human not to be a person? We might instead want to say, on grounds unrelated to abortion, that the special, morally protected sense of "person" comes from being human. Therefore, preserving the principle of not killing innocent humans at all would ensure that the goal of not killing innocent human persons is met. The opponent of abortion thus may respond by saying that the unrestricted version of premise 2 as originally given is actually a more independently plausible version than the revised premise 2. We are left, then, with the question of whether we should consider all (biological) humans as worthy of protection or whether only those humans who qualify as persons are due that protection. But how do we decide between these two stances without "begging the question" one way or another as to the conclusion of the whole argument about abortion?

The Stalemate and Some Ways to Move Past It

We can thus see how a kind of stalemate develops between the opponent and the defender of abortion. The abortion opponent needs the term *human* to have moral weight for the conclusion against abortion to go through. But the defender of abortion can't accept this broadly moral sense of *human* as it applies to the unborn. Meanwhile, the criterion of personhood that the abortion defender appeals to is just what he or she needs simply for the purpose of defending abortion—in other contexts, the motivation to restrict the moral sense of "human being" doesn't even arise. And someone who opposes abortion isn't going to agree with that restricted sense of *human*, because he or she already believes that abortion is seriously wrong just because it involves the killing of a human being, period.

Another Antiabortion Approach

The fact of there being a standoff between the most common approaches to attacking and defending abortion was pointed out by philosopher Don Marquis (1989). Marquis's approach was to argue for the immorality of abortion on a somewhat different basis, one that does not depend on potentially contentious uses of the terms *human* and *person*.

Instead, Marquis set out to show that in judging killing to be wrong in the most general sense, we are committed to a certain principle about exactly what it is that makes killing wrong. Suppose you were to beat someone badly, someone whom you simply did not like. This would clearly be wrong. Now imagine you actually killed the person. This would be even more wrong. What makes killing more wrong than merely harming someone? Is it just because you harmed the person even more severely? No. However you may harm someone, the difference seems to be not merely one of degree but of kind: in killing someone, you deprive that person of his or her life. Not the life that the person had up to now, which no one can take away, but his or her future life. On the other hand, some people may want their lives to end sooner rather than later—if they are terminally ill, for example. Without needing to take a firm stand against euthanasia (discussed in Chapter 10), we can at least say that depriving someone of a future life of value (that is, a life that is desirable and not dominated by terminal suffering) is wrong. Marquis said that this is precisely what makes all killing wrong; it is depriving a being of a future life of value.

Now, having adduced a perfectly general principle that explains why killing is wrong in all the cases in which we already think it's wrong, all that's left is to apply it to the case of abortion. Killing an unborn human is wrong, Marquis said, just because it has a future life of value. If that's the reason, then we don't even need to bring in the question of whether or not it is a person yet at the time it is killed. This approach is therefore potentially powerful, particularly because it promises to leapfrog the whole vexed question of personhood that led to the aforementioned stalemate; according to this approach, the matter of whether a fetus is a person *now* is not nearly so relevant as the kind of life that fetus will have in the future.

But is Marquis right about this principle about killing? Is the reason we find killing wrong in general that we're committed to the wrongness of depriving anything of a future life of value? In the case of killing an adult human, if some component of the individual's rights not to be deprived of a future life of value

plays a crucial role in making that killing wrong, then it could be that this result does not actually transfer over to the case of killing a fetus. It could be that, in the end, the wrongness of killing still derives from a violation of a person's rights; therefore, a fetus still does not have the right not to be killed that a "fully fledged person" does. So it may still come down to the moral status of the fetus. As we have seen, the antiabortion and pro-choice sides of the issue are going to disagree about this anyway.

A Novel Pro-Choice Approach

Another approach that could be said to be motivated by the desire to overcome the impasse, or stalemate, that has already been discussed is in Judith Jarvis Thomson's influential defense of abortion (1971). She noted that much opposition to abortion comes from a belief that a fetus has a "right to life." This is a similar argument to the one that has already been discussed, which ascribes moral personhood to the unborn, from which its moral rights would then be derived. Thomson notes a similar impasse to that which figured in Marquis's diagnosis of the usual sort of debate: once the issue is said to hang on the right to life, disagreement on whether abortion is wrong comes down to whether something has such a right. And what way is there to settle whether something actually has a right to life but to loudly proclaim "Yes, it does!" or "No, it doesn't!"

Thomson's solution, like Marquis's, seeks to transcend that debate by moving it onto different ground. But Thomson thinks the defender of abortion can simply grant that fetuses have a right to life. Not because she thinks they really do; in fact, she thinks it's highly debatable, and in any case impossible to determine in any systematic way. But the very debatability of the issue makes it advantageous to move past it and let the issue be decided on other grounds. This is what it means to grant something "for the sake of argument"—if you can make an argument that succeeds even if your opponent's key premises are granted, then you don't even have to worry about challenging those premises. If those premises—the right to life of the fetus, for example—are apparently impossible to establish without already agreeing with one side or the other as to the conclusion, then you can save yourself a lot of time to grant one or more of your opponent's premises, meaning that the conclusion doesn't actually depend on the truth or falsity of those premises.

So Thomson's strategy is to ask, "*Even if* the fetus has a right to life (whatever that may mean), would that guarantee that it should never be killed?" This is a startlingly original strategy, because it is a question that we would ordinarily never think to ask—without much thought, the answer would apparently be yes—in the context of abortion, at least, a right to life just means a right to not be killed in any circumstances. But in an ingenious way, Thomson challenges this assumption by trying to get to the bottom of just what a right to life is, independent of the abortion issue, and what it would entail for someone who has such a right.

An Imaginative Thought Experiment

Thomson tries to bring out some relevant principles to which we are supposedly already committed, as is done in any significant and well-crafted philosophical argument. The tricky part is that, as already noted, few people will have even thought explicitly of such principles, since we are used to thinking of having a right to life as entailing a protection from being killed no matter what. The principles all cluster around the idea that just because something or someone has a right to life does not entail that the life must be preserved at all costs. Thomson brings out this idea through a series of imaginative thought experiments. We are supposed to react to these experiments by intuitively agreeing with a certain conclusion about how to judge the case described. The fact that we agree with the verdict of the thought experiment is meant to show that we're already committed to that principle, even if we've never thought about it before.

The thought experiment that is most central to Thomson's case is as follows: Suppose a famous concert violinist is facing kidney failure and death, and you are the only one who can save her life, by hooking up her body to your own so you both share your kidneys for a certain period of time until the violinist recuperates from her disease. (Why a famous concert violinist? It goes back to the strategy of granting as much as possible to your opponent, if your argument can still succeed. We are supposed to think that a famous concert violinist is a valuable person whose life, all things considered, we would want to save, and then see what a right to life for that person would entail. If it didn't entail the desired conclusion for the right-to-lifer, then neither would the conclusion follow in the case of a being that may be considered much less valuable than the violinist.) A dedicated band of music lovers decides to take things into its own hands by kidnapping you and rendering you unconscious. You awake to find yourself sharing a hospital bed with the famous violinist, who is hooked up to your body so she can share your kidneys. If you disconnect yourself from the violinist, she will die. If you do disconnect and free yourself from this situation into which you were placed without your consent, are you in the wrong? We are supposing that, all things considered, the violinist has a right to life as much as anyone does. But the salient facts of this imaginary situation are supposed to point to the conclusion that even so, the violinist does not have a right to your body, even if that's the only thing that can keep her alive. Therefore, we are meant to react to this experiment by thinking, "No, you're not in the wrong if you disconnect yourself, even if the violinist dies as a result." We are meant to think that a person has a right to his or her body even if someone else's life depends on using it. And we are meant to think that the reason we easily conclude this is because we are committed to a certain principle, which is the whole point of the thought experiment.

The Resulting Argument

The specific principle Thomson is getting at here is as follows: if person A is dependent on person B for sustaining person A's life, the fact of this dependence does not, in and of itself, morally obligate person B to do everything in his or her power to sustain person A's life. The relevant factors of this thought experiment are meant to go right over into the case of abortion: the fetus is dependent on the mother's body for its life, but even if it has a right to life as much as anyone else, the mere fact of this dependence does not obligate the mother to do everything in her power to sustain the fetus's life—that is, carry the pregnancy to term.

To determine how much can be concluded from Thomson's argument, it is important to pay attention to exactly what the conclusion is and how it is reached. Here is how the argument goes in explicit form:

1. A fetus (who we are granting for the sake of argument is a person) is dependent on its mother for sustaining its life.

2. If person A is dependent on person B for sustaining person A's life, the fact of this dependence does not, in and of itself, morally obligate person B to do everything in his or her power to sustain person A's life.

Therefore, the fact of the fetus's dependence on its mother for its life does not, in and of itself, morally obligate the mother to do everything in her power to sustain the fetus's life.

The conclusion includes as an essential feature that the fact of the dependence of the fetus is not sufficient by itself to obligate the mother to carry the pregnancy to term, even if the fetus is granted a right to life. This is the main principle doing the work of the argument, premise 2. The point of the famous violinist and other thought experiments that Thomson spends a generous amount of time putting forward is to establish the truth of this premise (since it is one that would never have occurred to most people before). But it leaves the question open whether there may be some other reason that it would be wrong for the mother to have an abortion (remember that the failure of an argument does not necessarily mean that the conclusion is false—rather, it's that *that* argument did not prove it to be true). Also, the nature of the thought experiment is such that, as applied to pregnancy, it would apply directly to unwanted pregnancy (since the protagonist of the thought experiment was kidnapped and involuntarily attached to the violinist). So the argument could not be taken to show that abortion is always permissible. In fact, Thomson says that a woman who intentionally gets pregnant and then decides on an abortion merely because she subsequently decides to take a long cruise instead would definitely be in the wrong. Part of what gives Thomson's argument strength is that it only means to establish a limited conclusion, which is easier to establish but may not apply to every case where someone might want to have an abortion.

So the conclusion of Thomson's argument is simply meant to challenge the right-to-lifer to show what gives a fetus a right to have its life sustained by its mother no matter what. For, according to the conclusion of the argument, it cannot be because the fetus is dependent on its mother. If so, then we would have concluded that the kidnapped person would be morally obligated to keep sharing his or her kidneys with the famous violinist for as long as it took to get the violinist out of danger. And the conclusion of the argument is a limited one, since it cannot show that abortion is always permissible.

 ## Still Struggling

Any given argument for or against abortion doesn't set out only to establish the moral wrongness or rightness of abortion. It argues by a certain means, using some specific principle that carries over into the exact meaning of the conclusion of the argument. For example, Thomson's argument focuses squarely on whether the fact of a fetus's dependence on its mother's body gives it an absolute right not to be killed. Opponents could still argue against abortion by bringing other principles into play or resist Thomson's specific conclusion by focusing on the specific principles that make her argument work.

Chapter Summary

Arguments for the immorality or morality of abortion come in a variety of forms. Some of the most commonly made arguments seem to require the truth of premises that someone who does not already agree with the conclusion is not likely to accept. This leads to a standoff in the debate, since removing such a deadlock would seem to require the disputants to accept a different conclusion to begin with. Other types of arguments about abortion seek to go beyond the usual disagreements about personhood and the right to life and establish a conclusion in ways that are unrelated to what we may already be committed to simply on the basis of our preexisting position on abortion. As with all philosophical arguments, these may still be inconclusive, or, even if sound, establish only a limited conclusion that does not settle every aspect of the matter.

QUIZ

1. Since abortion is legal, what can we conclude?
   a. Most people think it is moral.
   b. There is likely to be substantial disagreement on the issue.
   c. No one has a good argument against abortion.
   d. Most people think it is immoral.

2. What arguments about abortion are the most effective?
   a. Those that have premises that we are likely to accept regardless of what we already think about abortion
   b. Those that have premises that we are likely to accept only if we already agree with the conclusion
   c. Those that have the strongest, most far-reaching conclusions
   d. Those that rely on a notion of moral personhood

3. For an argument against abortion that has as a premise that it is wrong to kill innocent human persons, a defender of abortion might most effectively respond to the argument by maintaining that _____.
   a. it is morally acceptable to kill innocent human persons
   b. it is not morally acceptable to kill innocent human persons
   c. fetuses are not persons, although they are human
   d. fetuses are not human, although they are persons

4. For an argument defending abortion that has a premise that not all humans are persons, an opponent of abortion might most effectively respond to the argument by maintaining that _____.
   a. fetuses are humans
   b. fetuses are persons
   c. something's being a person should be considered sufficient to protect it from being killed
   d. something's being human should be considered sufficient to protect it from being killed

5. Mary Anne Warren thinks that fetuses should not be considered persons because they _____.
   a. are not really human
   b. have not yet been born
   c. do not meet certain criteria that we associate with personhood
   d. are essentially the same as the unborn of any other species

6. **A stalemate develops in the abortion debate when the disputants can't agree on** _____.
   a. whether abortion is ever permissible
   b. whether the fetus has the moral rights of a person
   c. what makes something human
   d. the purposes for which abortion is performed

7. **Don Marquis thinks that what makes killing wrong in both ordinary cases and abortion is that it** _____.
   a. harms a person
   b. harms a human being
   c. deprives a person of his or her rights
   d. deprives something of the remainder of its life

8. **A weakness in Don Marquis's argument is the question of whether** _____.
   a. a fetus is really a person or not
   b. a fetus has a future life of value or not
   c. it is really wrong to deprive a person of a future life of value
   d. what makes killing wrong actually has to do with a person's rights

9. **The role of thought experiments in Judith Jarvis Thomson's argument defending abortion is to** _____.
   a. bring to light a principle to which we are supposedly already committed
   b. defend the permissibility of abortion in any circumstance
   c. show how not every human has a right to life
   d. show that a fetus is not a person

10. **Which of the following is the conclusion of Thomson's argument in defense of abortion?**
    a. A fetus does not have a right to life.
    b. A woman always has a right to an abortion.
    c. A mother is not obligated to carry every pregnancy to term.
    d. The right to life is forfeited if a woman becomes pregnant without her consent.

chapter 8

Capital Punishment

In this chapter, you will learn the following:

- The main motivations for capital punishment
- The most successful objection to the moral justifiability of capital punishment

Certain things are against the law not only because everyone agrees they are immoral, but because they are especially immoral. In particular, most people think that murder is about the worst sort of crime that can be committed. As long as the law requires punishment for crimes, almost anyone would agree that the worst sorts of crimes require the worst sorts of punishment. This is the main rationale for capital punishment, or the death penalty, the most severe punishment that any government today metes out. This chapter critically examines the primary motivations for capital punishment and discusses whether it fulfills the expectations that motivate it.

Two Faulty Objections to Capital Punishment

First, we need to address a couple of objections to get them out of the way, since they do not succeed as well as they may seem to at first. They fail either by assuming key points about the death penalty or by missing the point and failing to address the motivations for capital punishment.

The Hypocrisy Objection

One objection to capital punishment is that it is essentially hypocritical to condemn a person to death because the person committed murder. If the point of capital punishment is to recognize the seriousness of the crime of murder, so this objection goes, it is inconsistent to recognize the wrongness of murder by killing someone in retaliation—you will simply have added another death to the picture. As one pithy slogan has it, "Why do we kill people who kill people to show that killing people is wrong?" It could be thought of as deeply ironic to carry out a policy of killing people in order to recognize the serious immorality of killing.

But here's a big problem with that objection. If we took it seriously, we would have to apply it across the board to the punishment of every crime. The objection is that you cannot honor the value of life by sentencing a murderer to death. But applying that principle in the case of imprisonment would mean that authorities could not honor the value of personal liberty if they punished people with imprisonment. Nor could authorities fine people a monetary amount while also honoring the value of money as personal property. If the principle on which this objection seems to be based were applied generally (as principles must be), it would lead to some seemingly unacceptable conclusions and thus "prove too much" (Primoratz 1989). That is, to be consistent with the principle the objection cites, we would have to object to all kinds of other punishments on the basis of their taking away valuable things—in other words, simply on the basis of their being punishments. If the objector wants to cite this principle as a justification for his or her opposition only in the case of capital punishment, without applying it to other cases in which it could easily be applied, then he or she would be guilty of hypocrisy.

Another problem with the objection is that it at least seems to rely on a sense of wrongness about killing that makes capital punishment as wrong as straightforward cases of murder. The objector's claim that it is flatly inconsistent to kill people who commit murder seems to assume that capital punishment is the same thing as murder. But whether capital punishment is *morally equivalent* to murder is the whole issue that needs to be decided. Assuming in advance that the two are equivalent in order to argue against the death penalty would be begging the question (see Chapter 2). So opponents cannot sensibly assume in advance that capital punishment is equivalent to murder so they can say that capital punishment is the wrong way to deal with murder. The defender of the death penalty will simply not agree that capital punishment is equivalent to murder. And to someone who already agrees that capital punishment is equivalent to murder, there is no point in making the argument anyway.

The Risk of Wrongful Convictions

Another major point of resistance toward capital punishment is the threat of its being exercised on those who are wrongly convicted under the law, meaning that innocent people end up being killed unjustly. No one thinks it is acceptable for this to happen, and everyone thinks that every possible step should be taken to avoid unjust convictions under the death penalty. But care must be taken to see what bearing this issue has on the in-principle justifiability of capital punishment, because no matter how many innocent people were convicted and subject to the death penalty, this wouldn't do anything to show that capital punishment is not justifiable toward the guilty. This is the question that ultimately needs to be addressed: whether capital punishment is justifiable toward those who are, in fact, guilty of murder. Objecting to capital punishment purely on the basis of the fear that innocent people may be convicted and sentenced to death doesn't help us address this question. Now, you could conclude that the risk of sentencing the innocent to death is too great to even consider the death penalty to be viable, regardless of how it applies to the guilty. But again, this wouldn't address the issue of whether the motivations for the death penalty itself are sound.

The best approach is to grant the proponent of the death penalty that the risk of convicting the innocent is acceptable. (Because, if one or the other of the main justifications for the death penalty is solid, such a justification could well provide the basis for thinking that the risk of convicting the innocent *is* justifiable.) This can be seen as analogous with Judith Jarvis Thomson's strategy of granting the abortion opponent, for the sake of argument, that the fetus has a right to life (see Chapter 7). If capital punishment can be shown to be unjustified with this point (that capital punishment is justifiable even if a few innocents are condemned) granted to the defender, it will turn out that we didn't need to decide the issue based on the risk of executing the innocent anyway. And this would save the opponent of capital punishment a lot of time.

Two Motivations for Capital Punishment

Many people in the United States today support the death penalty. There are two main justifications. One is that having the ultimate penalty helps discourage crimes that merit that penalty. That is, maintaining the death penalty is beneficial overall because it acts as a deterrent to crime. There is also the more general, in-principle reason that the death penalty must be given in certain cases for justice to be upheld when dealing with perpetrators of those crimes. (Of course, some people who support the death penalty may be motivated by both ideas.) We will look at each of these justifications in turn.

The Deterrence Justification

In informal discussions about capital punishment, proponents often say that it acts as a deterrent to crime, or at least to crimes such as murder that would seem to warrant it. The thought seems to be that it is worthwhile and morally justifiable if it has the positive effect of decreasing the crime rate. This justification implies a commitment to consequentialism (see Chapter 4). However, the informal way in which such justifications are normally made makes it uncertain whether the person giving the justification is really committed to consequentialism in other areas as well.

One thing to note, of course, is that whether capital punishment *could* act as a deterrent to violent crime is open to question. It seems to imply that cases often arise in which people who might otherwise be tempted to commit murder will refrain from doing so once they realize the consequences should they get caught. Many murders do not seem to allow for much possibility of this happening, though, either because they are committed in the heat of passion, when the weighing of options is simply not done, or because the people committing murder are motivated enough to do so that they can convince themselves they will get away with it.

Another thing to note about the deterrent justification is even if we were to grant that capital punishment could plausibly act as a deterrent, it seems impossible in practice to *tell* whether capital punishment truly deters violent crime. To do so, you would need to do a controlled experiment, as you do in natural science, to tell whether the exercise of the death penalty lowers the incidence of violent crime from what it would be otherwise.

But it is impossible to settle the issue of what effects capital punishment has on the basis of a controlled experiment. We can compare crime rates between countries that do or do not carry out the death penalty, but too many other factors differ between countries to be able to tell for sure whether it is just the presence or absence of the death penalty that causes a difference in the crime rate. The best that we can say on behalf of this view seems to be that even if we grant the consequentialism needed to justify the death penalty on the basis of its deterrence in principle, it is inconclusive whether it is actually a deterrent.

Capital Punishment as a Requirement of Justice

The sort of justification that most philosophers who support the death penalty tend to give for capital punishment is a strictly "principled" one that does not depend on any deterrent or other outcome attached to it. This defense is based solely on the idea that capital punishment is required in certain cases for justice to be served. In sharp contrast with the consequentialism that seems to underlie the deterrent defense, this justification comes from a normative ethic that is strongly rooted in the notion of duty, such as that of which Immanuel Kant's works are suggestive (see Chapter 4). This ethic says that the way in which injustices have to be redressed—that is, wrongs somehow made right—is that those who are clearly morally wrong under the law need to be punished appropriately. Kant did, in fact, support the death penalty, and for the stated reason that the wrongness of the act of murder is so serious that carrying out capital punishment is the only way in which such an act could possibly be redressed (if anything can).

This defense sees the wrongness of murder as being redressed in the retributive idea of justice—that wrongs require punishment to be meted out to the perpetrator of the immoral act, not to deter future or hypothetical wrongs, but simply to serve the requirements of justice. In other words, if certain wrongs were not redressed with punishment, it would be an injustice. And the requirements of retributive justice are not just that wrongs be punished, but that they be assigned a punishment whose severity somehow matches the severity of the wrong committed. Since the wrongness of murder is thought to be so exceptional and matchless, it is therefore assigned a punishment that is correspondingly exceptional. According to the way in which the concept of justice is appealed to by this position, no other punishment would do; it would actually be unjust *not* to exercise the death penalty for cases that warrant it.

This view of justice places a uniquely high value on human life, which is why murder is assessed as so uniquely immoral as to warrant capital punishment. This justification for the death penalty often comes from traditional biblical views about human life that make it especially wrong to kill humans, because human beings are said to be created in the image of God. But although this tradition is one possible source for the unique value placed on human life that motivates the ultimate punishment for murder, it's not the only one. If a person does not subscribe to the overall Judeo-Christian view of life or does not even believe in God, it would not follow that he or she could not similarly view human life as having unique value (this would be to commit the fallacy of denying the antecedent; see Chapter 2). Such a view would have to come from some source other than religiously based principles. So a justification of the death penalty that involves a unique value placed on human life need not depend on whether this justification is derived from religious or other principles.

The Main Justification for Opposing Capital Punishment

Those who support capital punishment for the justice-driven reasons just discussed defend it on the basis of its being needed in order for justice to be served. The main issue of whether capital punishment is morally justified can be decided on the basis of whether it *is* needed. Because, if it isn't, then this would apparently mean that exercising the death penalty would be too severe, which would presumably be enough to show that it is not morally justified. So the opposition to capital punishment simply has to maintain that it is not needed to uphold justice. If this can be established, then it is a short step to the conclusion that the death penalty, far from being morally required, is actually morally wrong, since it involves taking a life without sufficient reason for doing so.

The justice-based support for capital punishment says it is needed because the redress of crimes such as murder require retributive justice. Moreover, specifically meeting murder with capital punishment would be required by a principle of *equal retribution*—assigning the same penalty for a crime that was involved in the commission of the crime itself. The main line of rebuttal to this point of view says that capital punishment is not needed because equal retribution generally is not necessary for justice to be served. To understand why equal retribution might not be called for, we have to look at the alternatives to it. An alternative would need to ensure that justice is served, even if it is not a case of equal retribution.

The Problem with Equal Retribution

As already stated, the main idea behind retributive justice is that punishments for crimes should be assigned in such a way that their severity matches the moral seriousness of the crimes they're supposed to redress—in other words, let the punishment fit the crime. Capital punishment is supposed to fit this philosophy of criminal punishment in that the guilty person is punished with something as equally bad as his or her crime. Thus, not just retributive justice, but more specifically the justice of *equal* retribution, requires it. The exceptional moral seriousness of murder, for example, is supposed to be due to the exceptional badness of taking human life by murder. The exceptional severity of capital punishment is meant to address and redress the violation of justice involved in a murder. The proponent of capital punishment claims that only the death penalty will do for severely morally bad crimes such as murder—without it, full justice would be left undone. The opponent of the death penalty, however, says that justice can still be done, recognizing and redressing crimes of exceptional moral badness, without exercising capital punishment.

Now the defender of capital punishment already has a reason for thinking it is warranted in at least some cases of murder—both capital punishment and murder involve an intentional depriving of life, so they are required by a justice of equal retribution that is supposed to make the punishment fit the crime. The question that the death penalty opponent must answer, then, is how justice is to be served on murderers if not by capital punishment. To answer this, we have to think about what it takes, in general, for justice to be served.

Recall what was said in Chapter 6 about justice. There is a difference principle involved, in which any difference in treatment between cases has to be justified in terms of some other relevant difference in those cases. It is for this reason that, for example, for two people who had committed the same crime, punishing one of them much more severely than the other would be a violation of justice. One way to correct the injustice would be to punish them both in the same way. Another way would be to show that there was, in fact, a significant difference between the crimes they committed. Justice requires that more severe crimes be punished more severely; this is the difference principle in action.

But does the difference principle specifically require equal retribution? If we look at the basic principle at work in retributive justice, we can certainly see how the theory that equal retribution is the only way to serve justice is open to question. In talking about equal retribution, Mahatma Gandhi has been quoted as saying that "an eye for an eye makes the whole world blind," meaning that retribution only adds to the list of immoral acts committed and does not solve any problems. But even if equal retribution *were* taken to be justified in some other sense, a more fundamental problem is that it seems impossible in principle to construct a complete and internally consistent system of punishment solely on the basis of equal retribution. Whatever principle we take to govern how we determine what punishments are given for which crimes, it has to apply equally to all cases; otherwise, it would not be a principle, but a justification given after the fact for how we want to deal with each case differently. But if we take equal retribution as the general principle for deciding on punishments for crimes, given some examples, we soon come to realize that applying it across the board as an operating principle is highly problematic. Equal retribution would require us to execute murderers, and many think that is perfectly just. But suppose we were to apply it to thieves: equal retribution would seem to require us to steal from thieves. Likewise, it would seem to require us to rape rapists, spy on spies, kidnap kidnappers . . . Does this seem right? Most of us would tend to think that such punishments are absurd, if not also immoral. Equal retribution also seems to give us no clue *how* to punish many other criminals, such as illegal drug users, prostitutes, and air polluters (Nathanson 1987). And not only is it impossible in a practical sense to implement equal retribution for many crimes, but thinking about what's wrong with the types of retributive punishments that we *could* implement seems to show that equal retribution, if taken as a general guiding principle, "tells us neither what people deserve nor how we should treat them when they have done wrong" (Nathanson 1987).

Proportional Justice

An alternative principle to equal retribution that upheld justice in respect of the difference principle would at least need to assign more severe punishments to worse crimes and less severe punishments to less serious crimes. There is, as it turns out, a suitable principle that accomplishes this but does not require equal retribution, or "an eye for an eye." This is *proportional justice*, which aims to assign punishments whose severity does not necessarily match the seriousness of the crime but is proportional to it. What is required for two things to be proportionally related to each other? They must each stand in some relation to a third thing against which they are measured. The additional thing required in each case is simply that there be a standard that says what crime and punishment are the most severe.

Figure 8.1 illustrates how this works. Proportional justice requires that there be a worst crime and a worst punishment and that the worst punishment be given for the worst crime. Beyond that, there is a "sliding scale" that assigns proportionally less severe punishments to proportionally less serious crimes. As long as the most severe crime is given the most severe punishment that the law allows for, the proportional system of justice is maintained, whether that most severe punishment is the death penalty or something else, such as life imprisonment. The difference principle can still be clearly maintained, regardless of what the most severe punishment may be. And such justice may still be considered retributive, as required by the pure need to redress immoral acts by punishing the perpetrator. But retributive justice does not in itself require equal retribution.

The proportional system of justice, unlike equal retribution, does seem to be a workable system for assigning punishments to crimes. It does not require

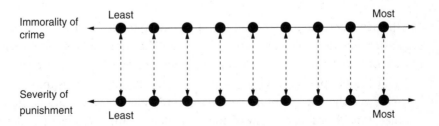

FIGURE 8.1   A proportional system of justice is on a sliding scale from least to most severe punishments, according to the immorality of the crime. Proportional justice in and of itself does not require that the death penalty be the worst punishment that is given out; the worst punishment could be something less severe.

that each crime be given a punishment that is the same as the crime itself. All it requires is a legal system that recognizes a range of crimes that can be ranked in order of degree of immorality and a system of punishments ranked from least to most severe. The punishments are then assigned according to their severity in proportion to the immorality of the crime.

But some people may still want to maintain that the death penalty is required, if not by equal retribution, then by the need to recognize the unique seriousness of murder. In that case, if you had the same punishment—life imprisonment—for murder as for some other crimes, then you would fail to address the crime of murder with due justice, because this would violate the difference principle. In response, you could still maintain, according to the needs of proportional justice, that we need an exceptional penalty for the exceptional crime of murder. But this alone still wouldn't require capital punishment; we would merely need to reserve the most serious punishment for the most serious crime. Proportional justice gives us grounds to do this but not specifically to justify capital punishment.

So the question remains as to whether there is some other reason to require the death penalty. The fact that proportional justice does not actually require the death penalty leaves it open that there *is* some other reason, but the onus is on the defender of capital punishment to clearly state what that reason is: that it is well motivated, comes from a general principle that applies to other areas besides capital punishment in particular, and that it really requires the death penalty specifically for certain crimes.

 Still Struggling

The need for retribution is a consideration having to do with justice. Retributive justice requires that criminals be punished for the immorality of certain actions just because they deserve it. According to this principle, it would be considered unjust not to punish criminals. Retributive justice only requires that there be *some* punishment. The principle of equal retribution, however, goes a step further. It maintains that by way of punishment, the same acts should be done to criminals as they themselves did to others. But authorities can carry out retributive justice without it having to be equal retribution.

Chapter Summary

Various arguments and justifications can be given for and against capital punishment, and some of them are better than others. With some controversial side issues granted for the sake of argument, the main justification for capital punishment is that it is needed to uphold justice. But the specific principle of justice that would require the death penalty in cases of murder is the principle of equal retribution. But when this principle is applied to other possible crimes, it does not seem to work. In light of this, it seems best to conclude that equal retribution is not the correct general guiding principle for governing what punishments are required by justice. Proportional justice, however, is a model that can be applied much more naturally as a general principle. But proportional justice does not require the death penalty—only that the most severe penalty, whatever that may be, be assigned to the most morally serious crime.

QUIZ

1. The hypocrisy objection to capital punishment is based on the inconsistency
   of _____.
   a. exercising the death penalty when we are not morally perfect ourselves
   b. giving equal retribution for murderers but not for other criminals
   c. treating criminals as though they had no rights
   d. exercising the death penalty to punish those who kill

2. One flaw in the hypocrisy objection to capital punishment is
   that _____.
   a. it does not give enough attention to the moral seriousness of murder
   b. it would be hypocritical to enforce other kinds of punishments
   c. the death penalty might be assessed for other reasons besides equal retribution
   d. it does not take into account the possibility of proportional justice

3. The main problem with objecting to capital punishment based on the risk of
   executing the innocent is that _____.
   a. there is no way to have a perfect system of justice
   b. the objection does not tell us whether it is right to execute the guilty
   c. it neglects the possibility that the justice system could be improved
   d. no one wants to execute the innocent anyway

4. Which of the following is *not* a problem with the deterrence justification for
   capital punishment?
   a. It is questionable whether capital punishment actually deters crime.
   b. It is impossible to tell whether capital punishment actually deters crime.
   c. It commits us to a principle of justice by equal retribution that cannot be
      generally applied.
   d. It commits us to a principle of consequentialism that we may not subscribe
      to in general.

5. The justice-driven justification for capital punishment says that the death penalty is needed _____.
   a. because wrongs need to be redressed
   b. to lower the overall crime rate
   c. because proportional justice requires it
   d. to serve as an example to other criminals

6. **Which of the following would *not* be motivated by retributive justice?**
   a. Criminals being given punishments equal to their crimes
   b. Criminals being given punishments proportional to their crimes
   c. Criminals being punished to make them better people
   d. Criminals being punished for the immorality of their crimes

7. **Which of the following objections to capital punishment is *not* based on a principle of justice?**
   a. Capital punishment is excessive and unnecessary.
   b. Capital punishment may result in convicting the innocent.
   c. Carrying out capital punishment on those who kill is hypocritical.
   d. Capital punishment is probably not effective as a deterrent to crime.

8. **What is the main problem with defending capital punishment on the basis of equal justice?**
   a. Equal justice does not necessarily require the death penalty for murderers.
   b. It is hypocritical to kill people in order to recognize the wrongness of murder.
   c. The principle on which it is based cannot serve as a general guideline for punishments.
   d. Equal justice cannot be used to exercise retribution.

9. **Proportional justice requires which of the following?**
   a. A scale of punishments of different severities
   b. Equal retribution for all serious crimes
   c. That criminals be made an example of for their crimes
   d. That the worst crimes be punished as severely as possible

10. **Why does proportional justice not require the death penalty?**
    a. Proportional justice does not require retribution.
    b. Retributive justice allows only for equal retribution.
    c. The death penalty is not possible under proportional justice.
    d. Proportional justice does not require that the death penalty be the most severe punishment.

chapter **9**

Torture

CHAPTER OBJECTIVES

In this chapter, you will learn the following:

- The reasons torture might be defended today and arguments that might be given in favor of its sometimes being morally permissible

- Consequences of considering torture morally permissible in certain cases

Torture, the deliberate inflicting of pain on a person to force his or her coop-
eration, seems obviously unethical. But hypothetical situations can arise in
which people can seriously consider the possibility that it might be necessary
to torture someone to prevent a greater evil from happening. In the face of
such possibilities, philosophers have to weigh whether it would ever, in principle, be morally permissible to use torture.

Reasons Torture Might Be Thought Necessary

The subject of torture is an ugly one for any civilized society and even an
unspeakable one to many people. No one wants to have to think about it. In
some earlier civilizations, victorious armies would torture their vanquished
foes just to show their power over them. This is obviously despicable. Torture was sometimes used in the past to force people to confess to crimes. But
every civilized country today has unequivocal laws against such practices.
Torture also used to be a fairly common form of punishing criminals, but
this is now widely regarded as abhorrent. The U.S. Constitution specifically
forbids it in the Eighth Amendment. But although the use of torture for punishment is ruled out by law, the Constitution does not specifically forbid it for
the purposes of extracting important information (interrogational torture).
The need to obtain facts that may be necessary to save a significant number
of lives provides for a unique setting and the only one in which our society
might ever consider the expedient of torture justifiable.

Interrogational torture is different from torture used to extract a confession in that confessing to a crime involves events in the past, whereas the
aim of interrogational torture is to obtain information about future events
(Luban 2006). Plans for events that will lead to many deaths (say, by an act
of terrorism or war) is the kind of thing that is bad enough to make many
people seriously consider the possibility of doing whatever it takes to prevent
it, should the opportunity arise (especially if only one person needs to be
involved).

To emphasize, the only possible justification for torture under consideration here is that it might be needed to prevent something even worse from
occurring. Even if it were deemed morally acceptable in this case, it would—
at the very best—be considered a "necessary evil." You might suggest that we
already accept other necessary evils that no one likes, because they have to
be done to prevent worse events from happening. So one way of determining

whether torture could be justified at all is to see whether it might fall under a principle we already accept about necessary evils. If this turned out to be the case, you could say, "We already accept such-and-such principle about why this thing, even though bad in and of itself, should nevertheless be allowed, so why not apply that principle to torture as well?" Then, even though no one likes to have to carry out torture, there may still be a way to justify it as acceptable.

A Suggested Parallel to Combat Killing

One example of a necessary evil that most of us already accept is the fact of war. Almost everyone abhors war and wishes there were none, yet we continue to engage in it. This must be because our society shares a collective belief that war, as terrible as it is, is sometimes necessary. You could try to make an argument that this is not just an analogy; perhaps whatever makes killing in wartime acceptable may also make interrogational torture acceptable. You could draw a number of suggestive parallels between the two cases. Philosopher Henry Shue examined this suggestion to see how good an argument could be made from it (Shue 1978).

In wartime, killing in combat takes place because it is necessary to achieve the aims of our own side over those of the other side. And it is assumed that war is only ever engaged in because those aims are very important, such that letting the other side have its way would be unacceptable (such as allowing our country to be conquered by a hostile nation). Similarly, you might think that interrogational torture, if it should be done, would have to be done in cases in which it is the only way to secure something that is all-important.

When there is war, it is only considered acceptable for soldiers to kill enemy combatants. Why is that acceptable? Perhaps because if you are one of those soldiers, you have to kill enemy combatants; otherwise, they will kill *you*. Each side has the opportunity to defend itself, and that is what differentiates combat killing from simply slaughtering defenseless people. Likewise, you might try to draw a parallel between combatants being able to defend themselves and a person being tortured under interrogation being able to stop the torture at any time by giving the torturers the information they want. If this parallel works, then it would allow you to conclude that if combat killing is permissible in time of war, so is interrogational torture, as long as lives are at stake. This conclusion might be reached by an argument like the following, of which a somewhat simpler version was examined in

Chapter 2. For the full version, though, we need an additional assumption: that being tortured is not as bad as being killed. This assumption is necessary because it would show that if a principle makes something bad acceptable, it should certainly make something *less* bad acceptable too. The argument, then, would run like this:

1. Combat killing in wartime is morally acceptable because the combatants are not defenseless.
2. Subjects of interrogational torture are not defenseless.
3. Being tortured is not as bad as being killed.

Therefore, interrogational torture is morally acceptable.

Premise 1 is plausible to anyone who is not a pacifist and who thinks there may be justified wars; it follows from this that soldiers in a war are not committing a flagrant moral indecency by killing enemy combatants. Premise 2 is based on the whole idea of interrogational torture, which is that it can stop or be prevented whenever the torturee gives up the information the enemy wants. Premise 3 assumes that being killed is the worst thing possible or at least that anything that stops short of killing is less bad.

Actually, all three of these premises are debatable. As for the first, you might argue that even conditions of war with an armed enemy does not, by itself, make killing permissible—it could be that some other condition is required (McMahan 2009). And whatever that condition may be, it may not transfer to the case of torture. For the second premise, the person giving up the valuable information may *not* be considered a form of self-defense, because based on that person's value system, such an action may represent losing everything important to him or her. For the third premise, it could be contended that being tortured is painful and traumatizing enough over the long term that it is worse than being killed in war.

But even if we grant the truth of all of these premises, debatable though they are, there is a further problem. As noted in Chapter 2, when a version of this argument was used as an example of the need for validity, the argument is still not quite valid. It needs at least one additional premise that spells out an assumption the argument has to make in order to be valid. It assumes, not only that combatants and torturees have an equal capacity to defend themselves, but that this fact applies to torture's moral acceptability in exactly the same way as it does to combat killing's moral acceptability. This additional premise (4) is stated in the following form of the argument:

1. Combat killing in wartime is morally acceptable because the combatants are not defenseless.

2. Subjects of interrogational torture are not defenseless.

3. Being tortured is not as bad as being killed.

4. Whatever makes combat killing in wartime morally acceptable is sufficient to make interrogational torture morally acceptable.

___

Therefore, interrogational torture is morally acceptable.

Premise 4 is not already included in any of the preceding premises. You could accept premises 1 through 3 but still think that interrogational torture is unacceptable because the capacity of torturees to defend themselves, unlike that of wartime combatants, is not sufficient to make torture morally acceptable.

But is premise 4 true? When we examine the different settings of combat on the one hand and interrogational torture on the other, we see that they are different from one another in many important ways. For one thing, the torturers have no way of knowing whether their captive actually has the information they want. For another, there really is no guarantee that the torture will stop right at the moment when the captive gives up the information. The torturer has absolute power over the captive in this situation, which makes it totally different from combat, where the enemies presumably have an equal opportunity of killing each other. Moreover, the "defense" that the captive has to prevent or stop torture must amount to a betrayal of principles on his or her part, which is totally different from defending oneself in combat. In short, there are many important ways in which the purported parallel between the cases of combat killing and interrogational torture does not hold up, such that it is hard to think of ways that anyone could defend the idea that they are similar enough for the exact same principle of self-defense to apply to both. The upshot to this argument is that a successful parallel between the acceptability of combat killing and of interrogational torture is hard to make.

The next step is to see, without trying to make an analogy or draw a parallel to anything else, whether torture could ever be morally justifiable on the specific grounds on which it is done.

Still Struggling

The argument in the preceding section tries to show how interrogational torture might sometimes be considered morally acceptable by applying the same principle to a case we already accept—combat killing. It is not assumed that either interrogational torture or combat killing are *good* things, just that they may be accepted as necessary evils. Nothing about this argument relies on issues specific to torture itself, which is its main weakness.

The Ticking Time Bomb Scenario

Earlier, the point was made that we only engage in war because its aims are of huge importance, such that not meeting those aims would be unacceptable. In a parallel sense, someone might consider torture to be necessary to prevent something unacceptable from happening. If the argument just considered, about a torturee not being defenseless, is put aside as unsuccessful, we may still be left with a possibility that torture may be morally justified in certain cases simply because it is necessary, never mind the abstract principles about how defenselessness applies.

The hypothetical case of needing to torture someone to get information that would prevent a large number of deaths is known as the "ticking time bomb" scenario. The idea is that there is a time bomb in a heavily populated area that is set to go off, and no one knows where it is except the terrorist who planted it. The terrorist is held captive by the authorities, and the only way to find out where the bomb is so it can be defused is to get the information from the terrorist, who naturally is unwilling to divulge the location. The scenario supposes that torture is the only way the authorities may be able to extract the information from the terrorist and thus save thousands of lives (if not more). The point of bringing up this hypothetical scenario is that if torture might be acceptable in any situation, this would be it.

Those who use the ticking time bomb scenario, in fact, are those who want to defend the in-principle acceptability of torture in some circumstances. Surely, they say, *if* you were faced with a ticking time bomb and had to torture a terrorist to get the information to keep it from exploding and killing masses of people, you would have to do so; you couldn't just stand by and let the bomb explode, when all you would have to do to prevent it is to harm one person. But remember the question with which we began: would it *ever* be permissible in principle to engage in interrogational torture? The ticking time bomb scenario is the most extreme case that can be devised and one that is specifically crafted to get you to answer yes to that question. As we shall see, though, while this may seem to be a natural way to address this question, there are problems with the entire approach to the question that the ticking time bomb scenario represents.

Consequences of Deeming Torture Morally Acceptable

The ticking time bomb scenario hinges on the number of people whose lives would be at stake. It is tempting, in the face of that hypothetical situation, to want to say that *any* lesser evil that could be committed to prevent that kind of loss of life would be acceptable. We have to note, however, what the normative commitments of such a view would be. Specifically, it requires some commitment to consequentialism (see Chapter 4), the view that whatever makes for the best outcome is the right thing to do. We could, instead, reject consequentialism entirely and hold that interrogational torture is always wrong, no matter how many lives are at stake. But the weight of sheer numbers of lives at risk from the "ticking time bomb" makes us seriously consider the permissibility of torture, which seems to indicate that many people are inclined to at least some degree of consequentialism. But even if we are willing to accept that the number of lives threatened by such a scenario outweighs any reluctance to engage in interrogational torture, this only raises a host of other urgent questions.

The Trouble with the Ticking Time Bomb Scenario

The "ticking time bomb," like so many other hypothetical scenarios, is highly idealized. It assumes (1) that authorities have a captive in custody who knows where the bomb is and will give them this information if put under enough torture, and (2) that this information will lead to saving perhaps thousands of lives. In the face of such a hypothetical scenario, we are almost forced to conclude, "Of course you would have to do whatever it takes in this situation. What do you have to lose?" But the problem with this is that in practice, you can never know if you are actually in such a situation. If you answer the ticking time bomb scenario by saying, yes, torture may sometimes be permissible, you then have to specify conditions under which you know in advance that it is permissible. The trouble with the ticking time bomb scenario is that since it is idealized and highly exceptional, it does not provide any assistance in setting general rules for knowing when torture will be warranted. All it can tell us is that *if* it succeeds in saving many lives, then it would be ethically proper to perform. But what if it *doesn't* succeed in saving many lives? Is it still acceptable if we just hope that it will? If so, then the whole force behind the ticking time bomb scenario—the *successful* saving of so many lives—becomes irrelevant.

In short, "hard cases make bad law" (Shue 1978: 141), which is to say that exceptional, idealized cases cannot provide general guidelines for dealing with difficult moral dilemmas.

Practical Moral Consequences of Accepting Torture

On the other hand, if we do allow that torture may be permitted in certain circumstances, then it becomes *legal*. In practice, this means that we are forced to craft an official policy governing it. Certain methods of torture become officially approved, and guidelines are given as to how to carry them out. As Shue puts it, "Torture gains the momentum of an ingrained element of a standard operating procedure" (1978: 138). Then, even if we wanted to reserve torture for exceptional circumstances, it would become easier to use. According to Shue, "Torture is the ultimate shortcut. If it were ever permitted under any conditions, the temptation to use it increasingly would be very strong" (1978: 141).

Therefore, using hypothetical, extreme cases cannot really help us answer the very general question of whether torture may sometimes be permissible. The only kind of answers such hypothetical cases can provide tend to open the door to torture as a widespread practice that will almost certainly go further than the "exceptional" cases for which it is to be held in reserve. Accepting torture sets a precedent that, once it is put in place, cannot be undone and will almost certainly ensure that torture will in fact be practiced and significantly more often than originally intended (Shue 1978).

Chapter Summary

The use of torture in and of itself is widely considered abhorrent. Yet there are times when it may be deemed a necessarily evil and defended even if it is considered a bad thing. That is, it may be necessary to prevent things that are even worse from occurring. Attempts to draw an analogy between torture and other necessary evils fail, however, because of the uniqueness of the setting in which torture takes place. We cannot easily say that torture meets the conditions that ensure that it would both (1) fulfill the purpose for which it was undertaken and (2) not overstep whatever bounds are placed on it.

Even so, we can put forward hypothetical cases for consideration that are constructed for the purpose of saying yes to the question "Would it be morally permissible to torture in this case?" But the trouble with extreme, ticking time bomb scenarios is that they are highly artificial and idealized, and they provide no real practical guidelines for determining in advance when torture may be permissible. People may, in the end, engage in torture if they feel they are in such an extreme situation, but they will have to answer to those who will later judge their actions and the consequences. Torture is an ethical territory for which there is no clear way to judge that it is anything besides atrocious.

QUIZ

1. The only reason that torture would be considered in our society
   is _____.
   a. to terrorize people
   b. to extract a confession
   c. to extract information
   d. for punishment

2. Which of the following does *not* form the basis of an argument for the permissibility of torture?
   a. It can be done without harming the captive.
   b. It may be necessary in some circumstances.
   c. It is similar to bad things that we already accept.
   d. The subject has the capacity to stop the torture.

3. Which of the following is *not* a weakness of the argument that makes an analogy between torture and combat killing?
   a. The subject's defense amounts to a betrayal of principles.
   b. The balance of power between torturer and torturee is vastly unequal.
   c. The subject may not have the information the torturer wants.
   d. The situation of combat killing is something that no one wants.

4. Torture may be defended on the basis of its _____.
   a. having been acceptable in earlier times
   b. being a necessary evil
   c. being permitted by the U.S. Constitution
   d. being a suitable form of punishment in some cases

5. Which of the following is *not* a feature of the ticking time bomb scenario?
   a. Many lives are at stake.
   b. Only one person has to be harmed.
   c. The subject may not know the needed information.
   d. There is no other way to prevent disaster from occurring.

6. The defense of torture requires a commitment to the claim
   that _____.
   a. saving many lives must outweigh the rights of one person
   b. torture may be justified for certain individuals
   c. duty may require the torture of someone for a greater good
   d. torture may not have to be legalized

7. **The setting in which torture occurs is a unique one in that** _____.

    a. everyone abhors its practice
    b. there can be no laws regulating its practice
    c. the torturee may end up being killed
    d. the torturee has no real defense against being tortured

8. **If torture is ever judged morally permissible in certain cases,** _____.

    a. its usage will be restricted to those cases
    b. it will have to become legal
    c. it will succeed in saving lives
    d. it will be ethical to do so in such cases

9. **If torture becomes allowable under the law,** _____.

    a. it will be restricted to wartime
    b. only the most humane methods will be used
    c. there will be official guidelines put in place for its use
    d. that will ensure that its use is limited

10. **If torture becomes allowable within legal limits,** _____.

    a. it will tend to be used more often than originally intended
    b. that will ensure that its practice is restricted
    c. everyone will approve of its practice
    d. subjects of torture will be treated humanely

chapter **10**

Euthanasia

CHAPTER OBJECTIVES

In this chapter, you will learn the following:

- The motivations for euthanasia and the single ethical hurdle that must be overcome in order to accept it

- Some sources of rational resistance to the acceptance of euthanasia

Euthanasia is the intentional and active termination of the life of someone who is deemed terminally ill and in too much pain to make the natural remainder of life worth living. The Greek roots of the word point directly to its significance: *eu* meaning "good," and *thanatos* meaning "death." Instances of euthanasia are supposed to represent "good death," because they cut short suffering for which there is no other relief. The possibility of euthanasia comes up when we judge that someone's death would be a good thing. And there's no particular problem with that, since we don't tend to think that prolonging everyone's life indefinitely is desirable.

But there's another essential component to euthanasia not contained in the word's etymology, which is that it involves, not just someone dying, but the active taking of a life—to put it bluntly, *killing*. Animals are euthanized all the time for terminal illnesses or things that are considered equivalent. But most people have an instinctive resistance to killing another human being, even when everyone agrees that the person's death would be a good thing. So those who support euthanasia because it brings about a decrease in suffering need to convince others that the fact that it involves killing a human does not make it any worse than letting the person continue suffering until dying a natural death. Supporters of euthanasia seek to establish not only this view, but also that euthanasia is to be *preferred* to letting the person die naturally, since it cuts short the length of time he or she suffers.

The Case for Euthanasia

There is no overriding principle in medical practice that people must be kept alive for as long as possible. The central purpose of medicine is to treat (or prevent) diseases so people will be cured of them (or remain healthy). When there is no possibility of a disease being cured, it must instead be treated as much as it can so the patient can live as well as possible. But if a disease is progressive and will cause the patient's death in the not-to-distant future, then there is no possibility of that person continuing to live a long and valuable life. And if a patient's life is shortened *and* is marked by an increasing amount of pain and/or disability due to the disease, there is considered to be no value in treating the disease at all. In such cases, withholding treatment is not only widely considered ethical, but it is also standard practice. When treatment is withheld, it is assumed that the disease will kill the patient *and* that it is better for that to happen sooner rather than later. Otherwise, treatment would be continued so as to postpone death for as long as possible. When death is no longer postponed but allowed to arrive as a result of a disease, it is assumed that this death would be welcomed.

At this point, someone may ask, if death would be welcomed, why not bring it about? The motivation would be to shorten the period of suffering even more than it would be with treatment withheld. We want suffering to be lessened out of compassion and mercy for the person experiencing it. If intentionally ending a life keeps suffering to a minimum, then there may be such a thing as "mercy killing." So if the whole motivation is to lessen suffering, why not lessen the suffering as much as possible by actively bringing about death, which we've decided would be a good thing anyway? The central obstacle to this conclusion is that it requires killing, which is repugnant to most people, especially in a medical setting. The difference between a scenario that is welcomed and one that is repugnant is simply the difference between "letting die" on the one hand and killing on the other. This difference is the single obstacle to euthanasia. Its opponents maintain that the difference is enough to make euthanasia unethical simply because it is an instance of killing. The defender of euthanasia has to convince the opponent that the difference between killing and letting die is not crucial or, indeed, that it makes no difference. The most influential attempt to do this was undertaken by philosopher James Rachels.

James Rachels's Challenge to the Medical Profession

Rachels published a paper in the *New England Journal of Medicine* (1975) that challenged the American Medical Association's (AMA's) official prohibition of "the intentional termination of the life of one human being by another." The point of this prohibition is the principle that doctors are not in the business of killing humans (at least, humans who have been born). The AMA policy goes on to state that such "is contrary to that for which the medical profession stands," meaning that actively taking a life is incompatible with the medical profession's purpose of healing. Rachels argued that such a doctrine should be discarded, because it is inconsistent with the actual medical practice of what he refers to as "passive euthanasia," discontinuing treatment so as to let the patient die sooner instead of later. Rachels argued that for the same reason we already accept passive euthanasia, we should also practice "active euthanasia," cutting a life short intentionally.

Rachels's case can be put like this. He observed that in practicing passive euthanasia, we already accept the following two principles:

Principle 1: When a life is doomed to unbearable pain, not prolonging that life is acceptable so as to shorten the amount of suffering.
Principle 2: Less pain is better than more pain.

Certainly, anyone who accepts passive euthanasia is committed to these principles, and they are the very basis for accepting the discontinuation of treatment so as not to prolong a patient's life. Rachels's challenge is that if we accept these principles, we should also accept this further principle.

Principle 3: Whatever shortens a life for the reasons given in principles 1 and 2 is at least as acceptable as a case where the same principles apply but in which we don't shorten a life as much.

Passive euthanasia does not shorten a life as much as active euthanasia. So Rachels's point is that if we already decide not to prolong someone's life because of the pain he or she is in, then to be consistent with that motivation, we should accept whatever shortens a life even more and for the same reason. Now, principles 1 and 2 don't quite add up to an airtight (that is, valid) argument that gives principle 3 as a conclusion. For one thing, people who accept principle 1 may do so simply because it specifically says "not prolong," whereas principle 3 says "shorten." The difference between not prolonging someone's life and shortening it is the difference between letting die and killing, which Rachels needs to overcome. We would not be flat-out inconsistent, then, to accept principles 1 and 2 but not 3. Shortening, however, at least entails not prolonging, so the challenge is that insofar as shortening a life accomplishes the purpose of not prolonging it, we should accept doing so, especially because it accomplishes the purpose of lessening suffering even more effectively than simply not prolonging life. In any case, if we had a word that was neutral between "not prolonging" and "shortening" so that either one would be an equal instance of it, principle 1 could be stated using that word, and it would put the point of the challenge in an especially stark way. Principle 3 could then simply be stated as, "If we want to decrease the amount of suffering, why not decrease the amount of suffering as much as we possibly can?"

As a philosopher, Rachels is looking at the principle by which the medical profession already supports passive euthanasia and trying to press the point that, to be fully consistent with that principle and actually accomplish its purpose even more effectively, active euthanasia should also be accepted. With this challenge in place, the onus is placed on opponents of euthanasia to justify exactly why they support principles 1 and 2 up to a point but no further. The way Rachels puts this challenge is to lay out three options showing how someone might take a stand on the issues, so as to see what might be most consistent:

> **Option 1:** Reject principle 1 and always prolong life as much as possible (that is, reject passive euthanasia).
> **Option 2:** Accept principle 1 but reject it in cases of *active* euthanasia.
> **Option 3:** Let principle 1 decide whether euthanasia is practiced, regardless of whether it is active or passive.

Option 1 has not yet been considered, and it is at least consistent. We could say that the single primary aim of the medical profession is to prolong life as much as possible and this is what forms the basis of its activity in the prevention and cure of disease. Dying is often accompanied by suffering, but if the dying (and accompanying suffering) is not prevented, then death must be postponed as much as possible, regardless of the suffering. The medical profession does not actually endorse this principle or practice in accordance with it, but it *could*, and it would be philosophically consistent to do so.

The stance that the medical profession actually takes is option 2, what Rachels calls the "traditional doctrine." Unlike option 1, it recognizes the value of lessening pain, regardless of whether there is even an imminent threat of death. Doctors regularly prescribe medicines that are meant *only* to help alleviate pain and that have no effect on the length of the patient's life. For terminal illnesses, where there is no hope of recovery, treating the pain with medications and allowing the disease to kill the patient is as far as the medical community is willing to go. Even if ending a life would lessen the amount of pain experienced, doctors will stop short of it. And it's not just that the AMA forbids them to do it—their consciences react strongly against it.

But according to Rachels, reason tells us that if there is a commitment to lessen pain, as is given by principles 1 and 2, the most consistent way to be committed to it is to take option 3: instead of letting a difference between killing and letting die be the overriding factor in whether or not to let pain continue unchecked, let principle 1 decide whether to kill or let die, since this principle is the whole motivation for passive euthanasia (which is already accepted). Rachels urges, in other words, that a thoroughgoing commitment to relieving suffering should prevent us from distinguishing between active and passive euthanasia.

The challenge is thus starkly put to those who hold to the traditional doctrine—if the only difference between decreasing the time of suffering somewhat and decreasing the time of suffering as much as possible is the difference between killing and letting die, then that difference had better be pretty important. But Rachels goes on to argue that this difference, contrary to popular belief, is of *no* moral importance.

The Equivalence Thesis

Rachels argues that for whatever moral differences there are between individual cases, if the *only* difference is that one case involves killing and the other letting die, then the two cases are morally equivalent. This is termed the *equivalence thesis*. If this is accepted, then it becomes urgent that Rachels's principle 1 be applied without restraint so that active euthanasia be carried out to minimize the suffering of the dying as much as possible. Rachels clearly believes strongly in the equivalence thesis; he published his argument in the *New England Journal of Medicine*, hoping that the entire medical profession would take notice, be persuaded that there is no moral difference between killing and letting die, and begin carrying out active euthanasia so as to reduce suffering. If everyone is deluded in thinking that there is an important moral difference between killing and letting die, then efforts need to be made to change people's minds so that, in the case of euthanasia, needless suffering can be prevented and cut short.

That's his claim and the motivation behind it. Now, for the actual argument behind the claim. To argue for this thesis, Rachels leans heavily on a certain thought experiment that he devised as an "intuition pump," as philosophers say, which is mean to prompt readers to thinking about things in a certain light. Like Judith Jarvis Thomson's thought experiment about the famous violinist that's meant to draw out your intuition a certain way about the extent of the right to life (see Chapter 7), Rachels's is highly artificial but focused on a specific point—there are two hypothetical cases, and the only difference between them is supposed to be that one is a case of killing and the other is of letting die. If Rachels is right, and that is the only difference, then they should be morally equivalent.

In the first case, a six-year-old inherits a large fortune, and his adult cousin, Smith, is next in line to receive the inheritance should anything happen to the child. So one evening while the child is in the bath, Smith sneaks in and drowns him, leaving evidence so that it will look like an accident.

In the other case, Jones is in the exact same situation: he will gain a large inheritance if his six-year-old cousin dies, and like Smith, plans to drown him. But as he sneaks into the bathroom, the child happens to slip and hit his head. He loses consciousness and falls facedown in the bathwater, drowning while Jones watches and is delighted at his amazing luck.

Rachels asks, "Is Jones's behavior less reprehensible than Smith's, merely because he let his cousin die and Smith actually killed him?" The point of this experiment is that we are supposed to answer no; going easier on Jones because he "merely" watched his cousin die seems absurd. The two cases isolate the bare difference of killing versus letting die; even the intentions of Smith and Jones were the same. The result was also the same, and the difference in how the result came about doesn't seem to make a moral difference.

Of course, this thought experiment is a completely different setting than that of euthanasia, but it is simply meant to establish this principle: there is no moral difference between killing and letting die—period. This is supposed to be a general principle that applies equally everywhere, and it is a key premise in Rachels's argument as it can now be explicitly laid out:

1. There is no moral difference between cases where the only difference is between killing and letting die.
2. The only difference between active and passive euthanasia is between killing and letting die.

Therefore, there is no moral difference between active and passive euthanasia. (Except, of course, that the former can be used to shorten suffering even more than the latter, in which case the former would actually be morally better than the latter.)

This is a valid argument. The bulk of the work in establishing its soundness is in establishing premise 1, which is the whole point of the Smith and Jones story.

It's also important to emphasize what Rachels is *not* claiming with his equivalence thesis. He is not saying that there can be no moral differences between cases of killing and cases of letting die. Certain individual cases of killing and letting die may be such that a certain case of killing is morally worse than a certain case of letting die, but Rachels believes that if that is so, it will be due to some other factor than killing. For example, most cases of killing are those in which the killer not only wants the victim to die but brings about that death against the victim's wish. Maintaining the equivalence thesis, Rachels says that what we object to in ordinary cases of killing as morally bad is the intention of the killer to harm the victim by ending his or her life and the fact that the victim does not want to be killed. But switching to a case of active euthanasia, if the intention of the "killer" is to cut suffering short, and the "victim" *wants* to die, the killing itself is supposed to be completely unobjectionable, and the fact that the aim of lessening suffering is accomplished effectively is supposed to be morally good.

Two Objections and Replies

One possible objection to killing per se is that being the cause of someone's death is a bad thing. The difference between active and passive euthanasia is that, in the former, some person is the cause of someone else's death, whereas in the latter, the disease is allowed to be the cause of that person's death. Doctors, so the objection goes, should never be the cause of someone's death. To this, Rachels says that it can't be bad to be the cause of someone's death in cases when we've already decided that death would be a good thing. If it's to be a good death (remember the etymology of *euthanasia*), then why wouldn't we want to bring it about? Is the death only good because the disease caused it? The reply goes that if death is good simply because it ends suffering, bringing it about can only be good, not bad.

The AMA's position that mercy killing is "contrary to that for which the medical profession stands" might be based on the notion that the medical profession stands for healing and not harming. If so, doctors have an overriding duty not to harm (if nothing else), so it could be held that for them to kill in *any* circumstance goes against this basic principle. But Rachels replies that this line of thought misses the whole point. Again, if we accept letting die—passive euthanasia—in cases of terminal illness and significant suffering, then it cannot be that letting die in such cases represents a failure on the physician's part to live up to his or her duty to heal. Rather than being a failure to heal, not postponing death would be a good thing because of the decrease in suffering that results. If this is accepted, then bringing about a death the patient would welcome cannot be a case of harming. Unless, that is, every case of killing is ipso facto considered harm because of its being an overt act and condemned as such, whereas letting die is never harming because it isn't active. But this is just the supposed moral difference between killing and letting die that Rachels argues is illusory, and that the objector has yet to establish.

Reasons Against Accepting the Equivalence Principle

As was emphasized back in Chapter 1, philosophers today focus mainly on uncovering to what principles people are committed and deducing to what other things they have to be committed in order to remain consistent with those principles. Most of us come already committed to the principle that says, "Do not kill humans," and think this is a general rule that should always be followed; the only exceptions, if any, are extraordinary cases of urgency, in which some other principle may override this rule. A dying person whose life cannot be saved and is in terrible pain is in a dire situation, but someone who holds to the do-not-kill-humans rule would not think it is urgent to kill the person, whether or not he or she is already dying. If we accept Rachels's equivalence thesis and embrace the practice of active euthanasia, this would require us to drop the do-not-kill-humans principle and replace it with something else that could yield the same or similar results in most situations where it might be applied.

But replace it with what? This question needs careful attention. In addition, we need to examine the principle that Rachels thinks is acceptable and strong enough to make us reject the do-not-kill-humans principle.

Euthanasia and Utilitarianism

The normative basis on which Rachels argues his conclusion on this issue could be derived most straightforwardly from utilitarianism (a species of consequentialism; see Chapter 4). That is, it is concerned with bringing about whatever maximizes happiness and minimizes suffering, however that might be accomplished. According to utilitarianism, whatever action brings about a net increase in overall happiness and a net decrease in suffering is what morally *ought* to be done, no matter what that action is, including killing. So if minimizing suffering requires ending a life, then that is what must be done. We may feel sympathetic with the idea of active euthanasia in its aim to mercifully cut suffering short, but if we accept this on utilitarian grounds, then to be philosophically consistent, we must be convinced of the rightness of active euthanasia not just because we feel compassion for the special plight of the dying, but because we accept the principle that tells us we *must* accept it.

Rachels himself emphasizes that our stance on euthanasia must be based on purely rational grounds. This is why he thinks doctors should allow their moral intuition to be changed by his argument on purely rational grounds and thereby agree with the ethics that wipe out any moral difference between active and passive euthanasia. So in trying to rationally find the right answer, if we should ignore any instinctual resistance to killing, we should also discount sheer compassion and just go by the pure principles at work. Philosophical consistency requires that, whatever principle we point to in order to justify active euthanasia, the principle be applied across the board and not just to special cases such as the possibility of euthanizing the terminally ill.

Any utilitarian would accept Rachels's principles in a heartbeat and probably already does accept active euthanasia. Principles 1 and 2 are directly entailed by utilitarianism. But it does not follow that to reject utilitarianism is to reject principles 1 and 2 (this would be to commit the fallacy of denying the antecedent; see Chapter 2). It is possible to hold to principles 1 and 2 for other reasons besides being a utilitarian—maybe they result from the more general principles that we should help those in distress (understood in such a way that it does not include the possibility of killing them) and that suffering is bad. What Rachels is really trying to do is to convince the reader of the equivalence thesis; accepting the equivalence thesis does not in itself entail a commitment to utilitarianism. But this requires doing away with traditional morality's principle of not killing humans, which is the single obstacle to be overcome for acceptance of active euthanasia. A person coming from the standpoint of traditional morality, then, needs to consider the consequences of accepting the equivalence thesis across the board, since this entails doing away with the do-not-kill-humans principle.

Consequences of Eliminating the Do-Not-Kill-Humans Principle

If we accept the equivalence thesis, this will be sufficient to establish the practice of active euthanasia, simply because it decreases the amount of suffering. But, of course, a philosophical principle like the equivalence thesis is not something that applies in only one kind of situation. In fact, there is no such thing: a normative principle, once accepted, is supposed to underlie all ethical decisions, and to accept the equivalence thesis is to accept that it applies in any situation. Therefore, if we accept it as the basis for accepting active euthanasia, we need to consider whether we are willing to be committed to it. If so, then to be consistent, we need to apply that principle in every applicable situation, not just that of euthanasia. If not, then we must reject utilitarianism wholesale, preventing it from being the basis of a sound argument for active euthanasia or anything else.

So what happens if we apply the utilitarian basis for accepting euthanasia to other situations? Utilitarianism simply says to decrease suffering and increase happiness. That means that if someone is living an unhappy life, then suicide might be a good thing for that person. Many utilitarians today are "preference utilitarians," meaning that *happiness* is defined in terms of "whatever people prefer," which will differ among individuals. So utilitarianism needn't mean that we kill unhappy people against their will. But it could mean that people would be given the right to choose suicide in the easiest way possible; euthanasia advocates have actually devised such a way in the form of the "peaceful pill." This is a radical departure from the current standard policy of authorities and health-care professionals to do everything possible to prevent people from committing suicide. But it could well be taken as perfectly consistent with (even required by) utilitarianism. One leading activist in the pro-euthanasia movement put it this way (Lopez 2001):

> If we are to remain consistent and we believe that the individual has the right to dispose of their life, we should not erect artificial barriers in the way of sub-groups who don't meet our criteria. This would mean that the so-called "peaceful pill" should be available in the supermarket so that those old enough to understand death could obtain death peacefully at the time of their choosing.

This is to say that if active euthanasia were accepted, there would be no apparent principled reason to restrict it to dire medical cases. If "rules" were struck down in favor of applying the utilitarian principle as far as possible, there would likely be consequences in other areas as well, certainly where suicide is concerned.

In the final analysis, the opponent to euthanasia maintains that killing humans is immoral and that this principle must be applied consistently everywhere. Resistance to euthanasia, then, comes from this simple argument:

1. Active euthanasia is a case of killing a human.

2. Killing a human is immoral.

Therefore, active euthanasia is immoral.

This is a valid argument, and premise 1 is obviously true. To hold back the conclusion, the euthanasia advocate needs to deny premise 2. Accepting the equivalence principle would allow us to say, instead of premise 2, that "Killing a human is not necessarily immoral." Instead, for most cases of killing that we think are immoral, we might judge them so simply because they increase suffering and decrease happiness. But in cases where we deem that killing humans will decrease suffering and/or increase happiness, such killing might be permissible (and utilitarianism would view it as, in fact, obligatory).

An alternative way to reject premise 2 would be to qualify it by saying, "Killing humans is immoral, unless _____." But what general principle do we put in the blank, such that we would want to be committed to it consistently? More to the point, simply listing types of situations in which killing a person would not be immoral wouldn't be to state a principle at all, but simply to list exceptions for capricious, and effectively arbitrary, reasons of our own. Really, anything with which we might fill in that blank, no matter how general, would require an answer to the question "What is wrong about killing ordinarily, and why *this* exception?" The choices overall are really between thoroughgoing utilitarianism and maintaining the rule that killing humans is wrong simply because it is killing.

Resisting the Equivalence Thesis

We could try to undermine the equivalence thesis—the position that there is no moral difference between killing and letting die—in the following ways. Consider again the Smith and Jones thought experiment, which is intended to establish the equivalence thesis. We might want to judge Smith and Jones as morally the same, not because letting die is no better than killing, but simply because their intentions are the same. Here's how we might try to show this. Tweak the thought experiment so Jones, instead of having planned to kill his cousin, had no prior thought of killing but happened to walk in just as the child hit his head and fell facedown in the bathwater; Jones then watched the boy die because he realized what he would gain from his cousin's death. In that case, it seems we might judge Jones at least somewhat less harshly than Smith (and perhaps for the same reason as premeditated murders, "in cold blood," are judged more harshly than crimes of passion with equivalent outcomes). If so, this cannot be because the outcome was different (it wasn't) but because their intentions were different: in this variant of the thought experiment, only Smith had the premeditated intention of killing his cousin. Jones let his cousin die, but had the boy not died on his own, Jones would not have killed him. So assuming that we use the same set of intuitions to judge this case as we do the original version of the thought experiment, that would mean we judge Smith and Jones equally reprehensible not because the outcome was the same, but because both men had the same intention.

Here's still another variant. Suppose Jones had no conscious intention of killing his cousin but did kill him while sleepwalking or under the influence of a hallucinogen or other mind-altering drug. Then, although both Smith and Jones killed their respective cousins, their conscious intentions would have been different; in that case, it seems that we would also judge Jones less harshly. This only serves to further support the idea that in the original thought experiment, we morally judge each of them by their intentions. If that's the case, then if both of them intended to kill, that's the reason we judge them to be equally bad—not because killing is no worse than letting die. *Yet*, Rachels could grant all this and still press this point: Why *don't* we judge Smith and Jones *differently* in the original version of the thought experiment, when the only difference between them is that one killed and the other let die? We could point to the variations in the case as perhaps indicating that we look to people's intentions to morally judge them rather than the outcome. If so, this could potentially undermine utilitarianism, but not necessarily undermine the equivalence thesis—not, anyway, if the equivalence thesis were maintained for some other reason than utilitarianism (since, as discussed above, maintaining the equivalence thesis does not in itself entail a commitment to utilitarianism).

There are also other, more direct reasons to think the equivalence thesis is false. Here's a simple thought experiment from Judith Jarvis Thomson (1976):

> Charles is a great transplant surgeon. One of his patients needs a new heart but has a relatively rare blood type. By chance, Charles learns of a healthy specimen with that very blood type. He can take the healthy specimen's heart, killing the man, and install it in his patient, saving him. Or he can refrain from taking the healthy specimen's heart, letting his patient die.

Clearly, we want to say, Charles must not kill; he must let die instead. The two patients are presumed to be of equal value; one of them will die, and the only difference is between killing and letting die. But the moral difference between killing and letting die in this case seems crystal clear. This is especially so if we vary the thought experiment, as Thomson goes on to do, so there are five patients in need of different new organs, and the surgeon finds a single "healthy specimen" who can provide all of them. The surgeon can kill the one person to save the five or let the five die. The verdict that our moral intuition gives is exactly the same—the surgeon must not kill one person; he must let five people die. This makes the point even stronger, because in this case, the stakes are much higher, yet it seems to make no difference to the principle at work: the duty not to kill overrides even the need to obtain a net result of several more lives saved. In fact, it seems that this moral verdict would have to remain the same no matter how many lives were at stake.

The duty not to kill seems to invalidate whatever good consequences killing might have. On the other hand, the utilitarian must say that if the five people *want* the transplant done by killing the one healthy person, their preference must outweigh that of the one, because the difference between killing and letting die is of no moral significance. The one not only can but must be sacrificed to save the five.

The resistance to the equivalence thesis, then, seems to come from a foundational place in our moral psychology, which is why most people are unable to accept it. One explanation for this, which Thomson goes on to cite, is that we have two kinds of duties: positive duties and negative ones. Positive duties are those that we are obligated to do. Negative duties are those that we are obligated *not* to do. Not killing is a negative duty. Not letting die (that is, saving or prolonging lives) is a positive duty. The important moral difference between killing and letting die seems to be an instance of the general fact that our negative duties are much stronger than our positive duties (Foot 1967). That is, it is much worse to neglect a negative duty and kill, for instance, than to neglect a positive duty and let die. Whatever more general reason there might be for this important moral difference between positive and negative duties remains to be seen. Noting the difference and that we seem to be strongly committed to it, however, suffices to show that our belief in an important moral difference between killing and letting die may be taken to have a foundation and cannot be thrown aside lightly. Moreover, this important difference between kinds of duties tells strongly against utilitarianism, which cannot even recognize a moral obligation to obey duties, let alone recognize an important moral difference between different kinds of duties.

Back to the case of euthanasia. The traditional resistance to active euthanasia but not passive euthanasia seems to be based on there being a duty not to kill. If a person overrides this duty in the case of euthanasia, then the do-not-kill-humans principle either has to be dropped or must be qualified with some set of exceptions. Utilitarianism is the most general and consistent reason to drop the principle, but then we have to think through whether we would want to be committed to utilitarianism in all cases, not just that of euthanasia.

Still Struggling

For any ethical dilemma, any proposed answer has to have some philosophical justification. So it isn't enough to say that active euthanasia ought to be done to relieve the suffering of the dying and leave it at that. It has to be due to a working principle that applies to every possible area. The most straightforward way to justify euthanasia is to say that killing is morally acceptable when it is done to relieve suffering. But then, we have to consider whether that principle should be applied in every case of suffering and not just to the terminally ill. If not, then to be consistent—accepting a principle only if we're willing to apply it everywhere—we should reject that principle, in which case euthanasia is still without justification.

Chapter Summary

The possibility of euthanasia arises when the sick and dying are in terrible pain and nothing can be done for them but to end their lives. To purposely end someone's life, however, is an instance of killing, against which most people have powerful moral instincts. Proponents of euthanasia have to convince its opponents that killing is of no importance, such that if killing is required to bring about a decrease in suffering, then it should be done. This requires doing away with the all-encompassing rule against killing, however, and it is hard to see what principle would replace it that does not run strongly counter to traditional morality, in a variety of areas besides euthanasia.

QUIZ

1. **What does James Rachels mean by "passive euthanasia"?**
   a. A patient killing himself or herself
   b. Allowing a patient to die of his or her disease
   c. Killing a patient when he or she asks
   d. Killing a patient when he or she is unconscious

2. **Which of the following positions does Rachels think is inconsistent?**
   a. Allowing a patient to die but not shortening the suffering even more by killing him or her
   b. Allowing terminal patients to die when they choose but not giving healthy patients the same choice
   c. Killing a patient when the patient requests it but not against the patient's wishes
   d. Prolonging life as much as possible in all circumstances

3. **Which of the following does Rachels think should be the basis of deciding whether and how euthanasia is carried out?**
   a. Discontinue treatment of the disease when it becomes incurable.
   b. Let a terminal patient die, but treat the pain for as long as possible.
   c. Let a terminal patient die, but do not kill the patient unless he or she requests it.
   d. When suffering is unbearable, shorten the patient's life as much as possible.

4. **The equivalence thesis states that _____.**
   a. killing is only wrong if the person being killed does not want to die
   b. since Smith and Jones have the same intention, they are equally wrong
   c. every case of killing is morally equivalent to every case of letting die
   d. if killing and letting die are the only difference between two cases, they are morally equivalent

5. **One objection to euthanasia is that doctors should not be the cause of some-one's death. What is Rachels's reply to this?**
   a. Doctors are already the cause of many deaths.
   b. Doctors cannot be expected to give the dying everything they need.
   c. This cannot be a bad thing if someone's death would be a good thing.
   d. Being the cause of someone's death is not immoral in and of itself.

6. **The best reason for accepting active euthanasia requires a commitment to _____.**
    a. duty-based ethics
    b. killing people against their will
    c. the principle that whatever it takes to decrease suffering must be done
    d. the principle that happiness is not possible unless people have the right to end their lives

7. **Passive euthanasia requires a commitment to _____.**
    a. utilitarianism
    b. duty-based ethics
    c. the principle that as much as possible should be done to keep people alive
    d. the principle that not keeping someone alive is acceptable if the person is dying and in great pain

8. **What is the main weakness of the Smith and Jones thought experiment?**
    a. It shows that there is no difference between killing and letting die.
    b. The situation it describes does not apply to euthanasia.
    c. It may be that we judge the situations the same because the protagonists have the same intentions.
    d. We do not know if Jones would have really killed his cousin.

9. **A utilitarian would say that _____.**
    a. active euthanasia is often obligatory
    b. passive euthanasia is always preferable to active euthanasia
    c. active euthanasia is acceptable in some circumstances but not obligatory
    d. the lives of suffering people should be ended regardless of their wishes

10. **What is one reason to think that killing is worse than letting die?**
    a. Every case of killing is worse than every case of letting die.
    b. The medical profession's ethical principles cannot be changed.
    c. Our duties to do certain things are stronger than our duties not to do certain things.
    d. Our duties not to do certain things are stronger than our duties to do certain things.

chapter **11**

Animal Rights

CHAPTER OBJECTIVES

In this chapter, you will learn the following:

- Contexts in which the problem of animal suffering at the hands of humans arises

- The most influential philosophical basis for taking animal suffering as a serious moral problem

- Other philosophical grounds that would generate moral obligations to animals

In ethics, the subject of the rights of animals not to be abused was not discussed much prior to the last two centuries. Humans use animals for a variety of purposes, and with that use comes the possibility of abuse. That is, animals have a capacity for suffering, and people have the power to cause them suffering, either on purpose or as a side effect. Most people today would agree that using animals in ways that disregard their suffering as unimportant is unethical, and would seek to eliminate any animal suffering that is "unnecessary"—that is, not connected with anything that has an otherwise positive outcome. Some ethicists take the somewhat more radical stance that we should prevent animal suffering for the same reason that we want to prevent human suffering. According to this view, there is nothing special about human beings in this regard; rather, the suffering of any animal—human or nonhuman—should be prevented unless it brings about some greater good. This chapter discusses the ethical issue of animal rights in various contexts and the philosophical implications of possible stances on it.

Issues in Animal Rights

Humans, although one of millions of animal species, have a unique place in the world. In addition to being able to create and use technology, alter our environment in a variety of ways, and relate to one another in a rich and complex cultural setting, we have power over the rest of the animal kingdom. We use this power over animals to do work, study them scientifically, experiment on them, and use them as important sources of food. With this power comes an almost unlimited capacity to cause animals pain and suffering. Almost no one wants to do that for its own sake, but there is always the possibility that animals may suffer as a by-product of being used for our purposes. Historically, most people were not in the habit of caring much about animal suffering. At least, there used to be no laws forbidding maltreatment of animals, so individuals could be as cruel as they liked without fear of official repercussions.

However, it is now widely believed that cruelty to animals is unethical enough to warrant serious punishment under the law. This raises the question of exactly what constitutes "cruelty" to animals. Certain ethicists think that many of the ways in which we continue to use animals today are deeply unethical, even though most people automatically accept such practices. If these ethicists are correct, then people centuries from now may well look back on our time with the same distaste we feel looking back at times before there were any laws against animal cruelty.

Cruelty to Animals in General

Cruelty generally means inflicting suffering such that you know you are inflicting suffering and have a total lack of compassion for the being that is suffering. People can certainly be cruel to each other, but opportunities for cruelty toward animals arise in special ways. Such cruelty can manifest in as many ways as humans have power over animals.

Before there were laws forbidding people to abuse animals, people owning a horse or a donkey, for example, could "punish" the animal as severely as they wanted for not working hard enough. A person might decide to beat a dog or a pack animal simply to act out on angry feelings that were completely unrelated to the animal. Or a person might torture an animal simply out of sadistic and evil pleasure. What makes all of this possible is human power over animals; the simple fact that they have such power may be what makes some people *want* to abuse them. Intentional abuse of animals could well be a source of pleasure for those who, for whatever reason, get pleasure out of exercising as much power as they can (perhaps because they feel powerless in other areas of life).

Another way in which human power over animals makes cruelty possible is that the animals we own depend on us totally for their care. Some kinds of child abuse are possible for the same reason. Children have certain needs, such as love and attention, and more fundamentally, food, clothing, and shelter. Neglecting these needs is a form of child abuse and is punishable by law. Neglect of animals' basic needs is also punishable by law. (Animal neglect is not considered as serious as child neglect, of course, because humans are considered more valuable than animals—more on that later.) Animal neglect can involve not feeding them enough, keeping them locked in small and/or dark spaces for long periods of time, and not providing them with adequate shelter.

Eventually, people came to the consensus that being cruel to animals in the ways described is seriously wrong enough that it should be illegal. Today, a person can receive a significant prison sentence for serious animal abuse. This indicates that humans generally recognize that they have a moral responsibility for the animals they own and use for whatever purposes. This moral responsibility is why animal neglect is considered serious enough to be punishable by law; the law recognizes that animal suffering is morally significant.

Today's major ethical challenges pertaining to animal rights involve contexts in which many people want to say that animals are abused in ways that are essentially just like those already described, which are illegal. Those who are concerned about the continuing "institutionalized" abuse of animals would say that the main difference is that illegal animal abuse seems to be perpetrated by individuals, while similar things done on a systematic scale by corporations are widely—and wrongly—considered acceptable. Dedicated activists are convinced that some generally accepted practices that are carried out on a large scale but not legally prosecuted are as wrong as the kind of animal abuses that almost everyone decries. In fact, those of this position would say that institutionalized abuse of animals is even more wrong than the individual abuses currently prosecuted under the law, because of the sheer number of animals abused on a corporate scale and the way that institutionalized abuse perpetuates itself.

Factory Farming

One of the widespread uses of animals today is in agribusiness, the commercial management of farming for maximum profit. After World War II, food production increased enormously around the world when major food producers realized that it was most efficient and cost-effective to grow crops and raise livestock on a large scale. In place of many small farms, a smaller number of large farms with a high density of animals and crops and more automated production processes made agriculture into big business. These so-called factory farms were, and are, able to produce food more quickly and at a lower cost than multiple smaller farms with the same total amount of resources. Generating food at a lower cost to the producer means offering it at a lower cost to the consumer. So competition between factory farms not only encourages keeping costs down but makes it essential for their survival so they can keep pace with consumers' desire for inexpensive food.

This means the living conditions of animals raised on such farms for slaughter are very different from those of "free-range" animals at traditional, smaller farms. Animals are kept indoors in tiny enclosures so as many as possible can be raised using as little space as possible. In one extreme example, chickens have been kept in such close quarters that their beaks are singed off as chicks to prevent their pecking each other to death. Pigs at factory farms are often kept in two-by-seven-foot stalls for their entire adult lives. Long-term confinement in enclosures that are so tight the animals cannot even turn around is commonly practiced in keeping many kinds of livestock, including calves.

Except for milk cows, animals raised on factory farms, just like any other farm, are there to be slaughtered at some point. On factory farms, where quantity and speed of production are paramount, animals are slaughtered in whatever is considered the most efficient way. During the killing process, this can easily involve treating the live animals as though they were inanimate raw materials being manufactured into products. At a factory farm, the use of automated machinery and conveyor belts is the usual sort of pattern for slaughtering animals. Such machinery, obviously, is geared simply toward efficiency and cost-effectiveness, not toward minimizing the animals' terror and suffering during the slaughtering process.

Some changes have been and are continuing to be made by factory farmers in response to concerns from a variety of quarters about animal treatment. As in the days when laws against animal abuse first became widespread, people are becoming aware of the ways in which animals live and die on factory farms, and they are raising serious ethical concerns. But because these practices are already well established on a large scale and food-production corporations have a profit-based incentive to produce food as quickly and inexpensively as possible but no intrinsically profit-based motive to treat animals humanely, it is an uphill battle for animal-rights advocates. The overwhelming number of people opposed to animal cruelty, on the other hand, makes it such that increased general awareness of slaughterhouse conditions at factory farms is itself good news for activists.

Animal Experimentation

Another area in which animals are used on a large corporate scale is in experimentation. Sometimes this involves experiments performed on animals to see how they respond physiologically to certain conditions. Such experiments may easily entail suffering for the animals involved, and they can be treated as though they are not experiencing suffering at all or that their suffering is irrelevant. In many instances, scientists experiment on animals to learn about human physiological reactions under the same conditions. Animals are used because it would be considered horrifically unethical to perform such experiments on humans; other animals besides humans, however, are considered by some to be fair game. The leading ethicist for animal rights, Peter Singer, describes one such case (Singer 1993: 66).

> In many countries, the armed forces perform atrocious experiments
> on animals that rarely come to light. To give just one example: at

the U.S. Armed Forces Radiobiology Institute, in Bethesda, Maryland, rhesus monkeys have been trained to run inside a large wheel. If they slow down too much, the wheel slows down, too, and the monkeys get an electric shock. Once the monkeys have been trained to run for long periods, they are given lethal doses of radiation. Then, while sick and vomiting, they are forced to continue to run until they drop. This is supposed to provide information on the capacities of soldiers to continue to fight after a nuclear attack.

The usual context in which most people think of animal experimentation, though, is that of medical or other health purposes. These kinds of experimentation are undoubtedly more common than physiological experimentation and are done on a much larger scale. For example, it is standard procedure to test new pharmaceuticals on animals to find out basic facts about how the drug metabolizes and any side effects it may cause. Again, a large part of the reason that animals such as mice or rats are used instead of humans is because if the drugs were to kill or maim the animals, it would be considered far less bad than if humans were subjected to these unexpected results. Of course, rodents are also used partly because they are far less expensive than paying humans to be experimented on—as with factory farming, the economic motive is a powerful one, which can easily make consideration of animal suffering go by the wayside.

In addition to using animals to test pharmaceuticals that can help people, manufacturers frequently use them to test how cosmetics and other personal-care items will affect humans, such as whether the skin and eyes will be irritated. For this kind of testing, the product is typically applied directly to the animals' eyes and skin in liberal amounts, so the experimenters can see what the effects are. Thus, significant amounts of discomfort and suffering are almost inevitable for animals undergoing this type of testing. Perhaps what's most objectionable to animal-rights activists about cosmetics testing is that the benefits to humans—being able to wear cosmetics with a minimum of discomfort—seem so negligible compared to its effects on the animals on which the products are tested. Animal-testing practices are the kind that might be expected if people regarded animal suffering as of no moral importance. But animal cruelty in general is illegal, which means that almost everyone thinks it *is* of significant moral importance. There is the pressing ethical problem, then, of how such practices could be morally justified or allowed to continue.

The Animal Liberation Movement and Utilitarianism

In the 1970s, a new social ethics movement arose. People concerned about animal treatment in cases such as those described in the preceding section united under a common cause and became activists. As just mentioned, some of the ways in which animals have been used and treated in recent times seem to imply that humans think nothing of animal suffering. But in general, people *do* tend to think that needless animal suffering is highly unethical and should be prevented. These facts seem to point to a serious disparity between the actual, generally accepted, ethical norms on one hand and continuing practices that often go directly against those norms on the other. Some people have taken note of that disparity and tried to raise public awareness of it, actively protesting the practices they condemn and even illegally breaking into facilities to free animals being kept for experimentation. The lengths to which strongly dedicated activists are willing to go to improve the lot of animals shows that they consider the maltreatment of animals to be the most serious and egregious moral wrong being perpetrated today. Consider how outraged most people would be if humans were treated as some animals are in factory farming or experimentation. The most dedicated animal-rights activists have behaved with almost that same level of outrage toward the treatment of animals. This reflects the fact that these activists consider the moral significance of animal suffering to be comparable to, if not the same as, that of human suffering.

The normative theory that most directly leads to such a view is one that has already come up repeatedly in applied ethics topics discussed in previous chapters: utilitarianism (see Chapter 4). It is the normative standpoint that says whatever increases happiness (or "utility") the most, for the most beings overall, is what is morally right and even morally obligatory. One of its advantages as a normative theory is that it is impartial as to who should benefit; anyone capable of experiencing utility, or the lack thereof, is morally owed as much of an increase in happiness as is compatible with happiness for the greatest number. (This is an advantage because you would want a normative theory to have basic considerations of fairness and evenhandedness built into it.) As it happens, this theory naturally extends to the whole of the animal kingdom, insofar as many animals are capable of significant utility or suffering. The most obvious reason that animal-rights activists could give for thinking animal abuse is of such grave moral seriousness is that the serious deprivation of utility for animals is ipso facto a decrease in overall utility, which is what a utilitarian is primarily concerned with.

The philosopher who has unquestionably been the foremost ethicist of the animal-rights movement is Peter Singer, who is a utilitarian. His book *Animal Liberation* is widely considered the movement's "bible." Originally published in the 1970s, its many updated editions have chronicled the progress of animal rights. Singer has done more than any philosopher to apply utilitarian ethics to every important contemporary issue, including abortion, poverty, and euthanasia.

 Still Struggling

Utilitarianism is discussed in this chapter because it is an influential reason for advocating animal rights. If you ask for a philosophical justification for advocating animal rights, one must be given. And if utilitarian ethics is the basis of advocating animal rights, you must then consider whether you are willing to be committed to utilitarianism consistently and not just in cases where its application already agrees with your own views. If you are not willing to accept utilitarianism across the board but still want to advocate animal rights, you have to think of another philosophical basis for doing so. These philosophical issues are discussed in the last section of this chapter.

Bringing About the Greater Good: Ends

It should be noted that talking about "rights" within utilitarianism is, strictly speaking, out of place, so when utilitarianism is the normative philosophical basis at work, "animal rights" is a bit of a misnomer for the issue at hand. A right tends to be thought of as an absolute, inviolable protection for some entity. But according to utilitarianism, there are no such things. It says that no one has the "right" to anything, no matter what: if the time should come when someone's "rights" need to be sacrificed for the greater good, that is what should be done. When utilitarianism is the underlying normative standpoint, the discussion of rights should be understood as the right not to be caused to suffer without regard for the moral significance of that pain.

Utilitarianism provides a motivation for keeping animals from unnecessary suffering. But the flipside is that the utilitarian has to say that suffering is acceptable if it results in a net increase in overall utility. So, the utilitarian must grant that animal experimentation or factory farming would be acceptable if it brought about some greater good. This could either be an enormous benefit to relatively few beings (humans, for instance) or at least some moderate amount of benefit to a vast number of beings—whatever is sufficient to mathematically outweigh the suffering that made it possible. For factory farming, the utilitarian can easily say that the pleasure some humans take in eating meat does not come close to outweighing the suffering experienced by the huge numbers of animals who are raised and killed on these farms. But there may be cases in which animal experimentation does provide a greater good; say, in helping to cure diseases from which many humans would otherwise suffer and die. So, to be consistent with the fundamental utilitarian principle that the greatest (net) good for the greatest number of beings is what is morally best, the utilitarian should approve of animal experimentation if it brings about a greater good. However, utilitarian animal-rights activists point out that a large number of cases of animal experimentation are carried out purely for research purposes, with negligible, if any, benefits to humans (consider the radiation experiments on monkeys mentioned earlier).

Bringing About the Greater Good: Means

According to utilitarianism, an animal-rights activist should want to do whatever works best over the long term to increase utility. Consistent with this principle, many activists accept that pushing for smaller improvements than they would eventually like to see, at least for the short term, will better serve their goals. In particular, animal suffering by factory farming and experimentation might at least be minimized without being able to do away with it entirely. Some animal-rights campaigners push for whatever improvements can be made, such as making factory-farm slaughter as humane as possible, simply because they are less bad for the animals than existing practices are. These activists could say that smaller steps of improvement are easier to obtain than trying to get everything they want all at once, which might never work and would result in no improvement in animal treatment.

But someone who is morally convinced that animal rights should be advocated may not believe so on the basis of utilitarian ethics. Instead, a person could take a position that animals literally have certain rights not to be harmed for human purposes and that these rights should be upheld no matter what. Such activists may feel that they should settle for nothing less than the elimination of all objectionable practices, because that is what a specific principle such as "Animals should not be subjected to suffering by humans, regardless of what good may come from it" would require. To an activist who stands on a principle other than utilitarianism, settling for a smaller, short-term improvement in animal treatment would make it seem as though this improvement was all that was morally required, as though the principle involved were just to reduce animal suffering *somewhat*, whereas it would really require the maltreatment of animals to be eliminated *entirely*. Some people may even stand on a principle like this at the expense of obtaining any limited, short-term betterment (and possible further long-term progress), which is in sharp contrast to the basis for animal rights given by utilitarianism.

But in pragmatic terms, accepting limited, stepwise improvements in animal treatment could be seen as a better way to eventually get to a total elimination of the practices that all animal-rights activists agree are morally wrong. One of the sources of resistance to change from those in the relevant industries is that the full extent of the changes advocated by activists is such a long way from current practice that they must seem drastic and radical to factory farmers and researchers. But if the pressed-for changes do not seem so drastic, then they are more likely to be seen as being in the interests of those using animals. Once a limited improvement is made, the stage is easily set for another improvement to be made at some point down the road and so on. Eventually, if usual practice at some future point becomes sufficiently close to the ideal of animal-rights activists, then at that point, the factory farmers and animal experimenters (if there still are such people) may be much more likely to agree to go on and make the changes that are exactly what the activists want. For these reasons, the animal-rights activist who pushes for more gradual change probably has the better (or more effective) strategy.

Speciesism

The overall utilitarian ethic that provides the normative philosophical grounds for the animal-rights movement can (and should, to be consistent) be applied in a broader way than just to nonhuman animals. Peter Singer has done this—going further than suggesting just that animals should be treated much better than they are now—by urging that improvements in animal treatment should be part of a bigger sea change in how we think about the issue of species overall. He notes that many of us tend to ignore contemporary instances of the maltreatment of animals but, in sharp contrast, tend to want to preserve human life at all costs. Singer proposes that this is because we put the human species on a certain pedestal above all other species on earth. This means that we not only think we have the right to use animals as we please, but we seem to believe that human life has a unique value that is different from that of any other species. Singer notes that traditional morality seems to have it that a human life has a special value just because it is human, and we accord this value to no other species; he calls this attitude *speciesism* (a term Singer did not coin himself). It is perfectly analogous to racism, the attitude that certain people are superior and others inferior just because of their respective races.

Singer believes that the best principled way to improve the lot of animals is to eradicate the attitude of speciesism. That is, people should not discount the moral significance of nonhuman animal suffering just because such animals are not human. Instead, people should take into account the capacity for suffering of each kind of animal. This is, in fact, the view that utilitarianism takes to figure out how to maximize overall utility for all beings. This means that if human life is considered to outweigh the life of some other species, it should only be because humans have a greater capacity to enjoy utility than other species do. This is still consistent with the rejection of speciesism. What is *not* consistent is for human life to be favored over nonhuman life just because it is human. So, a utilitarian may reject speciesism and not object to certain cases in which human lives are favored over nonhuman lives. As long as such cases are decided on the basis of maximizing overall utility, human life may be favored over nonhuman life in a particular case simply because, in that case, the human lives have more capacity for utility than the nonhuman lives.

Of course, it is generally true that beings of certain species may have more or less capacity for utility than other species, and that this necessarily goes along with the membership of their species. Human beings have more capacity for utility than any other species on the planet, and this is part of their natural human characteristics. So putting the moral significance of animals of different species on different levels may look like speciesism, when it is actually being done on the basis of capacity for utility. Where speciesism itself can most clearly come into play is in specific cases where a particular human—say, one who is severely disabled in some way—actually has a much lower capacity for utility than a particular normal, nonhuman animal. Treating the life of that severely disabled human as if it still had special value just because it is human, and treating the life of the normal nonhuman animal as of less value just because it is not human, would be a clear instance of speciesism. So part of rejecting speciesism means not only looking at nonhuman animals in a different light but regarding some humans in a different light as well.

Unsanctifying Human Life

Part and parcel of basing moral decisions only on the maximization of utility is that the lives of human beings who are *not* capable of experiencing much utility should not carry much moral weight. That is, to be philosophically consistent with the elimination of speciesism, Singer urges us to think of the human species differently than we do now. Traditional morality has it that human life has a kind of special sanctity to it, where all human lives are entitled to special protection, regardless of a particular human being's capacity to enjoy utility. Practices such as infanticide and euthanasia are widely abhorred, and most people would say that this is because killing human beings always violates the special sanctity of human life. But Singer says that believing in this special sanctity only gets in the way of maximizing utility: it makes us (1) favor the lives of humans even when they cannot enjoy much utility and (2) devalue the lives of animals, even when their capacity for utility is quite high. That is, a consistent ethic that would allow us to maximize utility for all human and nonhuman animals would require "unsanctifying" human life.

This means that the lives of animals whose capacity for utility is thought to be comparable to that of humans can, in principle, be compared to human lives for the basis of moral decisions. For example, suppose that a normal dog's capacity for utility is considered to be half that of a normal human. In that case, the lives of two normal dogs would be considered of equivalent moral value to that of one normal human. Of course, it's hard to see how we could make an exact quantitative comparison of utility capacity between kinds of beings, but if we can be assured of even a rough basis of comparison, it would allow us to make some moral decisions. For example, a chimpanzee's capacity for utility is thought to be nearly that of a human being. We could be assured in saying, then, that the lives of fifty chimpanzees outweigh that of one human. To make a value judgment like this seems outrageous to most people, since we tend to think that the life of one human being has a special value that outweighs that of the life of any number of nonhuman animals. But Singer would say that this is because we are in the grip of speciesism and that those of us who accept the speciesism that goes with traditional morality should retrain our moral thinking so as to leave behind any doctrine that gets in the way of maximizing utility for all beings.

Another corollary to unsanctifying human life that goes with the elimination of speciesism is that the value of human lives that do not have much capacity for utility can easily be outweighed by other competing interests. For example, Singer would say that the life of one chimpanzee is more valuable than the life of one profoundly retarded child. It would also mean that the value of human lives that have negligible capacity for enjoying utility, such as those of a profoundly retarded child or an elderly adult suffering from dementia, can easily be outweighed by the capacity for utility of those who are burdened with caring for these individuals over long periods of time. The lowered utility for the caregivers does not result in much increased utility for those needing their care. So to relieve the burden of such caregivers, Singer says that invalids in this position should be put to death. This hardly results in any decrease in utility for the invalids, who do not get much benefit from being alive in the first place, and it greatly frees up those who had to care for them to do more to increase utility in their own lives, which unlike those of the invalids *do* have a significant capacity for utility. So putting invalids to death leads directly to an increase in overall utility for everyone. This is all necessary to be consistent with the utilitarian ethic that is the basis for the elimination of speciesism, the ethic that also requires unsanctifying human life.

All of this is part of holding to a consistent philosophical basis for maximizing the overall utility for all animals, both human and nonhuman. Most people, however, would be outraged at the prospect of putting invalids and terminally ill people to death, and this is enough to show that utilitarianism is not consistent with the normative basis for the traditional morality that most of us hold. Thus, if someone argues for a conclusion in a way that seems to require a utilitarian principle, that person should be pressed on the point to find out whether he or she is really committed to utilitarianism in all cases. If not, then that person cannot consistently argue on the basis of utilitarian principles—not, in any case, if those principles are supposed to apply only in arbitrarily selected cases.

All in all, Singer emphasizes the point that people's existing commitment to speciesism leads to a much lower overall utility for both human and nonhuman animals than would otherwise be possible. Consistent with rejecting speciesism, he thinks we should unsanctify human life so we don't favor all human lives, even in cases where unsanctifying human life does not increase utility; regarding human life as having a special sanctity is itself an instance of speciesism. The best way to understand the significance of this proposal and what it entails is to look at it from the standpoint of consistency. Singer notes that once we fully reject speciesism and instead treat animals and humans as essentially on the same footing, there are three ways in which we could change our views to make them consistent with that rejection (Singer 2002b: 224):

- Keep our attitudes toward animals as they are and begin using humans, such as retarded infants and other individuals who cannot live productive lives, as we already use animals, for experimentation and food.

- Keep our attitudes toward our own species the way they are and begin treating animals the way we treat humans, making it wrong to kill them for food; to subject them to experimentation, even when it would be tremendously useful; and to euthanize them, even if they are in terrible pain or a burden for their caregivers.

- "[C]hange our attitudes to both humans and nonhumans so that they come together at some point in between the present extremes." In other words, we can increase utility for animals more than we already do and at the same time not save or protect human lives in instances where it does not lead to an increase in utility.

Singer naturally favors the last option, because he thinks this is the best way to maximize overall utility for all beings.

Still Struggling

The point of unsanctifying human life is not to compensate or give reparation for instances of animal suffering. Rather, it is part of a whole utilitarian ethic that leads to increased regard for animals. The elimination of speciesism means that we take into account particular animals' capacity for suffering and do not base our moral regard on an animal's species. The elimination of speciesism also requires that we not view all human life as specially protected; if we do protect human lives, it must be because they result in increased utility. So the motivation for unsanctifying human life is just to free us from protecting human lives that do not increase anyone's utility.

Other Philosophical Grounds for Preventing Maltreatment of Animals

Most people are not utilitarians, as reflected by the fact that most people would not be willing to swallow the conclusion that we should put invalids to death in order to maximize utility or that the lives of enough chimpanzees would outweigh the life of one human being. Utilitarianism does provide a robust basis for advocating animal as well as human rights. But if you are not a utilitarian, it doesn't follow that you cannot feel obliged to prevent animal suffering. (To infer the rejection of concern for animals from the rejection of utilitarianism would be to commit the fallacy of denying the antecedent, as described in Chapter 2.) There are other possible philosophical grounds on which you could argue that the lot of animals used by humans should be improved. If you were pressed to give a reason why we should improve conditions at factory farms or eliminate these farms altogether, for example, you wouldn't necessarily have to point to utilitarianism as the basis for normativity and then be committed to applying utilitarian ethics in all cases across the board. Instead, you could point to a principle to which you *would* be willing to be committed in other cases besides animal rights and thereby (1) have a principled reason to care about animal rights and (2) be able to uphold that principle consistently in other cases as well.

Duty to Prevent Suffering

It could be that preventing suffering is, in and of itself, one of our positive duties. Then insofar as animals are sentient (conscious in some sense) beings, they would have a right not to be abused. It could be taken as a duty that we prevent all suffering, whatever the cost of doing so or the benefits of not doing so. This would be a different normative ground than that of utilitarianism, which is interested only in the consequences. In fact, the duty-based normative ground might be a better way to prevent suffering, at least in the short term, since utilitarianism has to accept suffering or killing in cases where it brings about a greater good (that is, an overall increase in net utility).

With this normative ground, you could still regard human life as "sacred" in some sense and not necessarily be inconsistent with the duty to prevent suffering. Whereas utilitarianism could not provide any moral obligation to protect life in cases where it does not increase utility, holding to a duty to prevent suffering would be consistent with holding to a duty to protect human life.

Intrinsic Value of All Life

Another moral basis for objecting to animal abuse would be to place a high moral value on allowing all life to flourish. You could take as a fundamental principle that all life, no matter how seemingly insignificant, is intrinsically valuable. Recall from Chapter 3 that things can be valued either intrinsically or instrumentally. Something with intrinsic value has value all by itself. In contrast, something with instrumental value is valued because it can bring about some other good. With this distinction in place, treating something with intrinsic value as though it had only instrumental value would be wrong, because it devalues something that has real value independent of how we treat it. For something that has real intrinsic value, what determines whether our treatment of it is morally good or bad is the real value of the thing itself and whether we treat it in accordance with its real value. So if all life of any species has intrinsic value, then no form of life should ever be treated as though it just had instrumental value, which is exactly what leads to abuse of animals and disregard for their suffering. This would mean protecting all animal life, even life that is not sentient.

This duty to protect life would entail protecting animals from abuse on grounds that are actually independent of whether or not any given animal actually experiences suffering—it would apply the same way to a fly as to a chimpanzee. Some Eastern religions value life this way and require strict vegetarianism, because using any animal for food would mean treating that animal as if it had merely instrumental value, an abuse of its intrinsic value. Some practitioners of Jainism are said to go so far as to sweep the road ahead of them to make sure they do not tread on any insects.

Natural-Law Ethics

Another normative basis for objecting to the abuse of animals is the "natural-law" perspective. (This normative stance was not discussed in Chapter 4.) According to this view, all features of nature, including humans and other animals, have a built-in sort of normativity that is based on the given nature of the thing itself. Your behavior toward a being can be consistent with the nature of that being, or it can be inconsistent with the being's real nature, which is what this perspective calls abuse. For example, animals that are predators need to kill and eat other animals for food. But it isn't immoral for them to do this, because they have absolutely no choice in the matter. It's in their nature to be predators, and it's part of the natural ecology in which they reside and have evolved for them to have prey. In contrast, humans are not natural predators; we do not actually need to eat animals.

If you took the natural-law perspective at its most conservative and cautious aspect, you could make a case for vegetarianism. This application would say that since it may be immoral for us to eat animals at all, we should err on the side of caution and not do so, since it is unnecessary for us to do so; unlike for carnivorous animals, none of the foods that are known to be part of our natural and required diet include meat. Or if you applied the natural-law perspective on a more lenient, liberal basis, you might say that since certain animals are raised specifically for human consumption, it has become natural for us to eat them. Milk cows are bred so that they produce far more milk than their calves need, so they *need* to be milked by humans. You could still object to factory farming conditions on this basis, though, because you could still say that this manner of using animals is not natural for them.

You could apply the natural-law ethic more broadly and consider what we do with animals to be of moral significance for the entire planet. For humans, you may take into account health problems that are associated with eating at least certain types of meat and ask whether that is worth the pleasure people take in consuming these meats. You may also consider the environmental impact of large factory farms in terms of the huge amounts of animal waste produced and the greenhouse gases, such as methane, that cows produce. Using animals in ways that are deleterious to our health and to the health of the planet as a whole can be objected to on a natural-law basis.

Chapter Summary

It is only relatively recently in the history of ethics that the question of protecting animals from various kinds of abuse has entered many people's minds. To determine what changes need to be made, there has to be a consistent ethical basis that decides what should be done and why. Utilitarianism is one influential normative ethic that has been cited as an effective philosophical basis for animal rights. But holding to it consistently would require repealing many tenets of traditional morality, such as the sanctity of human life, that most people would be loath to give up. But there are other possible normative standpoints from which to defend animal rights besides that of utilitarianism. So it does not follow that if you are not a utilitarian, you cannot care about improving the treatment of animals.

QUIZ

1. Most people today object to animal cruelty because they
   think _____.
   a. animal suffering is morally significant
   b. animals have the same rights as humans
   c. it involves a decrease in overall net utility
   d. humans should not use animals for their own purposes

2. Most animal experimentation _____.
   a. is done on higher apes such as chimpanzees
   b. is limited to the cosmetics industry
   c. does not lead to many animal deaths
   d. does not lead to significant medical advances

3. Factory farming is objectionable to animal-rights activists mainly because
   it _____.
   a. involves the killing of many animals
   b. entails deplorable living conditions for animals
   c. leads to animals being viewed as insignificant
   d. entails a lot of meat being eaten by humans

4. "Animal rights" is actually a misnomer for the cause as pursued from a utilitarian standpoint, because utilitarians think _____.
   a. animals by nature cannot have rights
   b. no one has rights that have to be protected
   c. human rights always come before animal rights
   d. rights can only be given to animals that feel pain

5. Utilitarianism is an effective normative standpoint from which to defend animal rights because it _____.
   a. opposes all suffering in any species of animal
   b. especially favors the happiness of nonhuman animals
   c. advocates the happiness of any species of animal
   d. is especially concerned with matters of justice

6. **Which of the following would be an instance of speciesism?**
   a. Not eating the meat of any animal species
   b. The lives of fifty chimpanzees outweighing one human life
   c. Human lives outweighing rat lives because of humans' greater capacity for utility
   d. Keeping a severely retarded child alive at the expense of several elephants' lives

7. **Peter Singer urges unsanctifying human life because he thinks _____.**
   a. human life is not as valuable as most people think it is
   b. no individual's life should be treated as having intrinsic value
   c. no animal's life should be viewed as more important than any other
   d. all individuals should be treated only according to their capacity for utility

8. **Which of the following does Peter Singer think is not consistent?**
   a. To treat all human life as sacred and animals with little concern for their suffering
   b. To treat people's suffering with as little concern as we do that of animals
   c. To treat human and animal life according to their respective capacities
   d. To treat all human and animal life as sacred

9. **Which of the following might be a direct result of a natural-law ethic for determining how animals should be treated?**
   a. Protecting the lives of all living beings, no matter how small or seemingly insignificant
   b. Not raising dogs for meat because that is not what dogs are for
   c. Preventing the suffering of any conscious being
   d. Treating all animals with regard to their capacity for suffering

10. **Which of the following might be a direct result of recognizing an intrinsic value in all life on earth?**
    a. Campaigning for improved conditions in factory farms
    b. Objecting to animal experimentation that does not result in a greater good
    c. Eating only food that does not require the killing of a living thing
    d. Unsanctifying human life so the utility of all animals can be maximized

chapter 12

Poverty and Affluence

In this chapter, you will learn the following:

- Ways of thinking about the ethical significance of poverty
- Influential ethical challenges to those who have the means to help those in need

We have all become used to the idea that standards of living vary widely among different places around the world and even among areas of the same city. The exercise of charity, where those with greater resources than others give to those most in need, is now commonplace. Almost everyone thinks that giving to charity is a worthwhile cause and that it is praiseworthy to do so. But when we compare the luxuries that most of us take for granted with the ethical significance of people in other places in the world dying of starvation and preventable diseases, charitable giving can take on an ethical urgency. If we can demonstrate a principled ethical obligation on the part of those who are able to help relieve human suffering, giving just whatever we feel like giving may not be enough to meet this obligation.

Unequal Access to Resources

The Industrial Revolution of the nineteenth century gave humans the ability to use resources to produce products and food at a much greater rate than before. Those of us living in "developed," industrialized countries today enjoy the fruits of that industry, as we have productive economies that generate all kinds of comfort-enhancing goods. In most of these countries, more than enough food is produced for everyone living there, so the great majority of citizens never have to worry about having enough to eat.

We take many of these comforts for granted as our normal standard of living. But in many parts of the world, people do not have access to the same luxuries. Many scrape by on a day-to-day basis, growing their own food. Their livelihood is subject to things like the weather, political crises, and other things they cannot control. The means and economic environment of these less fortunate often do not provide them with enough basic resources on which to live. Whereas the economic environment of industrialized countries provides those living there with more than enough resources, people who live in places with poor economic environments often end up very needy from a variety of causes. Thus, the inequality of resources to which people have access is a fact of our world. This is much truer today than it has ever been in history, simply because more people in industrialized countries have access to more comforts and amenities than there ever existed before.

Poverty

Poverty is usually defined according to a lack of access to economic resources. Within a society, those making the least amount of money relative to their needs are considered "poor." But *poverty* isn't just a relative term defined in terms of who happens to have the least money. The basic needs of people everywhere are objectively the same, and anyone with the resources to meet only those needs and nothing more would be considered poor. Even if a certain region contained only poor people, they would not all be considered "middle class" just because they were at the same level. People who live in poverty probably have a roof over their heads, just enough food and clothing for their family, and not much else.

Poverty is caused by a variety of factors, most of them outside the direct control of the poor themselves. For example, most of them are born into the conditions in which they live, which serves to perpetuate the poverty. Hardly anyone would think that people are poor simply because they are not willing to work hard enough. Therefore, many people feel a need to use their excess resources to do whatever is possible to help people in poverty find their way to a better economic situation. In short, insofar as most people are not ethical egoists (see Chapter 4), our society's consensus view is that helping the poor is, in itself, an ethically good thing. In fact, some would go so far as to say that for those with the means to do so (especially the richest among us), giving charitably to help those less well-off is obligatory in some sense.

Affluence

At the other end of the scale of economic privilege is affluence, the possession of significantly more money and resources than you need to live on. Like poverty, *affluence* isn't simply measured in relative terms, defined as whoever is the richest in a given society. If it were, we could call the poor affluent if everyone else lived below the poverty line. The notion of affluence is based on the resources relative to what anyone would need to meet his or her basic needs. (In absolute dollar amounts, it could be—and often is—that it takes more money to have your basic needs met in one country than it does in another. Affluence and poverty *are* relative to a given nation's economy in that sense, but the objective measure of what kinds of goods you are in a position to buy with your resources remains the same.) So, in objective terms, anyone above the level of poverty, by any amount, could be considered affluent.

The notion of affluence covers a wider ground than the notion of poverty does. Poverty is defined according to a baseline of what you need to survive. In everyday speech, the term *affluent* is used to describe people who are far above the poverty line and have more money than they know what to do with. But where do you draw the line to determine who is really "affluent" and who isn't? Considering a certain set of people affluent doesn't mean that people in the same society who are *not* considered affluent don't have a great many luxuries, objectively speaking. Even if we don't think of ourselves as affluent, most of us are used to a certain standard of living and don't consider many of the things we have to be luxuries. But this is only because we are used to them, not because they aren't luxuries in objective terms. The objective terms are based on whatever the poverty line of income is for a given society, and in these terms, anyone above the poverty line, by whatever amount, could be described as affluent.

Starvation and Disease

Wherever there is a baseline of poverty, there can be people above that line and people below it. People below the poverty line may be in need of immediate assistance to meet their basic needs. In addition, such people are particularly vulnerable to disruptions in their means to make whatever living they can. Many people throughout the world do not have the means to easily survive a crisis situation, such as a natural disaster or mass migration due to political upheaval. People in these situations can easily be threatened by imminent death due to their inability to meet basic needs like food, clothing, shelter, and medicine. This raises the ethical issue of helping such people. It is pretty uncontroversial that they *should* be helped; the only questions that remain are *by whom* and *how much*.

Just as it is considered ethically good to help those who have fewer resources than we do, it should be considered all that much better, morally, to help those in imminent danger of dying. It is easy to see how we might consider it obligatory to do so. The ethical urgency increases even more when we consider how easy it is to supply the kinds of basic needs that would suffice to sustain people in dire need, especially relative to the level of resources the affluent have at their disposal. Essential items like food and shelter, and the most rudimentary of medicines such as antibiotics, are often all it would take to save the lives of those in danger of dying from starvation and disease.

Ethical Challenges to Our Accustomed Standards of Living

While there are significant numbers of people in need of basic aid, there are also many people with plenty of money and resources. Given the question of an ethical obligation to give such money and resources to prevent the deaths of many people, we have to compare what it would cost the affluent to help the very needy. In terms of the objective definition of poverty given previously, the kinds of things on which the affluent would spend money if they did not give charitably are of much less moral value than saving people's lives. This difference can potentially generate a very strong moral obligation.

Singer's Original Challenge

A powerful argument for the ethical obligations of the affluent to the needy was made by Peter Singer (1972), who examined the moral dimensions of the issues we've just discussed, given the current facts about our world and those who live in it. He observed that human beings starve or are killed by easily cured and preventable diseases all the time, while governments, organizations, and individuals spend money, not to save these lives, but on things of far less moral urgency. Singer also noted that we cannot plead ignorance of others' needs, because the worldwide news networks (and now, the Internet) give us reliable and up-to-date information on trouble spots everywhere, no matter how far away.

Peter Singer is a utilitarian (as noted in the previous chapter), and we can easily see how the utilitarian principle can be applied to make an argument for the moral obligation to help those in need. Recall that a utilitarian thinks all moral obligations derive from the need to maximize the total utility (roughly, happiness) for everyone, no matter who or where they are. When people are in danger of starvation or other forms of easily preventable death, anyone with the means to help them ought to do so. Who are those with the means to help them? The affluent. This is especially true for the wealthiest people, but it is also true for anyone living above the poverty line, according to the broad sense of the term *affluent*. Although the affluent are accustomed to spending their money on their own luxuries, they *could* give the money to charities that would feed starving people.

By far the most morally significant form of utility is that which suffering people lack. The affluent have excess utility without which, if they gave away some of their resources, they would not really suffer in objective terms; that is, they would still have all the basic needs of life. Holding on to their luxuries—with the term *luxury* understood in the objective sense of "any excess utility"—is nowhere near as important as using those resources to save lives. So on a utilitarian basis, the conclusion is straightforward: the fact that the affluent are in a position to save people's lives just by foregoing their own luxuries obligates them to do so. This means if they do not do so, they are morally blameworthy.

This is a challenging conclusion to most people's concept of morality, because they tend to think of charitable giving as praiseworthy but also, in some sense, as optional—generous but not obligatory. That is, charitable giving to the degree that Singer urges is something we tend to think of as supererogatory, or going above and beyond what is morally obligatory. But recall from Chapter 4 that on the normative basis of utilitarianism, any action that increases utility is not only morally good but obligatory; there seems to be no room for the supererogatory as such. The reasons why hardly anyone would ordinarily think that charitable giving is obligatory and not giving is morally bad will be discussed presently. First, it is necessary to be clear about exactly what the conclusion is and what extent of charitable giving is to be considered obligatory.

Marginal Utility: Those at, Below, and Above It

As already discussed, there is a way to objectively define poverty as whatever means are necessary to sustain basic physical human needs and no more. In utilitarian terms, Singer defines this as the level of *marginal utility*. And, as also discussed, there is an objective sense in which anyone who has means beyond the poverty level is considered affluent, even if they are not the richest in a society. The affluent can thus be defined as anyone living above the level of marginal utility. But maximizing utility overall doesn't just mean totaling it up among everyone. If it did, many people could be dying while others enjoyed huge excesses of utility, and that excess might be considered enough to maximize the overall utility. Rather, the primary goal of maximizing utility is to prevent suffering. While people are suffering, it's no good putting resources toward increasing the utility of those at or above marginal utility, because the suffering people need those resources much more. So the excess utility the affluent enjoy is not nearly as valuable as the utility those below the level of marginal utility lack. This is what generates the affluent's obligation to give to increase the utility of those who would otherwise die.

This primary need to decrease suffering is what makes it incumbent on anyone living above marginal utility to do whatever he or she can to bring others up to the point of marginal utility. Figure 12.1 shows one way in which this might work. It is probably not possible to measure utility quantitatively, but we can compare relative utility roughly in relative terms, using marginal utility as a "100%" baseline. Suppose an affluent person (the giver) is at point A in the diagram, well above the level of marginal utility. If there are people below the level of marginal utility (the needy), the affluent are obligated to

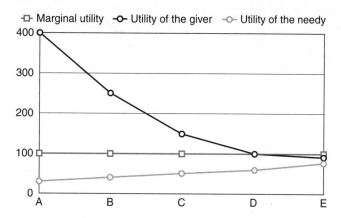

FIGURE 12.1   As measured in utilitarian terms, it is unjust for the affluent, who live above the level of marginal utility (defined as "100%" in this graph and the next), not to give money and resources to help those who are living (or dying) below the level of marginal utility. According to this ethic, as long as there are people living below marginal utility (the needy), anyone whose means are above marginal utility (the giver) is obligated to give until he or she reaches the point of marginal utility (point D) but no further (point E).

help relieve this group's suffering—that is, they are blameworthy if they do not. So suppose an affluent person gives to where she is at point B, having relieved some suffering. The giver is still well above marginal utility, and there are still people below marginal utility, so if the giver stops here, she is still blameworthy (although presumably not as much as if she had given nothing). Point C is an improvement over point B but still not enough to relieve the giver of all of her moral obligation. At point D, finally, she has given enough that she herself is right at the level of marginal utility. Then, even if there are still people below marginal utility at that point, the giver is not obligated to proceed to point E and sacrifice some of her own marginal utility. In fact, under utilitarianism, it is not even praiseworthy to do so, because utilitarianism does not care whether it's you or someone else who is below the level of marginal utility. Regardless of how many people are below marginal utility or how far, if you've given until you are at marginal utility yourself, you have discharged all your moral obligations.

Another example of how the basic utilitarian principle works with respect to marginal utility is shown in Figure 12.2. An affluent giver starting at point A can give through points B and C and still be obligated to give more. But if everyone should reach at least marginal utility (point D), the affluent are not obligated to give any more. (This is a highly unlikely scenario, but it is discussed

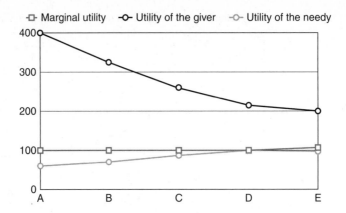

FIGURE 12.2   In another utilitarian scenario, as long as there is anyone below marginal utility (the needy), the affluent (the giver) are obligated to give to increase the needy's utility. If everyone's utility were brought up to the marginal level (point D), the affluent would not be obligated to give anything further (point E), even if they are still well above marginal utility themselves.

merely to illustrate how the principle works.) The fact that the affluent still have more wealth than others at point D is not, by itself, sufficient to obligate the affluent to proceed to point E, because the need to relieve suffering has already been met at point D. Again, the entire goal of maximizing utility in this setting is *not* to keep giving until everyone is at the same level or to otherwise effect a total redistribution of the amount of wealth; it is simply to aid those who are below marginal utility so that everyone can at least live.

 Still Struggling

Utilitarianism says that moral obligations come from the need to increase utility, first and foremost to prevent suffering. Comparisons of levels of utility can be made with respect to an objective standard, and this standard is given by marginal utility—having just what you need to survive. Resources can be put toward increasing utility for anyone. But utilitarianism says that given a choice of how to use available resources, they *must* be put first toward relieving suffering, no matter whose resources they are. If resources are put toward other things that are far less morally urgent, then any person making that decision would be considered ethically wrong.

The Psychological Problem of Distance

It is hard to argue against the idea that saving lives is far more important than having things we can easily live without. So why don't more people give to relief organizations, when it would be so easy to do and would result in such tangible benefits to those in need? The answer has to be that the affluent do not think much of the suffering of people who happen to live in faraway places. Furthermore, the affluent do not know the needy personally, so whether those people live or die has no direct impact on their lives.

Peter Singer proposes a simple thought experiment to help us explore our moral intuitions about our obligation to help others. Suppose you are walking by a shallow pond. You notice that a small child, who obviously cannot swim, is splashing around in the pond and drowning. You are wearing nice, new clothes that you don't want to get wet, so instead of going into the pond to save the child, you stand by while he dies. Anyone would say that your actions are monstrous. Wading into the pond to save the child would not only be a good thing, it would be morally obligatory for anyone; thus, it should be considered impermissible *not* to help. The value of your nice, new clothes is certainly negligible next to the value of someone's life.

Singer says that this is, in fact, analogous to how many of us act when we are in a position to save the lives of people far away; we prefer to spend money on our own luxuries instead—eating out, going to a movie, buying fashionable clothes or the latest electronic gadget, and so on. As in the drowning child scenario, we don't know or have anything to do with the people in need, but that certainly doesn't lessen our obligation to help. And by sending a check to a relief organization (or even more easily, donating online), we are just as capable of helping as those nearby. The only remaining difference, then, is the distance between ourselves and those in need. "Out of sight, out of mind" might be how we think about people in distant places who are in dire need of help.

But how could mere physical distance relieve us of the obligation to help? It can't, Singer insists: mere physical distance cannot make a moral difference. He makes the interesting suggestion that distance may make a significant *psychological* difference because our ordinary moral code evolved to apply to our behavior toward others in our own society, not toward outsiders. But ethical impartiality (which utilitarianism, at least, succeeds in establishing) requires that we help *anyone* in need if we are able. And, so the argument goes, that is what makes our inaction in not saving faraway people morally the same as the inaction in not saving a drowning child.

The Argument

Singer's argument overall goes as follows:

1. If we are able to save people from dying without sacrificing something of comparable moral value, we are morally obligated to do so.
2. We can save people far away from dying of starvation or easily treatable diseases without sacrificing something of comparable moral value.

Therefore, we are morally obligated to save people far away from dying of starvation or easily treatable diseases.

The drowning child scenario described earlier is supposed to establish the truth of premise 1. Any of us in that situation is obligated to save the drowning child, regardless of whether we would get wet, ruin our clothes, or anything of the kind. The scenario is *not*, however, meant to establish that we would be obligated to put our own life at risk (that's why the pond in the example is shallow), much less sacrifice our life for a stranger, but that much isn't necessary for the given purpose. All that's needed is to show that if all it costs us is much less than our own life, we are morally obligated to save the stranger's life. This also illustrates the difference (as already discussed) between the moral value of what the affluent usually spend money on and the moral value of the things that those who are below marginal utility need.

Since distance cannot plausibly be said to make a moral difference, it certainly seems that we *can* save the lives of people in faraway places without sacrificing something of comparable moral value; that is, premise 2 is true. The argument's form is straightforwardly valid. In that case, the conclusion of the argument has to be true: the affluent—anyone whose means are above the level of marginal utility—are morally obligated to give to help people in imminent danger of dying, no matter how far away or unfamiliar they are. But even of those who do give, very few give to the point at which they are at marginal utility themselves. So, since it is part of the definition of moral obligation that failing to meet that obligation is impermissible (that is to say, immoral), then almost everyone who is above marginal utility lives immorally by spending resources on themselves instead of to save lives. A hard pill to swallow, to be sure, but to resist the conclusion, we would have to find something wrong with one of the premises. The premises themselves are not explicitly based on any utilitarian principles; all that's needed to accept premise 1 is to agree with the point of the drowning child case. The argument represents a stark challenge indeed to those of us who would think it perfectly ethical simply to spend our own money on ourselves regardless of the needs of people far away.

The "Jack Palance" Thought Experiment

In failing to save people from dying, we are letting them die. If it is in our power to prevent people's deaths and we do not, we are failing to meet a moral obligation and therefore are morally wrong to let those people die. It is possible to take the moral obligation that Singer's argument appeals to in an even stronger sense, as in an argument by James Rachels (Rachels 1979). Recall from Chapter 10 that Rachels urged the acceptance of "active euthanasia" (or mercy killing) primarily on the basis that, contrary to popular belief, there is no moral difference between killing and letting die. (More precisely, if the only difference between two cases is the difference between killing and letting die, there is no moral difference between those cases.) In the context of arguing for euthanasia, the main task was to convince that killing in itself is no worse than letting die. As it happens, there is a flipside to that coin: if killing and letting die are morally equivalent, that also means that letting die is *no better* than killing. In that case, it is not only bad that we let starving people die, it is no better than if we killed them ourselves!

To illustrate this point, Rachels invites us to consider a thought experiment wherein the movie actor Jack Palance is in a room with several starving children. He has a plate stacked with sandwiches and chooses to eat them all himself, slowly savoring each one while the starving children watch, desperately needing just a bite. (Jack Palance seems to be the one chosen for this scenario because he was known as the epitome of the "tough guy." This makes the image vivid because it is relatively easy to picture such a person going beyond being tough into being flat-out callous.) What would we say of Palance in that situation? That he is something of a moral monster. This is supposed to represent a situation in which someone is so morally bad that we can hardly imagine a worse person. Palance all but killed those children himself; would he be any worse if he *had* killed them himself? Hardly, we are supposed to think.

The point of this thought experiment is to underwrite the purported moral equivalence of killing and letting die. The scenario applies to saving the lives of people overseas just as the drowning child case does. We "have nothing to do with" the people overseas dying of disease or starvation, just as Palance has nothing to do with the starving children; he just happens to be in the same room with them. The added force of the Jack Palance experiment is that if we do not help, we are not just like someone who fails to help a drowning or starving child; if killing and letting die are morally equivalent, we are morally like someone who kills the child ourselves. This takes the application of the utilitarian point of view to its full conclusion: if only the results matter, regardless of whether people are killed or we let them die, then if we do not save lives by giving away our excess "sandwiches," we may as well have killed the starving people ourselves.

Singer's Updated Proposal

We might think that such a conclusion is so extreme and runs so counter to our usual moral intuitions that few would accept it. This is, in fact, the case; at least, very few people have actually taken Singer's advice and given away all their resources above the level of marginal utility to help those in need. Singer has considered this fact in light of his utilitarianism and reconsidered a philosophical approach that might be more likely to result in some of the hoped-for increase in utility for suffering people. After all, utilitarianism requires not that we just argue for utilitarian conclusions but that we do whatever works to increase utility.

In his recent book, *The Life You Can Save* (Singer 2009), Singer concedes that to insist that everyone give everything they have above the level of marginal utility is perhaps not the best way to get the most relief aid to those who need it. People tend to be more taken aback than anything else by this advice, and even those who do agree and act on it will be more likely to make other people defensive and intimidated than to win them over by example. A seed of that worry was expressed in Singer's original paper (Singer 1972: 237), where he confronts the following possible objection to his argument's conclusion.

> It has been argued by some writers . . . that we need to have a basic moral code which is not too far beyond the capacities of the ordinary man, for otherwise there will be a general breakdown of compliance with the moral code. Crudely stated, this argument suggests that if we tell people that they ought to refrain from murder and give everything they do not really need to famine relief, they will do neither, whereas if we tell them that they ought to refrain from murder and that it is good to give to famine relief but not wrong not to do so, they will at least refrain from murder. The issue here is: Where should we [draw] the line between conduct that is required and conduct that is good although not required, so as to get the best possible result?

The objection he cited here says that if people have to add a burdensome obligation that is hard to put into practice to their morality, that might make them dismiss their entire morality out of hand. Singer's reply to this is that the possibility that all moral obligations might be rejected if one of them is too hard to accept "seems remote" (Singer 1972: 238), especially relative to the pressing need to give to relieve suffering. But the point could be modified to aim more specifically at the very idea of giving to charity. Imagine being a very affluent individual and being told that you are obligated to give all of your resources above marginal utility to feed starving people. You might be most inclined to react by putting any thought of people needing help out of your mind entirely. That way, you wouldn't have to think about the moral obligations you're not meeting by not giving. In effect, having Singer's original argument put to them could well make many people *less* likely to give to save lives.

Singer's modified recommendation is that everyone donate 1 percent of his income to humanitarian relief. This is a far cry from the stark conclusion that anything above marginal utility ought to be given away. But Singer defends this recommendation strictly from the consequentialist terms allowed by his utilitarianism, saying that this may result in more funds being given for relief. The idea is that if people adopt a modest expectation and don't push it on others, avoiding any suggestion of guilt that might make them defensive, others will be much more likely to adopt the same practice. If all goes well, the practice of donating 1 percent of their income could be adopted as a general expectation that more and more people take on, and this would result in more aid being given than otherwise would be. Singer's book is immensely practical in its approach; there is even an associated website where you can find out how best to help and hear testimonials from others.

A Nonutilitarian Approach

Yet another recent approach to the problem of affluence and need is that of Peter Unger. Unlike Singer or Rachels, Unger is not a utilitarian or even a consequentialist. But in his book *Living High and Letting Die: Our Illusion of Innocence* (Unger 1996), he argues for essentially the same sort of conclusion as that of Singer and Rachels. The difference is the basis on which he argues for it. Singer seemed to think that the entire ethic on which he based his original argument was revisionary in nature: that is, that it not only required people to accept a conclusion they hadn't before, but that to do so, it was necessary to revise the whole standard of morality they used to accept. As part of his original proposal, Singer urged that "the whole way we look at moral issues—our moral conceptual scheme—needs to be altered, and with it, the way of life that has come to be taken for granted in our society" (Singer 1972).

Unger, however, thinks that although our way of life should be altered, we can argue to that conclusion without having to revise our whole moral conceptual scheme (the set of assumptions with which we reason ethically). Rather, we can simply start with the standards of our ordinary morality and apply them consistently and without confusion. Unger's main idea is that irrelevant psychological distractions such as distance, which were also pointed out by Singer and Rachels, tend to skew the application of our existing moral intuitions. This is different from saying that our whole morality needs revision. As the title of Unger's book suggests, his conclusion is that we are not actually "innocent" to use our resources on our luxuries while others die, and that this can be demonstrated starting with the standards of the morality we already accept. We simply tend not to realize it, because we don't apply our existing moral principles as consistently as we ought to.

So although it might seem that conclusions like Singer's require utilitarianism as a starting principle and are not reachable without it, Unger states that the same kind of conclusion can be reached on the basis of ordinary morality. This makes the conclusion more accessible and widely applicable than it would be if we first had to be convinced of utilitarianism to accept that we are obligated to prevent people from dying. In other words, even though the conclusion is essentially the same, the basis of Unger's argument makes it easier to accept.

What the Challenges to the Affluent Do and Do Not Entail

Now let's address some possible objections and misconceptions that might arise about the conclusions we've discussed. First, it should be emphasized that the moral obligation to give that Singer and others argue for applies to people collectively as well as individually. The obligation to the individual arises from the obligation to the collective of which each individual is a part. Some people might try to deflect the obligation off of themselves because anyone else could also give but doesn't. But the fact that any number of people can also give of their resources does not lessen any individual's obligation to do so. To see why this is so, imagine you are back at the shallow pond, and a number of other people are no farther from the drowning child than you are: does the fact that they could do something lessen your obligation to do what *you* can? It certainly doesn't seem to. Since the responsibility to help is collective, the moral onus falls on anyone who doesn't do whatever he or she can—just as it would on anyone who stands by while the child drowns in the pond. Of course, it doesn't take *all* of them to save the child. But if no one does, *everyone* is culpable, because each person could equally have done something (Singer 1972).

Also, the obligation to give to relief efforts does not entail a total redistribution of wealth until everyone is equally poor. The ethical obligation discussed here comes not from the fact that some people are "poor," but that people will die unless they receive timely help. The obligation is simply for those with disposable income (as measured by being anywhere above marginal utility) to save lives that will be lost to starvation or disease. This should not require the total liquidation of capital and everyone descending to the level of marginal utility. Actually, Singer originally thought this would be a good thing (Singer 1972: 241). However, not only would saving the lives of those most in need not be so expensive as to require all excess utility to be liquidated, but doing so would actually be counterproductive. Without capital being invested in commerce in the first place, the resources needed to transfer goods and supplies to needy people would simply not exist. In that case, there could obviously be no humanitarian relief of the kind that Singer urges.

Another possible objection to investing in aid to those in need is that it does not solve the underlying problems that cause such crises. Pouring money into Band-Aid solutions, so this objection goes, does not do anything to prevent the need from continuing to arise in the future. In that case, it might not just be overly expensive to pour money into charity; it also might not be the best way to accomplish humanitarian betterment over the long term. To this, the reply should be that charitable relief is not supposed to be a long-term economic solution, but it also isn't incompatible with concurrently looking for more fundamental, long-term changes as well. It's true that humanitarian aid does not prevent crises from happening in the future. But by the same token, while trying to address underlying problems is a worthy cause, it doesn't save the lives of those suffering now. So being urged to give to humanitarian aid shouldn't be taken as a suggestion that we should focus on that *instead* of working for long-term solutions. It should be "both–and," not "either–or."

Finally, in being urged to give charitably and reacting to the argument that doing so is morally obligatory, it can be hard to know how to draw a line in order to tell whether we have done enough. In practice, this could keep people from making the move to give at all, since that would open the door to the uncomfortable question of whether they have done all that they are obligated to do. But this shouldn't be a barrier, because even if it is hard to tell when such an obligation has been discharged, we can still tell that *something* ought to be done. We can definitely tell if we're not doing anything and have excess utility. Any ethicist would certainly agree that doing something is a praiseworthy improvement over doing nothing.

Chapter Summary

Although charitable giving is normally thought of as an act of generosity, it has been influentially argued by leading ethicists that giving to those in dire need is obligatory. Who is obligated to give and how much can be defined according to whatever means are not as morally significant as the need to save lives. This can lead to a startling conclusion, which is that anyone above the poverty line who does not give to relieve suffering is immoral. When comparing the needs of the dying with the means of the affluent, some straightforward moral principles generate a strong obligation for the affluent to give to save lives. On whatever basis this obligation is argued for, however counterintuitive the conclusion is, it is not obvious how we might resist it. At the very least, it seems likely that the moral obligation to give to save the lives of faraway people is quite a bit stronger than we might ordinarily think.

QUIZ

1. **Poverty can be objectively defined in terms of** _____.
   a. whoever does not give away extra money to charity
   b. whoever makes the least amount of money in a society
   c. whatever means are required to sustain basic human needs
   d. whatever amount of money is given away by the affluent to charity

2. **Affluence can be objectively defined in terms of** _____.
   a. whoever does not give away extra money to charity
   b. whoever makes the largest amount of money in a society
   c. whatever means are required to sustain basic human needs
   d. whatever amount of money is needed by those in danger of dying

3. **People normally think of charitable giving as** _____.
   a. an act of generosity
   b. likely to induce guilt in others
   c. morally obligatory for anyone who can
   d. something in which only governments should be involved

4. **Singer's example of the child drowning in the shallow pond is meant to show that** _____.
   a. we are morally obligated to help those in need, even if we do not know them
   b. we are morally obligated to help those in need if we can easily do so
   c. distance from those in need of help cannot make any moral difference
   d. most people are morally worse than they think they are

5. **Singer believes that we are obligated to give to charities up to the point at which we** _____.
   a. feel better about ourselves
   b. are worse off than those already in need
   c. don't have all the luxuries that we might otherwise be able to afford
   d. have given up everything that is not as important as preventing suffering

6. **With regard to poverty and affluence, maximizing utility means** _____.
   a. getting everyone to the same level of utility
   b. getting everyone above the level of marginal utility
   c. preventing anyone from having any excess utility
   d. preventing anyone from being below the level of marginal utility

7. **The Jack Palance thought experiment is meant to show that** _____.
   a. we are morally obligated to help those in need, even if we do not know them
   b. distance from those in need of help cannot make any moral difference
   c. letting people die when we could easily help them is morally worse than most of us think it is
   d. movie actors can be some of the most callous people imaginable

8. **Singer's newest proposal about charitable giving is motivated primarily by** _____.
   a. not making people feel guilty
   b. getting the most relief aid to those who need it
   c. making an argument that most people will accept
   d. creating a community of like-minded people

9. **The difference between Peter Unger's case for charitable giving and that of utilitarians is that Unger thinks** _____.
   a. our existing morality already requires it
   b. a revision in our moral conceptual scheme is required
   c. the moral obligation to give extends to more people
   d. most people are morally worse than they think they are

10. **Seeing the task of relieving suffering as morally obligatory entails all of the following** *except* _____.
    a. people giving more than they might have thought they needed to
    b. giving charitably as long as there are people below marginal utility
    c. viewing luxuries as not of comparable moral value to saving lives
    d. everyone giving away everything above the level of marginal utility

chapter 13

Affirmative Action

CHAPTER OBJECTIVES

In this chapter, you will learn the following:

- The social inequities that the practice of affirmative action is meant to address and the ways in which it is intended to correct those inequities

- Some criticisms and defenses of the justice of affirmative action

People of minority races in any country tend to be subject to discriminatory practices that limit their opportunities simply because of their race. Ethicists, as well as most people in developed nations, are virtually unanimous in condemning such discrimination as unjust. However, unjust discrimination continues to occur, whether people consciously intend it or not. Also, people of minority races are often born into underprivileged circumstances that result from past discrimination toward their forebears. This tends to ensure that people born into these circumstances will also have limited opportunities, even if they are not discriminated against, and their offspring will presumably end up in a similar situation.

Since the civil rights movement of the 1960s, there have been attempts to correct these inequities by means of *affirmative action*—specific efforts to increase the opportunities of minorities that have historically been discriminated against. Typically, this has involved some form of preferential selection that increases the representation of minorities in various professions and educational institutions to where that representation is greater than it would be otherwise. There are those who say this is necessary to address the present circumstances and inevitable discrimination that minorities actually face. Others insist that affirmative action only adds new injustices to past ones and that it may even be counterproductive toward the goal of improving the status of minorities.

The Case for Affirmative Action

For centuries, at least, there have been stark inequalities in how people of different races living in the same country have lived. The worst sort of example is that of the people who were wrested from their homes in Africa, forcibly brought to the Americas and Europe, and owned as slaves. It has been a century and a half since slavery was officially found unjust and abolished. But it is only in the last few decades that the injustice of the differences in opportunity for people of different races has been widely recognized as such. Since then, action has been taken to correct this problem and improve the station of minorities. The general term for such corrective measures is "affirmative action." Throughout this chapter, this term will refer to preferential selection practices on behalf of minorities. There are various normative standpoints from which the practice of affirmative action can be, and has been, defended. But as with any particular ethical issue, its advocates and critics do not always communicate, or even think, clearly about what their general normative commitments are or, specifically, how they bear on the issue of affirmative action.

Addressing Past Injustices

Perhaps the most basic motivation for affirmative action among its advocates is that *something* has to be done to recognize current inequalities and the injustices of the past that have led to them. Recall from Chapter 6 the difference principle that governs the most basic requirements of justice and fairness. It says that if two people are treated differently, it must be because there are salient differences about them or their circumstances. Likewise, if two people are basically the same and in exactly the same kind of circumstances, they should be treated the same. By this measure, it would be unjust for people in the same circumstances to be treated differently. Likewise, it would be unjust for people in different circumstances to be treated the same, as if their circumstances were the same. This is where the need for measures like affirmative action comes in. From the standpoint of ensuring that justice is served, *not* putting something like affirmative action into practice would be seen as unjust on the basic grounds of treating people the same when their circumstances are different. In other words, to do nothing would be to act as if there had never been any long-standing racial discrimination and differences in opportunity in the past; it would be consistent with pretending that past injustices never happened.

As it happens, this concern about justice in terms of the difference principle can also be appealed to as grounds for finding racism in general to be unjust. The assumption is that discriminating against people on the basis of race is to treat people differently when the difference should make no difference at all. People of any race are human beings with the same basic capacities and rights, so race is not supposed to be a relevant difference in how people are treated and cannot be the basis for justifying treating certain people differently. But even though affirmative action is also racial discrimination in favor of minorities, it can be viewed as a necessary measure to correct the results of past unjust discrimination. That is, given this past discrimination, minorities are in a different position from the majority and therefore should now receive different treatment that is in their favor.

Thus, it is possible to defend affirmative action simply from the standpoint of justice—looking at the injustices of the past and seeking to do something about them now. If the only principle at work were the difference principle, affirmative action might simply have the goal of making reparations to those who have been discriminated against or perhaps even whose ancestors were mistreated on the basis of race. The added advantage to those who benefit from affirmative action would be thought of as helping to balance out historical wrongs. This minimalist notion of justice may not even provide a reason to care particularly what the *results* of affirmative action are.

If the primary motivation for affirmative action were the results expected from it, the most straightforward way to justify this would be from the standpoint of consequentialism (see Chapter 4). But concerns about pure justice are outside the scope of consequentialism itself; justice or injustice per se is not directly relevant to this theory, which is only concerned with bringing about good results regardless of whether the means to that end are just or unjust. It is not that proponents of a purely justice-based normativity cannot be concerned about future consequences; it's just that they don't necessarily have to bring them into consideration. On the other hand, from a normative stance of pure consequentialism, any appeal to considerations of justice requires some explanation as to how they bear on the consequentialist dictum to simply bring about the best results.

Not many people would likely defend affirmative action purely on the basis of applying the difference principle to address past injustices. Few would tend to think justice simply requires doing something to compensate for past wrongs, regardless of what benefits it might bring to minorities now and in the future. On the other hand, a justice-driven motivation might be concerned with correcting for the historical disadvantages under which minorities have lived. In that case, affirmative action might be thought to address—and perhaps redress—past injustices and, by doing so, improve the lot of minorities today. Enhancing minorities' current opportunities would thus help fix the results of past injustices that are the reason for their present disadvantaged station in life. When people defend affirmative action on the basis of correcting past injustices, they probably mean that justice also requires that those corrections improve the status of minorities now and in the future too. The natural connection between past inequalities and present ones provides the most likely basis for this sort of justification.

Correcting Present Discrimination

Prejudiced views of people of minority races—ascribing certain characteristics to them simply on the basis of their race—have been long-standing and accepted in the past. Since the civil rights changes made throughout the 1950s and 1960s, discriminating against people simply on the basis of race has come to be widely thought of as unethical and actively discouraged. It is hard to deny, though, that prejudice against minorities still occurs. Much of it may happen at the unconscious level, whereby people make certain assumptions or judgments about people based on their race, without actually entertaining conscious thoughts of minority races having certain characteristics. In an article in defense of affirmative action, the literary critic Stanley Fish (1993), who is white, cites an episode of a network news program in which standing racial prejudices of people in their daily lives was examined "in the field":

> In a stunning fifteen minute segment, reporters and a camera crew followed two young men of equal education, cultural sophistication, level of apparent influence, and so forth around St. Louis, a city where neither was known. The two differed in only a single respect: one was white, the other black. But that small difference turned out to mean everything. In a series of encounters with shoe salesmen, record-store employees, rental agents, landlords, employment agencies, taxicab drivers, and ordinary citizens, the black member of the pair was either ignored or given a special and suspicious attention. He was asked to pay more for the same goods or come up with a larger down payment for the same car, was turned away as a prospective tenant, was rejected as a prospective taxicab fare, was treated with contempt and irritation by clerks and bureaucrats, and in every way possible was made to feel inferior and unwanted.

Thus, the reality of racial discrimination and prejudice today could be taken as sufficient reason for the need for affirmative action. The idea would be that, given the prevalence of racial discrimination, it is insufficient simply to expect or even ask people to be evenhanded in their treatment of everyone. Racial discrimination can be played out on an unconscious basis—much of what Fish describes could be the result of purely unconscious prejudice—so affirmative action could be seen as necessary to correct for the inevitable differential treatment of minorities that puts them at a significant and unfair disadvantage. If nothing can be done to eradicate prejudicial attitudes, this motivation for affirmative action seeks to recognize frankly the fact that they exist and compensate for the reduced opportunities arising from discriminatory selection practices by giving minorities enhanced opportunities in a different way.

Ensuring Future Opportunities

The facts of inequality in racial treatment are not only current but also rooted in the past. Many minorities are poor and disadvantaged today because they were born into a situation like that in which they presently live. Their parents were in a similar situation because they were born into it too, and that was because of *their* parents' status and living situation, and so on. For blacks, for example, this is traceable all the way back to when people from Africa were kidnapped and traded as slaves overseas. Even when blacks were freed from slavery, they did not suddenly find themselves with opportunities equal to those of whites, because they essentially had to start over from scratch; even as free people, they found themselves at the bottom rung of the social ladder. In addition, they continued to face pervasive maltreatment and discrimination. When official policies of discrimination and segregation were finally abolished, blacks found themselves in a situation analogous to that of their ancestors when they were freed from slavery—equal to whites in principle but still severely hampered by the past circumstances that brought them to that point. Historical limitations such as poverty and poor access to education prevent minorities from enjoying the full range of possible opportunities to fulfill their potential.

It might be hoped that affirmative action policies will give minorities a needed boost out of the historical precedents with which they are burdened. Thus, affirmative action can be defended as a means to ensure that racial inequalities rooted in historical status differences do not continue to perpetuate themselves. Without such measures, minorities could easily continue to form an underclass on a permanent basis, even with equal treatment under the law. If the goal of overcoming racial discrimination is to bring about equality in real terms such as opportunity and socioeconomic status, affirmative action might be deemed necessary to provide opportunities for success that would not otherwise be available. The most straightforward way to defend affirmative action toward this end is with consequentialism: whatever it takes to help minorities overcome the disadvantaged position in which they find themselves should be done. But if that is the basis for the argument, then the advocate of affirmative action needs to be certain the practice really does help minorities overcome their disadvantaged position. There is no way to tell in advance whether it will succeed, so if the practice of affirmative action is justified on the basis of its positive consequences for minorities that could not be accomplished otherwise, there should be quantifiable terms by which to measure the success of this aim. If it is not successful, it should be discontinued.

If pressed on the matter and asked whether they are willing to be consistent in their commitments, relatively few of us will opt for thoroughgoing consequentialism. But if pure consequentialism is not our chosen normative basis, we must choose another instead and be committed to *that* consistently. Arguing for certain ethical conclusions on one normative basis and conclusions on other matters based on a different normative standard is not philosophically consistent: the whole point of having a normative basis for an argument for a certain ethical conclusion is to see what generally applicable normative theory yields that conclusion. Otherwise, we may be choosing a normative standpoint for a given argument on an ad hoc basis just to ensure that an argument reaches a specific conclusion to which we are already committed. But this is backward; it turns philosophy on its head and gives an after-the-fact rationalization of what we want to believe in the first place. This is the challenge that a systematic pursuit of ethical philosophy presents to those thinking about any ethical issue. With regard to affirmative action, advocates need a consistent philosophical basis for arguing that it is an ethically just policy, and the same basic ethical standpoint needs to be used to defend it against potential objections.

Objections to Affirmative Action

Obviously, anyone who thinks that blacks or other minorities should not be afforded the same opportunities as others in our society will object to affirmative action. Such a person would object to minorities reaching equality of status or to any measure that might be undertaken with this as an aim. But it doesn't follow from this that any objection to affirmative action *must* come from a desire to limit the opportunities of minorities. Objections to affirmative action itself can arise from other motivations. Anyone, including minorities, might object to affirmative action—in spite of its good intentions and to the assumption that it will bring about a desired outcome—purely on the grounds that it does not bring about its desired results or that it is unjust. Criticisms of affirmative action can come from a variety of angles.

More Discrimination?

Perhaps the most apparent feature of affirmative action is that it works by favoring those of minority races. To do that, it has to discriminate between people on the basis of race. This can certainly seem ironic, given that it is supposed to correct long-standing and unjust differential treatment based on race. This irony is one of the most common criticisms of affirmative action. Opponents suggest that advocating affirmative action is hypocritical, since its practice tries to correct for discrimination on the basis of race by engaging in *more* discrimination and actually institutionalizing it, thereby ensuring that racial discrimination happens. We often hear such objections put like this: where it is granted that discrimination against minorities is objectionable, discrimination in *favor* of minorities is just "reverse discrimination."

"Reverse Discrimination"

The word *reverse* in the term "reverse discrimination" evidently means the direction in whose favor the discrimination is applied—discriminating in favor of minorities instead of against them. But if *reverse* is taken only as a modifier for *discrimination*, then its usage can seem a bit peculiar. In that sense, the expression "reverse discrimination" would be fitting if *discrimination* simply meant discrimination against minorities; then "reverse discrimination" would mean discrimination in favor of minorities. But why is discrimination against minorities objectionable? Those against affirmative action may say simply because it is an instance of discrimination. So they would hold that discrimination is discrimination, whichever way you cut it; in which case, they *should* say there's no such thing as reverse discrimination.

But the defender of affirmative action will probably want to say that what is wrong with discrimination against minorities is that it leads to unjust deprivation of opportunities for them. Acting against this specific sort of injustice is certainly the point of affirmative action. So is it discrimination per se that is unacceptable? If so, then the critic may have a sound objection to affirmative action. Or is it unjust deprivation of opportunities for minorities that makes racial discrimination objectionable? In this case, the proponent of affirmative action may have a sound defense of discrimination in favor of minorities. As it happens, addressing injustices toward minorities is the motivation behind the practice of affirmative action. So it doesn't necessarily hold that, in advocating a certain form of discrimination in favor of minorities, the affirmative action proponent is being contradictory. The reason for decrying discrimination against minorities as unjust is because of the unjust circumstances to which it leads. In that case, if racial discrimination could be used in minorities' favor and to correct the effects of discrimination against them, an advocate of affirmative action would not be hypocritical.

However, if advocates of affirmative action take this stance, they are committed to saying that racial discrimination is not wrong in and of itself, but only because and when it leads to a disadvantaged position for minorities who are discriminated against. In other words, to defend against the charge of hypocrisy, a commitment to consequentialism seems necessary; consequentialism views all wrong actions as wrong only because of the harm they bring about. The situation is analogous to the utilitarian who views killing as wrong in typical cases only because and when it brings about the death of people against their will; if killing is needed to bring about a greater good, such as a significant decrease in suffering, then it would be morally necessary. (See Chapter 10 for the application of this theory to the topic of euthanasia.) This is not, of course, to draw a comparison between the acts of discrimination and people killing themselves. The parallel is in how consequentialism applies to either case; the moral goodness or badness is assessed purely in terms of the consequences. Meanwhile, if someone objects to discrimination against minorities only because it is a case of racial discrimination (which always hurts somebody by putting him or her at a disadvantage), that person will also have to object to affirmative action purely because it is an instance of discrimination too; such a person would be inconsistent not to object to affirmative action for this reason.

Reply: Affirmative Action as a Necessary Measure

In the article cited earlier, Stanley Fish said the following about the need for affirmative action even if it involves discrimination:

> "Reverse [discrimination]" is a cogent description of affirmative action only if one considers the cancer of racism to be morally and medically indistinguishable from the therapy we apply to it. A cancer is an invasion of the body's equilibrium, and so is chemotherapy; but we do not decline to fight the disease because the medicine we employ is also disruptive of normal functioning. Strong illness, strong remedy: the formula is as appropriate to the health of the body politic as it is to that of the body proper.

Someone may object to affirmative action by saying something like, "The cure is worse than the disease." But a defender of affirmative action, in the spirit of Fish's quote, would reply that the cure surely can't be worse than the disease. Rather, looking at the magnitude of the injustices suffered by minorities in the past and the tremendous obstacles they have to overcome now, preferential hiring or admissions policies are certainly not worse than the injustice of those disadvantages. They may also be regarded as the least society can do on behalf of minorities in the interest of rectifying inequality.

If we assume that affirmative action is much less bad than racial injustice against minorities and that it effectively corrects such injustice, Fish's defense of it seems to come from a consequentialist standpoint; at least, if we were to look for an underlying normative ethic, consequentialism would make perfect sense of what Fish says. If the analogy were exact, we could say that whatever means were necessary to bring about real racial equality in practice would have to be accepted. But of course, the analogy isn't exact for nonconsequentialists: hardly anyone would object to chemotherapy if it were necessary to save the life of someone with cancer, but outside of medicine, people can and do justifiably scrutinize the means to see whether they are a justifiable way to ensure a given end. Furthermore, in the case of affirmative action, there is no way to ensure that it will bring about its intended consequences. So even if consequentialism were granted, the ethical propriety of affirmative action would still be debatable. And if consequentialism is not granted, there may certainly be grounds for objecting to affirmative action per se. In that case, even if we grant that it *would* be successful in bringing about an improved status for minorities, we may not agree that it is a justifiable means of reaching that end.

There is another "disanalogy" between affirmative action and chemotherapy, which is chemotherapy is normally used because it is necessary to save someone's life. But even if it is granted that affirmative action is *sufficient* to bring about the desired end, it might not be *necessary* to bring about that end. In informal reasoning, people often confuse necessary and sufficient conditions: they tend to think that if x is a sufficient condition to bring about y, then it is also necessary to bring about x in order to bring about y; that is, y could not be achieved without undertaking x. But granting that x is a sufficient condition for y says nothing about what will happen if x does *not* happen. Although it may be a sufficient condition for y, something else may also be a sufficient condition for y. If that is so, then even if x is a sufficient condition for y, it will not be necessary. Concluding x's necessity from its sufficiency is equivalent to the fallacy of denying the antecedent (see Chapter 2). If x is a sufficient condition for y, this means "if x, then y." But if not-x, not-y does not follow: y might be true for some other reason. Conversely, if x *is* a necessary condition for y, this means that "if y, then x." In other words, if y has happened, then you know that x must have happened too because it is a necessary condition for y. This inference happens in a reverse direction from x being a sufficient condition for y. Although x may be a sufficient and necessary condition for y (in which case, we would say "x if and only if y"), sufficiency and necessity are still two different things: a condition being sufficient to bring about its effects does not by itself entail that condition x is also necessary for bringing about the effect y.

Specifically with regard to affirmative action, it could be that racial equality will be achieved naturally over time as the equilibrium gradually shifts away from inequality. This may take at least several generations, but given this possibility, a fully successful defense of affirmative action would have to show either that equality cannot be achieved without affirmative action (that is, affirmative action is both sufficient *and necessary* for bringing about equality) or that enacting affirmative action policies now will bring about such results much more quickly than otherwise, making it justifiable for that reason.

Unjust Justice?

Opponents may object to affirmative action purely from the standpoint of justice—for example, because it is an instance of discrimination. This seems to be what is intended by use of the phrase "reverse discrimination." Another way of putting it would be in terms of the ethical folk wisdom that says two wrongs don't make a right. If discrimination against minorities is unfair, so this objection goes, then so is discrimination in favor of minorities (which is ipso facto a case of discrimination against those of the majority race in a society).

Stanley Fish points out that the discrimination involved in affirmative action can only be regarded as unfair if we considered both sides as starting from a level playing field. But obviously they don't, and this is the reason affirmative action is practiced. Additionally, the injustices minorities such as blacks have historically suffered go well beyond unfairness. According to Fish, "When the deck is stacked against you in more ways than you can count, it is a small consolation to hear that you are now free to enter the game and take your chances."

Affirmative action may also be defended on a principle of justice. Given the difference principle (as cited earlier; see Chapter 6), it may be regarded as unjust to treat minorities as though their historically disadvantaged position never happened. Even if we grant that doing nothing to boost the historically disadvantaged is unjust, it does not follow that *anything* done to help them would be just. Some methods might appropriately correct for past injustices, such as those that do not hurt others' opportunities. As noted previously, though, discrimination in favor of minorities is necessarily a case of discriminating against those of the majority. But if this is thought unjust, a defender of affirmative action may reply that current opportunities for whites were arrived at unjustly—as minorities are now unjustly hampered by past discrimination and inequality, those in the majority now enjoy privilege and opportunities that result from historical discrimination in their favor. To those of the majority who are passed over for positions in favor of a minority candidate, the affirmative action advocate will say, "Don't take it personally" (Fish 1993); it's not a slight against any given person and his or her race, just an attempt to compensate for historical patterns of inequality to tip the scales back toward an overall, long-term realization of justice. The critics and defenders of affirmative action may generally both support their position by an appeal to justice, but they do it in different ways: the proponent is primarily motivated by correcting the injustice of historical patterns of inequality, and the opponent is primarily motivated by criticizing the justice of affirmative action itself.

Presuming Victimhood? Perpetuating Discrimination?

Another way to object to affirmative action is in seeing another sort of irony that is intrinsic to the way it works. To implement affirmative action policies is to assume that minorities need such policies and will not be able to succeed without them. Affirmative action addresses existing inequalities, but as long as it is in place, it carries with it the presumption that there are inequalities and that minorities cannot realistically be expected to succeed without the extra boost from its policies. Affirmative action recognizes that minorities have been the victims of unjust discrimination and inequalities of opportunities, but there is a flipside: in explicitly addressing the problem this way, individuals of minority races are assigned a special status as victims, which still sets them apart from those of the majority, even if it is in a way intended to further the interests of minorities by helping them overcome unequal status.

Shelby Steele, a former professor of African-American studies, says, "Under affirmative action the quality that earns us preferential treatment is an implied inferiority" (Steele 1991: 116). In other words, affirmative action is not used only to correct for discrimination, but also to recognize the fact that their disadvantaged background actually makes minorities less qualified. Steele says this is enough of a problem in itself, but it is also

> . . . compounded by the cultural myth of black inferiority that blacks have always lived with. What this means in practical terms is that when blacks deliver themselves into integrated situations, they encounter a nasty little reflex in whites, a mindless, atavistic reflex that responds to the color black with alarm. Attributions may follow this alarm if the whites care to indulge them, and if they do, they will most likely be negative—one such attribution is intellectual ineptness. . . . [T]he black will be aware of the reflex his color triggers and will feel a stab of horror at seeing himself reflected in this way. He, too, will do a quick repression, but a lifetime of such stabbings is what constitutes his inner realm of racial doubt (117).

The attitudes, even unconscious ones, of whites toward blacks that Steele describes is part of what motivates the need for affirmative action. But Steele goes on to say that, ironically, "the implication of inferiority that racial preferences engender in both the white and black mind expands rather than contracts this doubt." The end result of this seems to be that even if affirmative action gives minorities a needed boost, without which they would continue to have limited opportunities available, they can never be certain if they have succeeded on the basis of their own merits.

Of course, one reason that affirmative action is considered necessary is to correct for existing discrimination purely on the basis of race. Thus, even if minorities had every reason to think of themselves as qualified and generally not disadvantaged, objectively speaking, they may still need the help of affirmative action to correct for the effects of conscious or unconscious racial prejudice that people of the majority may have. But for how long should it be necessary to assume that minorities will be unjustly discriminated against? Most advocates recognize that affirmative action is only a temporary measure. But if that is so, conditions for reaching an endpoint, at least in theory, should be specified. Otherwise, even if it is considered temporary, it may go on indefinitely in practice. One way of specifying an endpoint is to keep affirmative action policies in place until measurable social equality is achieved. The potential problem with this is that it is possible that affirmative action only keeps minorities from striving for real excellence or that it perpetuates discrimination against minorities by leading people to assume that minority individuals have reached certain positions only because of their race and not their qualifications (as suggested by Shelby Steele). In that case, affirmative action's stated goals would never be achieved, yet it would continue to be practiced, even though it perpetuates the very inequalities it seeks to correct. Above all, affirmative action advocates need a good reply to this worry.

Summarizing the Overall Picture

The most basic difference between the views of the defender and critic of affirmative action is that the defender wants to avoid doing *nothing*, while the critic is most troubled by the possible injustice by which affirmative action advocates want to do *something*. In the most cynical light, the comparison could be put in the terms of the nineteenth-century satirist Ambrose Bierce, who has been quoted as saying, "A conservative is enamored of existing evils; a liberal wants to replace them with new ones." What can be said, at least, is that if the critic of affirmative action is primarily focused on avoiding the potential evils that may come from correcting for racial inequalities, and the defender of affirmative action is primarily occupied with avoiding the evils of *not* correcting for racial inequalities, there is a real danger of the critic and advocate talking past each other. That is, if each side sticks to its respective guns in its focus, each may seek to defend the interests of justice but will never be able to see eye-to-eye with the other.

It may be unjust to do nothing to correct racial inequalities. But it doesn't follow that *anything* done to correct those inequalities will automatically be justifiable. It could still be unjust to discriminate on the basis of race even to help minorities and even if affirmative action is successful in its mission. There may be other ways of fixing underlying socioeconomic problems to address inequalities, and doing so wouldn't be doing nothing.

In any case, for defenders and critics of affirmative action to communicate meaningfully with one another, they should both address the concerns of the other and try to incorporate those concerns into their own position. Almost no critics of affirmative action don't want to see minorities do well, and almost no advocates of affirmative action actually wish bad things on the majority. There ought to be frank acknowledgment of these facts by both sides, and each should make efforts to reach an agreement that accommodates the concerns of both sides, justifiable as they are. Otherwise, there is little hope of society coming to a consensus on this issue.

Chapter Summary

Practically everyone in society today decries the past injustices that have been done to minorities on account of their race. People still disagree as to what, if anything, should be done to correct current circumstances that are rooted in past injustices and to compensate for continuing discrimination. The practice of affirmative action takes intentional steps to correct inequalities of opportunity by enacting preferential selection in favor of minorities who have faced significant disadvantages in the past. But the practice of affirmative action raises another set of potential difficulties related to discrimination in favor of minorities. Critics may be concerned that affirmative action itself is unjust, in spite of being motivated by the desire to correct injustices against minorities. They may also worry that affirmative action might not even succeed in bringing about its intended aims; ironically enough, it could perpetuate the very inequalities it seeks to address. Our society assumes that everyone wants an equal opportunity for all; even so, care must be taken to ensure that whatever means are undertaken to achieve this end are both necessary and sufficient to bring them about. Otherwise, the side effects of such means may not be worthwhile.

1. **Which of the following is not one of the motivations for affirmative action?**
   a. Relying less on merit in hiring decisions
   b. Improving historic socioeconomic status
   c. Correcting for discrimation against minorities
   d. Compensating for past injustices

2. **Which of the following motivations for affirmative action would be most strongly supported by a commitment to consequentialism?**
   a. Minorities have to deal with a playing field that is not level to begin with.
   b. Without affirmative action, minorities would not be able to have equality of opportunity.
   c. Minorities continue to be discriminated against unjustly.
   d. Injustices of the past must be redressed by compensating minorities today.

3. **Supposing that affirmative action brings about an increase in opportunity for minorities, which of the following would be the most effective criticism of affirmative action?**
   a. Affirmative action may result in a decrease in historically based white privilege.
   b. Affirmative action has to involve racial discrimination in order to work.
   c. It may be possible for equality for minorities to be achieved without the use of affirmative action.
   d. Minorities should not have the same opportunities as those of the majority.

4. **Assuming that minorities have capacities that are equal to those of the majority and that no one today will discriminate against minorities on account of their race, why might affirmative action still be considered necessary?**
   a. Discrimination in favor of minorities is needed to balance out past discrimination against them.
   b. Affirmative action sets an example as to how to treat minorities.
   c. Without affirmative action, minorities would be treated just as if they were of the majority.
   d. Past inequalities have led to a position of unjust disadvantages for minorities today.

5. **If affirmative action is regarded as a temporary measure, then _____.**
   a. its effects will need to be limited in scope
   b. conditions for its cessation will need to be set in advance
   c. it does not have to be demonstrated that it will succeed
   d. it should be tried to at least ensure that it works

6. Discrimination in favor of minorities entails _____.
   a. past injustices being put right
   b. improved economic status for minorities
   c. discrimination against those of the majority
   d. compensation for past discrimination against minorities

7. To the charge of hypocrisy for addressing past discrimination by enacting new forms of discrimination, the defender of affirmative action should say that discrimination is _____.
   a. necessary to right past wrongs
   b. necessary to ensure equal opportunities
   c. only wrong when it puts minorities at a disadvantage
   d. not really discrimination if it is done to the advantage of minorities

8. A critic of affirmative action may say that it's unfair to discriminate against anyone by race. What would be the most direct response to that charge from a defender of affirmative action?
   a. For centuries, blacks have not simply been treated "unfairly"; they were oppressed in every way.
   b. Anything that improves the status of minorities is fair.
   c. Two wrongs don't make a right.
   d. Few things in life are fair.

9. To someone of the majority who complains about being passed over for an opportunity because of affirmative action policies, the most effective response a defender of affirmative action can make is to say that _____.
   a. the person of the majority probably deserves it
   b. if a minority individual was given the opportunity instead, he or she is probably more qualified
   c. the minority individual will be able to appreciate the opportunity much more than the majority person
   d. the opportunities of the majority were arrived at unfairly and need to be compensated for

10. The fundamental reason that the advocate and critic of affirmative action may never agree is that they _____.
   a. cannot agree on the definition of justice
   b. come from different normative standpoints
   c. are concerned with correcting injustices in different areas
   d. disagree on whether minorities should have equal opportunities

chapter 14

Business Ethics

CHAPTER OBJECTIVES

In this chapter, you will learn the following:

- How ethical problems arise in business contexts
- How a corporation can be thought to have moral responsibilities similar to those of an individual

The operation of a business involves the potential for various people's self-interests to be furthered. This is, in fact, the reason for businesses' existence in a free-market economy: people start businesses to make money. A business can make profits and grow, employees can make money, and consumers and the public can benefit from the products or services the business sells. But while these interests ideally, and often do, come together harmoniously, there are instances when they may not. This is where the potential for ethical problems comes in.

If it were the case that everyone could do whatever he or she pleased without hurting anyone, there would be no such subject as ethics. (Or it would be purely hypothetical and have no application.) But since this is not the case, ethical decisions sometimes have to be made to prevent morally bad things from happening when people pursue their own interests. The realm of business carries with it a characteristic set of possibilities for some interests being pursued at the expense of others. This is what the category of applied ethics known as *business ethics* deals with.

Conflicts of Interest

In a free-market, capitalist economy, businesses are started for the purpose of making money. Of course, employees make money by selling whatever products or services the business deals in. The business itself makes profits that it can use to pay the investors who made start-up possible and also to put back into the cost of doing business. The aims of the employee and the business as such overlap considerably, such that typically where one's interest is furthered, so is the other. But they are not the same. It is possible for an employee to benefit at the expense of the business, and it is possible for a business to benefit at the expense of the employee.

Some may think that to do business ethically, they merely have to avoid doing anything illegal. Illegal acts are certainly unethical. But not breaking the law is no guarantee that you are acting ethically (see Chapter 6). Normative ethics can provide a way to look at business ethics in a way that explains both why illegal acts are illegal and why certain other acts might be unethical even if not illegal. The central ethical issues that arise in business practice can mainly be cast in terms of *conflicts of interest*—situations in which the interests of one entity (either a person or a corporation) are furthered at the expense of another's.

The existence and operation of a business require that the entities involved coordinate with each other so all of their interests can be furthered, which is exactly why each of the entities is involved in the business in the first place. This coordination generates ethical norms, which require that the interests of each involved entity are pursued toward the mutual coordination that makes business possible. If the interests of one entity are pursued at the expense of another's, this disrupts the coordination of interests between the entities. If one entity's interests are furthered in such a way that the coordination of interests is disrupted, this may involve one entity's being "hurt" in some way. But even if no visible harm comes of it, actions that go against what is required for all the entities to operate harmoniously will violate the norms of coordination involved in a business. Therefore, consequentialism (see Chapter 4) is not, by itself, an adequate guide for determining when a violation of ethics has taken place in the business context. That is, the norms of business arrangements are such that you cannot just ask "what difference does it make?" or "does anyone actually get hurt?" to determine whether an action constitutes a breach of ethics. The notion of conflict of interest provides a more generally appropriate scheme in terms of which to understand violations of business ethics.

The Sources of Normativity in Business

Perhaps the best way to understand the idea of a conflict of interest in terms of normative ethics is by means of Immanuel Kant's idea that we have a duty to only perform acts that conform to a categorical imperative (see Chapter 4), which states a kind of action and a reason for acting that are closely connected. The connection between them is that the action will successfully accomplish the goals of the reason for acting. For the two to form a categorical imperative, the action would accomplish its goals if *everybody* acted the same way for the same reason. According to this normative theory, lying, for example, is wrong because no categorical imperative can be constructed for it: if everyone lied all the time, then no one would believe anyone, so no one would be able to lie successfully. Thus, the goal of lying cannot be accomplished in terms of a categorical imperative. Rational behavior must always conform to a categorical imperative, because it is irrational to act in a way that will not fulfill the aim of the action. Kant's normative theory thus explains immoral actions in terms of their irrationality: immoral actions are irrational because they cannot conform to a categorical imperative.

The special way in which the categorical imperative can be applied to the realm of business comes from the fact that the different entities involved in a business are all in it to obtain certain ends. Normal business operations give each entity a rational means to accomplish its ends, such that all the entities involved benefit mutually. This is the source of normativity for participants in a business. The norms in business ethics can be thought to derive from the proper functioning of a business in terms of all the involved entities. If one of the entities acts in such a way that it benefits by undercutting the benefit to one of the other entities, then a norm has been violated; if all such entities acted that way, then no business could function properly, in which case no one would be able to benefit from business at all, let alone to mutual benefit.

There are basically three kinds of entities that work together in the operation of a business and are essential to it: the corporation itself, employees of the corporation, and the consumers who are the corporation's customers. The specific interests of any of these entities can be pursued in such a way that they conflict with the interests of one of the others. The fundamental ethical problems with such situations come from the fact that they go against the norms that dictate what is required for a business to operate.

The Corporation and the Consumer

A corporation can be thought of as having interests insofar as it exists for a purpose. Some things pertaining to it will further those interests, while others won't. A corporation's main interest is to do business in such a way as to make profits, to sell goods or services to make more money than it spends to purvey those goods and services. This interest comes from the fact that making profits are necessary for the corporation's existence. Investors help start up a for-profit company because they expect a return on their investment in the form of a share in the profits. A corporation that is not profitable cannot continue to exist, because it cannot pay back its investors and ongoing shareholders.

The consumer's interests, as they pertain to the corporation, are to obtain whatever goods or services the corporation sells. Presumably, the consumer could not obtain those goods and services any other way, and the corporation could not exist without consumers who want to buy its goods or services. This coordination between corporation and consumer is what makes for the mutually beneficial relationship involving both of their interests being furthered. It is also what constitutes the ethical norm that regulates their association and makes for the possibility of a conflict between these interests.

The Corporation's Interests at the Expense of the Consumer

To exist and operate, a corporation has to sell goods or services that the consumer wants. This norm is violated whenever the corporation tries to sell something to consumers in such a way that consumers don't *really* get what they *think* they're going to get. When this happens, it seems obvious that something unethical has happened, because it is an instance of deceit—consumers need to have accurate information about what they are buying, and businesses have a responsibility to provide this information. Failing in that responsibility is unethical in a business context because it is a violation of the norm established by the need for consumers to get what they think they're getting—after all, that's why they patronize the businesses they do.

One example is if a company puts a label on a food product that designates it as a "healthy" food, even if it is not what most people would consider healthy. A consumer could simply see that label, think it provides information as to the food's healthfulness without having to bother to look at the ingredients, and assume certain things about its ingredients that would be false. The company's interest is furthered by selling more products that way, but it is against the consumer's interest in getting what he or she anticipates. The expected arrangement between consumer and business is that the consumer will patronize the business and thereby get what he or she wants. But being given false or misleading information about a product is, as philosophers sometimes put it, "parasitic" on that arrangement—meaning that it exists at the expense of the consumer's expectation to get reliable information from the corporation about its products—which is what makes it unethical. In terms of a categorical imperative, if all companies routinely misled consumers about their products or services, consumers would no longer trust any company's information and would presumably not buy from them; the mutually beneficial coordination between companies and consumers would be scrapped. Although it is rational for each to benefit mutually by their business transaction, those rational aims could not be met if consumers couldn't count on reliable product information from a company.

Another way in which corporations may be said to benefit from consumers is by getting money from shareholders who invest in the company's stock. The shareholders do not necessarily consume the company's products, but the corporation depends on them just as it depends on consumers who do buy its products. So the arrangement between corporation and shareholder and its resulting norms are analogous to the corporation-consumer relationship: the corporation benefits from the up-front funds it receives from shareholders, who in turn receive a benefit later from dividends. This puts the shareholders in a vulnerable position, however, because they have to trust that the money will be put toward profitable aims so they can get an expected return on investment. (Even if the corporation does use the funds appropriately, it still may not be profitable enough to give investors a sufficient return, so shareholders are at risk anyway.) Normally, the arrangement is beneficial to both entities, and the rationality of the arrangement—that is, its mutual benefit—is what makes for its characteristic ethical norms. The norms of that arrangement are violated if the corporation uses its shareholders' money for some form of gain that does not benefit the shareholders.

A conspicuous example from the recent past is the highly publicized 2001 financial scandal of the energy corporation Enron. By making financial decisions that made it look as though it had assets that it really didn't, the corporation's directors cheated the stockholders out of investments they had made in good faith. The company's stock price rose, and the corporation's executives lined their pockets, but the shareholders lost all the money they had put into the corporation when reality set in and it became clear that the soaring stock price had no foundation. Part of the reason the directors' behavior was so blatantly unethical is that it was also utterly irrational of them to manage the corporation that way—their accounting practices were unsustainable, which doomed the corporation itself to failure. So Enron acted irrationally in terms of a categorical imperative, because all corporations could not successfully manage their funds that way. In addition, without even needing to bring in the notion of a categorical imperative, it failed the rationality test for achieving even its own ends.

A similar situation that occurred over a longer period of time and was perhaps not as blatant was the "housing bubble" that crashed toward the end of the 2000s. People made housing investments they couldn't really afford, yet consumers had good faith that if they could get a mortgage, then it was permissible by the banks' standards for them to do so. Too much money was invested in mortgages that could not be paid back; as a result, not only did many consumers face foreclosure and eviction from their homes, but the investing banks lost large amounts of money. The situation could be described as a climate of unwise investments that were, in the final analysis, unethical insofar as they were irrational.

The Consumer's Interests at the Expense of the Corporation

A conflict of interest in the other direction is possible too. From the point of view of the corporation, the basic arrangement between consumer and corporation is entirely based on the expectation that the corporation will get paid for providing what the consumer wants. If the consumer gets what he or she wants from the corporation without its benefiting in the expected way, then a conflict of interest arises. If they didn't benefit from their transactions with consumers, corporations could not do business, and then consumers couldn't get what they wanted from corporations. This is the source of the particular norm that obligates a consumer to behave only in certain ways toward the corporation with which he or she wants to do business.

The most obvious violation of this norm is stealing, in which a consumer gets what he or she wants from the corporation without paying for it. Stealing is wrong in general precisely because it is a conflict of interest. Further, it can be understood in a business context in terms of violating the norm that corporation-consumer transactions must benefit *both* parties. If they don't, then there can't be any such transactions. The same rule would apply to any other instance of deceit on the part of the consumer (in addition to stealing) in which the consumer gets what he or she wants while shortchanging the corporation in some way.

The Corporation and the Employee

A corporation's interests having already been described, an employee's role is to perform an assigned job in such a way that it furthers the corporation's ability to make money. The employee's interests, *as an employee*, are to receive payment, benefits, and possible intangible rewards directly associated with the work in exchange for assisting in the corporation's goal of profits. The corporation and employee are both in business to further their respective interests. But if one of them pursues his or her own interests while impeding the other's, the norms given by the nature of the arrangement will be violated.

The association between employee and corporation is an especially close one; each depends on the other in a much more far-reaching way than either depends on consumers. The balance between them can be delicate, so it can be particularly easy for conflicts of interest to arise between them. For the arrangement between employee and corporation to work to mutual benefit, their respective interests must be balanced carefully.

The Employee's Interests at the Expense of the Corporation

The interests of an employee with respect to a corporation are unique in that the personal interests of most employees, *as people*, range far outside those pertaining to the corporation. Pursuing those interests as part of their lives usually will not affect the interests of the corporation one way or another, as long as the employee's job gets done. Conflicts of interest can arise, however, when an employee's personal, "extracurricular" interests do interfere with his or her role as an employee of the corporation.

Corporations have available whatever resources are necessary for employees to do their essential jobs and expect those resources to be used for assigned jobs. Strictly speaking, if corporate resources are used for employees' personal interests, this is a conflict of interest against the corporation. Even if no "harm" comes to the corporation, meaning that its ability to make money remains unchanged, using corporate resources for personal ends violates the norm of corporate resources being used for corporate ends—that is their purpose. If all employees used corporate resources only for personal ends, there would be no corporations and no corporate resources to be used for anything, including personal ends. However, most companies make it permissible for employees to use corporate resources for personal ends on a limited basis, such as making a few copies or limited use of the Internet at work. This is an example of the delicate balance mentioned before; corporations recognize that a certain amount of flexibility is needed in their association with employees. Since employees have interests outside the corporation that do not go away during their time at work, to make employees feel that their personal interests are recognized, many corporations allow them to use a reasonably insignificant amount of resources for personal ends.

Likewise, corporations allow their employees vacation and sick time; some of them even give time off for children's school performances. Such policies are not implemented because they are in the corporation's direct interest; in fact, they could be thought of as being *against* the corporation's interests. But these policies are in the employees' personal interest and do not prevent the corporation from reaching its goals, so since they are a way of keeping employees happy, they end up being in the corporation's interest in the long run. But if an employee does not do his or her job well because of taking too much time off or otherwise letting personal interests get in the way of work, then it is a violation of the norm of the obligation of the employee to the corporation, since the employee continues to get paid while not yielding acceptable work in the interests of the company. Corporations make certain allowances to keep employees happy and have regulations by which they stipulate what amount of time off would constitute a real conflict of interest. Any cutoff has to be somewhat arbitrary, which is why policies vary between corporations. This give-and-take relationship reflects the delicate balance between employee and corporation interests that has to be regulated carefully so the arrangement will work optimally.

The ease with which the norm of obligation of the employee to the corporation can be technically violated prompts most corporations to allow some wiggle room just so they do not have to be too strict. But there are ways in which that norm can be violated flagrantly. For example, if an employee is paid by an outside source, perhaps a competing organization, to sabotage the corporation's operations or steal its trade secrets, then the employee benefits by his or her employment by being paid to actually prevent that corporation from succeeding. To call this a conflict of interest is an understatement, of course, but its wrongness from a business ethics standpoint is easily explained in terms of the model of the categorical imperative: if everyone acted that way, there would be no corporations left for employees to get paid for undermining.

The Corporation's Interests at the Expense of the Employee

A corporation can seek to benefit at the expense of its employees, and again, due to the closeness of the relationship between corporation and employee, this can happen fairly easily. When it does, corporations always lose, because they cannot do without their employees—especially talented, experienced ones. So if corporations seek to benefit in ways that harm their employees, they will be acting irrationally. This is not only because of the categorical imperative that states that all corporations cannot behave that way, but more urgently, because no corporations can, in the long run, afford to behave that way. This norm is respected when corporations give their employees good pay, benefits, and perks to keep them happy; a company gets a return on its investment by keeping good employees who are motivated to give back to the company, and the rationality of the arrangement is thereby sustained.

In cases like Enron's, the corporation "benefits" (although actually, it doesn't) at the expense of both its shareholders and the employees on whom it depends. In Enron's case, unfortunately, one of the employee benefits was stock ownership, so employees lost money just as the nonemployee shareholders did. Employees lost their money when the corporation went bust, but they also lost their jobs, which is the more general consequence of a corporation's undermining its own aims. The corporation and its employees are so closely associated that whatever harms the corporation harms the employees, which certainly applies when the corporation acts against its own long-term interest.

The Employee and the Consumer

An employee of a corporation and a consumer who buys from the corporation also have a characteristic mutual business interest. When consumers buy from a corporation, they get what they want while employees benefit by being paid. The benefits to the employee and corporation from consumer business are closely associated, since income to the corporation is income that pays employee wages. In many cases, the norms between corporation and consumer are intimately tied to those between employee and consumer: any ethics violation by the consumer hurts both corporation and employee, and any ethics violation by the corporation toward the consumer will likely be traceable to an unethical decision made by an employee (but not necessarily any one employee, as we'll discuss soon).

There are also many cases in which the consumer has to do business directly with employees to buy goods and services from the corporation. The most obvious example of this is salespeople who sell directly to the corporation's customers. Many of the most commonly recognized kinds of business ethics violations come from the possibility of salespeople dealing unethically with customers in order to get their business. One example of this is a ploy known as the "bait and switch." This term describes any attempt to attract business by advertising or promising a product that the customer will perceive as an excellent deal and, when the customer expresses interest, trying to sell him or her something else that would be more profitable to the salesperson. The bait is what the customer thinks he or she will be able to get and what puts the customer in a "ready to buy" frame of mind. The switch is what the salesperson really wants to sell the customer instead. There may not be anything illegal or even any outright lying involved, but this sort of tactic violates the norm between salesperson and customer that makes business between them possible. The salesperson-customer arrangement is one in which the customer *has* to trust the salesperson's communicated intentions in order to buy a product the customer wants. This trust, and thereby the characteristic norm between them, is violated if a salesperson simply says whatever is required to get the customer into a frame of mind in which he or she is more likely to buy the product the salesperson actually wants to sell than if the actual product and all its attributes were advertised up front. The bait-and-switch tactic is unethical because it disrespects the customer's need to take the salesperson's communications at face value. If all salespeople behaved this way just to get a quick sale, customers could not trust salespeople very far, and this would greatly hamper the ability of salespeople to get sales. To do business at all, salespeople have to expect that customers will want to buy from them. To maintain that arrangement, salespeople must, in return, be trustworthy in their interactions with customers. In this way, the arrangement between them is kept stable over the long term to the mutual benefit of each. It is irrational, and thereby also unethical, for any of the parties involved to disrupt this arrangement for short-term gain.

There are many other ways in which salespeople can try to do business unethically with customers. The personal interest of getting sales and associated commissions is strong, so salespeople have to be self-conscious and mindful of many factors when doing business so as to ensure that the way in which they pursue their self-interest is aboveboard and not at the expense of their customers' right to be treated fairly. The general rule that salespeople and other employees who deal directly with customers should follow is to treat a consumer as they would appreciate being treated if they were in the consumer's position.

When employees do business with customers unethically, both the corporation and employee stand to benefit at the consumer's expense. A corporation could just ignore these abuses because it benefits from them by getting extra revenue, but most corporations want to take care that they and their employees do business ethically. Many companies have a policy of requiring special ethics training for their salespeople on a regular basis to keep the principles fresh so the employees will be ready to apply them. Corporations pay special attention to ethics for its own sake, but ultimately, as in the corporation-consumer and corporation-employee relationships, there are business-driven reasons to ensure that business norms are respected. When business norms are respected by all concerned, the mutually beneficial arrangement between all involved entities is at its most stable and sustainable.

Still Struggling

All business arrangements involve both parties benefiting mutually from the arrangement. For example, consumers get products and services they want at the right price, and corporations make a profit by selling those products and services to consumers. Any business arrangement includes the possibility of abuse so that one party benefits while another is harmed or otherwise does not benefit. Business arrangements cannot be made to work this way in general, because both parties have to benefit. This is what makes conflicts of interest unethical.

Thinking of a Corporation as if It Were a Person

You may have noticed that when looking at the various entities involved in a business, it is easy to think of the employees and customers as having interests and moral responsibilities, while the corporation seems to be the odd one out. We can see how employees and consumers have interests because they are people, but the idea that corporations have interests and can act ethically or unethically may seem strange. It is, in fact, commonplace in business theory and legal terms to refer to corporations as if they were people. The remainder of this chapter will explain in what sense a corporation can be considered a person and what the ethical implications are of seeing a corporation in this way.

Corporate Personhood

Of course, a corporation cannot be an independent person in the sense that a human being is. A corporation's existence is sustained by the activities of people. One might think that when we think of a corporation as though it were a person, we are actually talking about the person who heads the corporation or a group of people, such as the corporation's board of directors. However, there are reasons not to identify corporate personhood with any particular person or group.

Consider a team of corporate executives voting on a certain decision. In the simplest cases, we may simply identify the corporate decision with whatever the majority decision was. Thus, the corporation's decision could be represented by any of the executives who voted with the majority. But in slightly more complicated decisions, it may not be possible to identify the corporate decision with that of any individual person nor even with a majority or unanimity. Here is one instance that shows how. Consider three executive board members—P, Q, and R—voting on three separate measures—A, B, and C. All but P vote in favor of A; all but Q vote in favor of B; and all but R vote in favor of C. The end result will be that all three measures pass by a majority, meaning that the corporate decision is to approve all three measures. Yet none of P, Q, or R voted in favor of all of A, B, and C. So the corporation's decision cannot be identified with that of any one of its executives; no majority, or even any, of the executives voted that all three measures should be enacted (Pettit 2007). (Table 14.1 represents the individual contributors and the corporate outcome of the situation.) The lesson here is supposed to be that a corporation can make decisions that no majority of individuals, or even any particular individual, actually makes.

TABLE 14.1	A Corporate Decision That Is Not Reducible to Individual Decisions			
	Board Member P's Votes	**Board Member Q's Votes**	**Board Member R's Votes**	**Corporate Decision**
A	No	Yes	Yes	**Yes**
B	Yes	No	Yes	**Yes**
C	Yes	Yes	No	**Yes**
All of A, B, and C	*No*	*No*	*No*	**Yes**

Here is an example of the kind of case just described, adapted from one from Alex Oliver (Warburton and Edmonds 2008): Suppose three people are on a job interview panel and are considering a certain candidate who has just talked with them. The three qualifications necessary for the job are to have sufficient sales experience, a winning personality, and management potential. The three panel members vote separately on each qualification. For each qualification, a two-thirds majority thinks the candidate meets that qualification. But a different person votes no on each of the qualifications, so the upshot is that no *one* of the panel members thinks the candidate has all three necessary qualifications. Yet given the fact that the decision of the panel is based on the votes of each of its members, the majority result for each vote added together means the *panel itself* decides that the candidate does have all three necessary qualifications. The panel, then, can be thought of as having a "mind" that makes decisions to which the panel members contribute but that are not the same as those of any one of the members.

In addition to decision making, there are other ways to approach the idea of corporate personhood, such as in terms of states of mind. There is no need to discuss all such aspects here; suffice it to say that the relevance of corporate personhood to ethics is that where there is corporate personhood, there must be ethical corporate responsibility. This means that in addition to individuals and groups of individuals as such, corporations must be held ethically responsible for their actions. Philip Pettit (2007: 117) gives the following example, which illustrates why this is important:

> The *Herald of Free Enterprise*, a ferry operating in the English Channel, sank on March 6, 1987, drowning nearly two hundred people. The official inquiry found that the company running the ferry was extremely sloppy, with poor routines of checking and management.

"From top to bottom the body corporate was infected with the disease of sloppiness." But the courts did not penalize anyone in what might seem to be an appropriate measure, failing to identify individuals in the company or on the ship itself who were seriously enough at fault. As one commentator put it, "The primary requirement of finding an individual who was liable . . . stood in the way of attaching any significance to the organizational sloppiness that had been found by the official inquiry."

Failing to find any one person responsible for this tragedy meant that *no one* was held responsible, so this situation shows the need to be able to hold a corporation responsible. Again, consider the three board members who were presented with three measures. Suppose the decision to enact all of A, B, and C led to an ethically bad outcome. Each of the board members could defend himself or herself by saying that he or she did not agree to all of A, B, and C. But if corporate responsibility is recognized, then corporations can be penalized for their bad decision making by fines, restrictions on operation, and other punishments suitable to hamper its operations. To take this responsibility in advance, ethically bad outcomes can be prevented if the members who contribute to decisions take responsibility not only for their own votes or decisions, but collectively for the corporation's decisions. In other words, if it is clear that enacting all of A, B, and C would be a bad decision, the members should collectively take responsibility by preventing all three from being enacted, even if their individual votes would have resulted in all of A, B, and C being enacted.

The Ethical and Social Responsibilities of a Corporation

If a corporation can make decisions, it can be held ethically responsible for them. This explains why, as discussed in the first part of this chapter, a corporation can be considered one of the contributing business entities that can act unethically. The responsibilities of a corporation come, in part, from the norms that arise from the arrangement between itself and the shareholders, employees, and consumers that make its existence possible. The concept of the social responsibility of a corporation, however, goes beyond the arrangements discussed previously in this chapter. A corporation's *social responsibility* would include ethical responsibilities to entities besides consumers, employees, and shareholders. The norms from which those responsibilities derive would therefore have to be based on relationships other than those required for the corporation to operate as a business. These can include ethical responsibilities to any number of entities with which the corporation shares space in the world, including the natural environment, the community in which it does business, and even the world at large.

The Social Responsibility of Business to Increase Its Profits

In an influential and much-discussed essay, the Nobel Prize–winning economist Milton Friedman (1970) argued that the social responsibility of a business is to increase its profits—and *only* to increase profits. This is a stark challenge to those who would think that all corporations must have social responsibilities besides pure moneymaking. Stated formally and in the simplest form, the argument goes as follows:

1. Any decision a corporation makes that does not increase its profits fails to advance the interests of its shareholders.

2. If a corporation makes decisions that fail to advance the interests of its shareholders, it fails to meet its (social and ethical) responsibilities.

Therefore, if a corporation makes decisions that fail to increase its profits, it fails to meet its (social and ethical) responsibilities.

This is a valid argument, so the only thing left to do is look at the premises to see whether they are true. The whole reason for a company's existence is to make profits. This much is hard to contradict. Friedman thinks this means that ethical norms for a corporation can *only* arise from the shareholders' interests. The norms of the corporation-shareholder relationship are such that each must uphold its responsibility to the other—that is the condition on which the relationship is based. So Friedman thinks that if a corporation fails to look after its moneymaking interests by donating money to charity or otherwise engaging in activities that do not have profit as their goal, it is acting irresponsibly and unethically; this is the reason behind thinking premise 2 is true. There is a parallel here with the normative doctrine of ethical egoism (see Chapter 4). According to this doctrine, the ultimate good for an individual is his or her *own* good. From this comes each person's sole and ultimate normative duty; failing to further your own good violates your ethical obligation to yourself. Likewise, Friedman stresses that the only reason for a corporation's existence is its profitability; therefore, the only norm that could obligate a corporation is its profitability, so for a corporation to act toward any other end violates its ethical responsibility to itself and its shareholders.

Friedman supports premise 1 of the argument in terms of a paradigm case in which the head of a corporation makes more or less "lone ranger–style" decisions against the wishes of the stockholders (Mulligan 1986). The shareholders invest money in good faith that it will be put toward making a profit so they can get a return on their investment. Instead, it gets put toward other things that do not make a profit ("spends the money in a different way than [the shareholders] would have spent it") (Friedman 1970), which violates the norm arising from the shareholder-corporation relationship. Friedman urges that this is, in fact, a case of "taxation without representation," since the shareholders' capital is being "taxed" for purposes that they did not agree to. Furthermore, he says that since taxation is a governmental function, then if spending that amounts to taxation of shareholders is to be enacted independently by corporations with no vested mandate to spend money to such ends, then what results is "pure, unadulterated socialism."

But of course, it isn't necessarily the case that if a corporation invests in "social responsibility" it is against the wishes of the shareholders. Friedman's favored paradigm is highly oversimplified and does not reflect actual business operations, which involve checks and balances at various levels, so that a corporation's decisions all involve collaborative buy-in from all stakeholders, as is the nature of corporate personhood (Mulligan 1986). This is to say there is reason to think that premise 1 of the argument is incorrect as stated. But Friedman thinks that, in any case, doing business while trying to invest in nonbusiness social benefits is just "hypocritical window dressing"—just as we would view the actions of a man who helps an old lady cross the street because he knows a woman he wants to impress is watching (an analogy made by Alex Oliver [Warburton and Edmonds 2008]). Charitable pursuits must be left up to individuals, Friedman emphasizes, because if corporations try to spend money in such a way, the "socialism" entailed poses a real threat to the free-market society on which corporations depend in order to do business.

Social Responsibilities of Business Besides Moneymaking

The condemnation of a corporation's socially unethical actions does not necessarily go against Friedman's stance. He would have to say that in a case like that of the ferry that sank, the corporation did act unethically in allowing the conditions that led to the ferry's sinking, but *only* insofar as it failed to meet its business obligations in running a sustainable business, which the ferry disaster no doubt ruined. If a corporation could make money by killing people, however, and it was part of its expected business plan to do so, it would seem that

Friedman's conclusion would have to be that a corporation is obligated to do so and would be unethical if it did not.

But of course, we must say in response, a corporation is also obligated to obey the laws of wherever it does business (which would prohibit killing people and a great deal else besides). This norm derives from the relationship between a corporation and the community in which it does business, which is a different one from those discussed earlier. This opens up a new set of possibilities for what other norms might be ethically binding on a corporation besides the aim of pure profit. The community gives a corporation a place in which it has the freedom to do business, for which it pays taxes. The relationship between a corporation and its community goes deeper than this simple transaction, however—the corporation benefits from the community's provision of places for the corporation's employees to live and the surroundings in which the employees work. The employees may also be pleased to know they are working at a corporation that gives back to the community or otherwise contributes to charitable causes, so socially responsible activity on the part of the corporation can be seen as a means to the rational end of keeping its employees happy (Mulligan 1986). Thus, if there is a norm deriving from the relationship between the corporation and the community, it could certainly be seen as ethically good, if not obligatory, for a corporation to spend money and resources in a socially mindful way to serve that norm.

Also, many corporations' "socially responsible" activities may well be done merely for appearance's sake; it would then be merely a form of advertising and thus could be criticized as "hypocritical window dressing." But it is hard to scrutinize a corporation's intentions (assuming it has them) to ascertain this. Even if such activities are just window dressing, many people may still be glad of their results, and in any case, a corporation can easily take part in these activities without violating the business norms that obligate it to generate profits; in fact, if it helps the corporation's image and that helps the business do better, it could be seen entirely as a rational corporate investment, even if it is hypocritical.

But there are so many ways in which corporations can benefit from parties other than those with which it does business directly that, in many cases, there is reason enough to think that a corporation actually behaves ethically *as* a corporation and benefits from its social investments. A corporation as a person is not located in an isolated space in which it interacts only with shareholders, employees, and consumers. Ecologically and socially sustainable practices are socially responsible goals that are actually in a corporation's own interests to pursue. A paper company, for example, cannot continue to do business over the long term unless it ensures that sound forestry practices are standard policy, so it will not run out of trees. There are myriad ways, then, in which it is in a corporation's interest as a profit-making entity to act in ways that benefit the world around it. In the end, the world of corporations and humans and environments is interconnected in so many ways that many corporate activities we would automatically place under the heading of "social responsibility" need not be thought of as sheer charity at all. Rather, if corporations take a holistic view of the world around them, they will find many business-related motivations to act in ways that benefit other parties besides their shareholders. They may also find this to be a more effective way of being profitable over time than if they invested solely in whatever directly made the most profits in the short term. Thus, far from being deleterious to a corporation's profit-making goals, social responsibility can actually serve those goals better, and in a broader sense than if profits were the only goal the corporation ever directly aimed at.

Chapter Summary

The realm of business includes various relationships between entities that are sustained for their mutual benefit. Individually, all the entities are "in it" for themselves and for the characteristic gain they receive from being involved in business. But each party involved has to respect the needs of the other to gain in the transaction. Each party's own self-interest may lead to its wanting to unethically gain more than it should and by doing so harm another party's ability to gain from the business transaction. According to one view of the sources of normativity whereby ethical violations occur in business, the ethical wrongness comes from the violation's irrationality, in its disrupting the coordination of interests in which all involved parties are supposed to be able to gain. Corporations can be considered persons in their ability to decide and act without these decisions and actions being determined by any one person within the organization. A corporation has a responsibility to the investors and shareholders who enable it to do business, as well as to the wider world around them in which, as persons in the world, they are situated and on which they depend.

QUIZ

1. The normativity specific to a business situation arises from the need to _____.
   a. avoid hurting anyone
   b. keep profits at a reasonable level
   c. make as much money as possible
   d. ensure that all parties have an opportunity to benefit

2. Which of the following would *not* keep a consumer from benefiting from a business transaction?
   a. Misleading information
   b. A price that is too high
   c. The necessity of buying via mail order
   d. A product that is not safety tested

3. Which of the following does a corporation need from a consumer?
   a. Repeat business
   b. Start-up investment money
   c. A return on investment
   d. A job done well

4. Unethical business transactions can be thought of as irrational. What is the most general source of this irrationality?
   a. A failure to benefit from the transaction
   b. A desire to profit from the transaction
   c. An action that prevents the other party from benefiting
   d. A desire to hurt oneself in the process

5. Corporations have a vested interest in _____.
   a. paying employees as little as possible
   b. attracting and keeping good employees
   c. doing whatever their employees want them to do
   d. getting as much work out of their employees as possible

6. A corporation's status as a person derives from the fact that _____.
   a. it affects the world around it
   b. there are laws that regulate its practices
   c. it exists for the purpose of making profits
   d. it makes decisions that are not the same as those of any one individual or group

7. Executives can take responsibility for a corporation's decisions by taking responsibility for _____.
   a. their decisions
   b. the collective outcome of their decisions
   c. the actions of their employees
   d. their customers' well-being

8. Milton Friedman thought the only social responsibility of a corporation is to make profits because _____.
   a. any other goal would be against the interests of the shareholders
   b. the shareholders will be the most socially conscious members of the corporation
   c. the social responsibility of a corporation is to its employees
   d. socialism requires that corporations make profits to survive

9. A weakness in Friedman's argument is the fact that _____.
   a. corporations have to make products that consumers will buy
   b. corporations can act ethically without benefiting their shareholders
   c. a corporation need not act against its shareholders' interests in being socially responsible
   d. the sense of social responsibility Friedman is talking about is purely economic, not ethical

10. The norms that obligate a corporation arise from its duty to _____.
    a. give charitably
    b. beat out competitors
    c. sell goods and services that consumers want
    d. benefit the various entities that make it possible for it to do business

PART THREE TEST

1. **A positive definition of liberty _____.**
   a. puts liberty in as positive a light as possible
   b. defines liberty in terms of what it is good for
   c. states what conditions have to be obtained to make liberty possible
   d. is one on which everyone in society can agree

2. **The concept of liberty may include any of the following,**
   except _____.
   a. freedom to do as one pleases
   b. freedom from restraint or coercion
   c. freedom to maximize one's potential
   d. freedom to obtain as much power as possible

3. **According to John Rawls's theory of justice, what is needed in order to tell if**
   someone is being treated justly?
   a. Ask the person whether he or she thinks his or her rights have been violated.
   b. Compare the situation to how someone else in a similar situation has been treated.
   c. Make sure the person has as much liberty as possible.
   d. Determine what the person deserves.

4. **Which of the following is *not* typically used as a basis for arguing against abortion?**
   a. Abortion kills a human being.
   b. Abortion kills a being that has a right to life.
   c. Abortion robs a being of a future life of value.
   d. Abortion takes a life that must be protected at all costs.

5. **A stalemate between those arguing for and against abortion is likely to arise**
   over the definition of _____.
   a. *human*
   b. *person*
   c. *rights*
   d. *killing*

6. **Which of the following is Judith Jarvis Thomson's position on abortion?**
   a. Fetuses do not have a right to life.
   b. Abortion is permissible whenever a woman wants one.
   c. A fetus does not have an unconditional right to its mother's body.
   d. It is always immoral to prevent a woman from obtaining an abortion.

7. Capital punishment today is _____.
   a. reserved for the most serious crimes
   b. used in almost every developed country
   c. defended by most philosophers
   d. protected by the Constitution

8. The most effective basis for opposing capital punishment is to argue that _____.
   a. it is not an effective deterrent to crime
   b. there is too much risk of executing the innocent
   c. it is inconsistent to kill to show that murder is wrong
   d. justice cannot generally be based on equal retribution

9. Proportional justice requires that _____.
   a. the worst possible crime be given the worst possible punishment
   b. there be a most serious crime and a most serious punishment
   c. murderers be sentenced to life imprisonment
   d. the death penalty never be used

10. The argument that defends torture through an analogy with combat killing assumes that _____.
    a. many lives may be saved by the use of torture
    b. wartime conditions are such that torture may be necessary
    c. whatever makes combat killing acceptable may also make torture acceptable
    d. the person being tortured will not be permanently injured

11. The danger of legalizing torture is that _____.
    a. most people will think it is a good thing
    b. it will lead to people being killed accidentally
    c. it will set a precedent that ensures torture will be used more often
    d. more and more severe methods will be used in its execution

12. Even if torture is allowed in certain cases, there is a significant danger of all of the following *except* _____.
    a. a disaster may not be prevented
    b. the torturee may not be tortured severely enough
    c. the torturee may not know the desired information
    d. the torturee may not give up the desired information

13. **James Rachels says that in making decisions on euthanasia, we should be guided by _____.**
    a. compassion
    b. rational principles
    c. consequentialism
    d. current medical ethics

14. **Rachels's Smith and Jones thought experiment is meant to show that _____.**
    a. the difference between killing and letting die is not morally significant
    b. the difference between killing and letting die is hardly ever morally significant
    c. every case of killing is morally equivalent to every case of letting die
    d. euthanasia is required regardless of whether it is active or passive

15. **To accept Rachels's argument for active euthanasia, one has to be committed to _____.**
    a. utilitarianism
    b. duty-based ethics
    c. the idea that killing is sometimes permissible
    d. the idea that letting die is always preferable to killing

16. **Utilitarians cannot object to animal experimentation in cases when it _____.**
    a. is also performed on human beings
    b. is done with as little pain as possible to the animals
    c. leads to greater public awareness of animal maltreatment
    d. leads to important and far-reaching benefits to other beings

17. **Which of the following is the best definition of *speciesism*?**
    a. Treating certain animals of different species differently
    b. Maximizing only the utility of animals of a certain species
    c. Treating certain animals differently from other animals only because of their species
    d. Singling out animals of certain species as inferior to those of other species

18. **According to utilitarianism, animals should be treated better than we currently treat them because _____.**
    a. humans have no right to use animals for instrumental purposes
    b. the ethical significance of animal suffering is comparable to that of human suffering
    c. the lives of animals are as sacred as those of human beings
    d. animals have the right not to be abused

19. According to Peter Singer, it is unjust for anyone _____.
    a. to be poor
    b. to be affluent
    c. to have luxuries while others starve to death
    d. to spend money on their own needs

20. In which of the following situations is someone obligated to give of their resources, according to utilitarianism?
    a. A person has more resources than someone else.
    b. There are people who are affluent.
    c. There are people who are below the level of marginal utility.
    d. There are people who are below marginal utility while others are above it.

21. Peter Unger's conclusion about giving to those in need _____ that of Peter Singer or James Rachels.
    a. is stronger than
    b. applies to fewer people than
    c. applies to more people than
    d. is argued on a different basis from

22. Someone who favors affirmative action can defend the practice of racial discrimination in favor of minorities by _____.
    a. arguing that it is only discrimination *against* minorities that is wrong
    b. affirming that all racial discrimination is wrong
    c. holding that racial discrimination is never wrong
    d. being hypocritical

23. Assuming that affirmative action succeeds in helping minorities achieve equality, it is still possible to object to it on the basis that _____.
    a. affirmative action is not sufficient to achieve its ends
    b. affirmative action is not necessary to achieve its ends
    c. minorities do not have the same capacities as others
    d. it puts the majority at an unfair disadvantage

24. Conflicts of interest in business arise from _____.
    a. the failure of a corporation to succeed in its goals
    b. the desire of each party to profit from business transactions
    c. attempts to benefit from a business arrangement in a way that does not benefit the other party involved
    d. a corporation's employees profiting from the corporation's success

25. **On which of the following ideas did Milton Friedman base his argument that the social responsibility of a business is to increase its profits?**
    a. The only responsibility a corporation has is to its shareholders.
    b. Socialism is not compatible with social responsibility.
    c. Corporations can sometimes make profits unethically.
    d. A corporation exists only to serve its customers.

Final Exam

1. Which of the following is a philosophical question?

   a. How do bees communicate?

   b. What exists besides elementary particles?

   c. Why is Pluto not considered a planet?

   d. Why do people behave a certain way in groups?

2. Which of the following is entailed by having made a commitment to a principle?

   a. Having a sound argument

   b. Having a valid argument

   c. Applying a principle wherever it is applicable

   d. Believing in a principle that most people believe in

3. Which of the following is an ethical question?

   a. Should marijuana be decriminalized?

   b. How did morality differ three generations ago?

   c. What are the effects of life imprisonment on a person?

   d. Why do some parents neglect their children?

4. **Which of the following is an epistemological question?**

   a. How do young children learn so quickly?

   b. How much does the average teenager know about the world?

   c. Why do humans want to learn so much about outer space?

   d. What part does evidence play in establishing knowledge?

5. **Which of the following is a metaphysical question?**

   a. Why do children make up imaginary friends?

   b. How many earthlike planets exist in our galaxy?

   c. Do colors exist in the world or only in our perception?

   d. What kinds of evergreen trees exist?

6. **Which of the following questions is best addressed by value theory?**

   a. Why should you get out of bed in the morning?

   b. Which career will make the best use of your degree?

   c. Should two people live together before they get married?

   d. Should you buy a new car or a used one?

7. **Which of the following questions is best addressed by normative ethics?**

   a. Do people commit crimes with full cognizance of the consequences?

   b. Why should you feel bound by a written contract?

   c. Why was slavery once permitted?

   d. Why do some wealthy people resort to crime?

8. **Which of the following questions is best addressed by metaethics?**

   a. In what circumstances do moral disagreements arise?

   b. Is there any way, in principle, to resolve moral disagreements?

   c. Should people be excused for acting harmfully out of ignorance?

   d. How do people in indigenous Australian cultures make moral judgments?

9. **Which of the following questions is a concern of applied ethics?**

   a. When does human life begin?

   b. Why do some people gradually change their morality?

   c. Should you invest money in the stock market?

   d. How should juveniles be punished for crimes?

10. **Philosophy is a discipline that anyone can engage in at any time, because it _____.**

   a. is very easy

   b. costs nothing

   c. deals with universal issues

   d. has connections with many other disciplines

11. **In philosophy, logic refers to _____.**

   a. valid structures of inference

   b. what makes statements true or false

   c. what is needed to make a sound argument

   d. whether premises of an argument are based on fact

12. **A conditional is a statement that _____.**

   a. might be true

   b. is a valid argument

   c. depends on another statement's being true

   d. expresses a relation of consequence between statements

13. **A true conditional is a statement that _____.**

   a. has a true antecedent and a true consequent

   b. is such that if the consequent is true, the antecedent must also be true

   c. is such that if the antecedent is true, the consequent must also be true

   d. is such that if the antecedent is false, the consequent must also be false

14. **A conditional is false just if _____.**

   a. its antecedent is false

   b. its consequent is false

   c. its antecedent and its consequent might be false

   d. it is possible for its antecedent to be true while its consequent is false

15. Consider the following argument:

    1. Mammals have hair.

    2. Barack Obama is a mammal.

    _____

    Therefore, Barack Obama has hair.

    This argument is _____.

    a. invalid

    b. valid and sound

    c. sound but invalid

    d. valid but unsound

16. Consider the following argument:

    1. If apples come from trees, then farmers can grow apples.

    2. Apples do come from trees.

    _____

    Therefore, most people like apples.

    This argument is _____.

    a. invalid

    b. valid and sound

    c. sound but invalid

    d. valid but unsound

17. Consider the following argument:

    1. If root beer has no sugar, no one will drink it.

    2. Root beer has no sugar.

    _____

    Therefore, no one drinks root beer.

    This argument is _____.

    a. invalid

    b. valid and sound

    c. sound but invalid

    d. valid but unsound

18. Consider the following argument:

    1. If it had been sunny yesterday, then we would have gone to the beach.

    2. We did not go to the beach yesterday.

    _____

    Therefore, it was not sunny yesterday.

    This argument is _____.

    a. invalid

    b. valid and sound

    c. sound but invalid

    d. valid but unsound

19. A logical fallacy is _____.

    a. a false conclusion

    b. an argument with one or more false premises

    c. an invalid inference

    d. an invalid argument

20. Consider the following piece of reasoning: "If it rained last night, the streets will be wet. It rained last night. Therefore, the streets will be wet." This inference is _____.

    a. a valid use of modus ponens

    b. a valid use of modus tollens

    c. an instance of the fallacy of denying the antecedent

    d. an instance of the fallacy of affirming the consequent

21. Consider the following piece of reasoning: "If you'd made a lot of money last year, you would have bought a house. You did buy a house. Therefore, you must have made a lot of money last year." This inference is _____.

    a. a valid use of modus ponens

    b. a valid use of modus tollens

    c. an instance of the fallacy of denying the antecedent

    d. an instance of the fallacy of affirming the consequent

22. Consider the following piece of reasoning: "If ten is greater than nine, then I don't like spinach. I do like spinach. Therefore, ten is not greater than nine." This inference is _____.

    a. a valid use of modus ponens

    b. a valid use of modus tollens

    c. an instance of the fallacy of denying the antecedent

    d. an instance of the fallacy of affirming the consequent

23. Consider the following piece of reasoning: "If cows could fly, it would be difficult for farmers to keep them. Cows can't fly. Therefore, it is not difficult for farmers to keep cows." This inference is _____.

    a. a valid use of modus ponens

    b. a valid use of modus tollens

    c. an instance of the fallacy of denying the antecedent

    d. an instance of the fallacy of affirming the consequent

24. Value theory is most analogous to _____.

    a. music appreciation

    b. scientific experimentation

    c. a fundamental physical theory of the universe

    d. explaining why a certain color is your favorite

25. Aristotle thinks that every rational person must have _____.

    a. a number of intrinsically valued goals in life

    b. a single activity that he or she values the most

    c. a variety of interests that make life worthwhile

    d. a single ultimate value in life

26. The experience-machine thought experiment includes which of the following?

    a. The experience of having reached all of our goals

    b. Experiencing everything that is intrinsically good

    c. Experiencing feelings of subjective well-being

    d. Finding out what experiences are intrinsically valuable

27. The point of the experience-machine thought experiment is that _____.

    a. nothing we experience is objectively good

    b. a subjective state of well-being cannot be the ultimate value

    c. happiness is potentially easy to reach, if only we knew how

    d. objective values that we cannot experience are ultimately irrelevant

28. The Stoics of ancient Greece believed that _____.

    a. happiness is compatible with the absence of pleasure

    b. pleasure is to be avoided whenever possible

    c. every physical pleasure ought to be pursued

    d. being virtuous is of instrumental value

29. A hedonist is committed to which of the following claims?

    a. Objectively valuable goods are those with intrinsic value.

    b. Objectively valuable goods will bring us the most pleasure.

    c. Subjective states of well-being are instrumentally valuable.

    d. Subjective states of well-being are the ultimate good.

30. Which of the following is *not* a reason for thinking that hedonism is false?

    a. Other things besides pain can harm us.

    b. Virtue is good because it tends to bring pleasure.

    c. We aim our activities at achieving a state of well-being.

    d. Other things besides pleasure are intrinsically good.

31. *Eudaimonia* might best be defined as _____.

    a. happiness

    b. well-being

    c. pleasure

    d. virtue

32. In normative theory, utilitarianism is a species of _____.

    a. value theory

    b. virtue ethics

    c. consequentialism

    d. ethical egoism

33. One of the advantages of utilitarianism is that it is _____.

    a. undemanding

    b. consequentialist

    c. impartial

    d. just

34. Which of the following is a weakness of divine command theory?

    a. Some people are not religious.

    b. People can disobey divine commands.

    c. It makes moral facts independent of our moral judgments.

    d. It does not guarantee that God's commands will be good.

35. Which of the following would divine command theory entail?

    a. There are moral facts that are independent of our judgments.

    b. Moral facts are rooted in human sentiments.

    c. God's character is good.

    d. God is rational.

36. Consequentialism is the normative theory that states that _____.

    a. every action has moral consequences

    b. the moral consequences of an action are determined by its intent

    c. the consequences of an action are what makes it right or wrong

    d. it is unethical to undertake an action without thought of its consequences

37. Aristotle thought that virtuous actions can be defined in terms of _____.

    a. whatever the most rational actions are

    b. whatever is done with the best of intentions

    c. what can only be learned by experience

    d. what a virtuous person would do

38. According to virtue ethics, _____.

    a. virtue will always bring about pleasure

    b. the virtues are learned by habit and experience

    c. the virtues come naturally to a good person

    d. happiness can potentially be found by anyone

39. The priority problem for virtue ethics is that it _____.

    a. only explains good actions in terms of the kind of person who would perform them

    b. cannot explain how a person learns to be virtuous

    c. cannot explain how the virtues aim at the good

    d. puts a priority on the virtues rather than morality

40. Immanuel Kant thought the most moral actions are those that are done _____.

    a. with the most knowledge of their consequences

    b. that are done with others' interests in mind

    c. that result in the greatest good

    d. purely out of a good will

41. Kant maintained that an action is rational only if _____.

    a. it is done with the best intentions

    b. its purpose could be accomplished if everyone acted that way

    c. it would achieve its goal in an ideal situation

    d. it actually achieves its goal

42. Which of the following is an example of a categorical imperative?

    a. Honesty is always the best policy.

    b. If you want others to behave charitably toward you, you should behave charitably toward others.

    c. If you need to rob a bank for a greater good, then it is morally acceptable.

    d. Breaking promises is inconsistent with having a good character.

43. Which of the following is part of Kant's concept of the good will?

    a. Generosity

    b. Integrity

    c. Duty

    d. The Golden Rule

44. Which of the following would be incompatible with ethical egoism?
    a. Looking primarily after your own interests
    b. Doing something that benefits another person
    c. Doing something that is not in your own interests
    d. Following a rule that someone else has made

45. Which of the following is the fundamental reason for accepting ethical egoism?
    a. People can only pursue their own well-being.
    b. It can be rational to sacrifice yourself.
    c. You should be just and fair to others.
    d. Your own life is the ultimate value.

46. Moral realism has trouble accounting for _____.
    a. what kind of facts moral facts would be
    b. why people believe in their moral judgments so strongly
    c. why people think their moral judgments are correct
    d. how people learn what norms are accepted in their culture

47. Which view holds that moral truths are independent of our judgments about them?
    a. Error theory
    b. Expressivism
    c. Relativism
    d. Realism

48. David Hume believed that the reason we think of morality as pertaining to objective facts is because _____.
    a. our moral judgments are all in error
    b. we think of our feelings as being about things apart from us
    c. we perceive the objective facts about morality
    d. we are motivated by objective facts

49. Both individual relativism and cultural relativism hold that _____.
    a. morality is subjective
    b. human feelings determine the possible moral judgments
    c. there are no moral facts that apply equally to everyone
    d. moral facts are relative to the individual making the judgment

50. Which of the following is *not* a reason to believe in expressivism?

  a. People seem to think their moral judgments are correct.

  b. Moral judgments are heavily laden with emotion.

  c. It is hard to say what kind of facts moral facts might be.

  d. People disagree about the correct moral stance on issues.

51. Sentimentalism is the metaethical view that _____.

  a. there are no facts about human sentiments

  b. morality has to be defined with reference to human sentiments

  c. every moral sentiment is fitting for the person who has it

  d. sentiments are things about which everyone can come to an agreement

52. According to error theory in metaethics, _____.

  a. no moral judgments are correct

  b. no moral judgments are correct or incorrect

  c. moral judgments are really about our feelings

  d. moral judgments may be correct or incorrect depending on the observer

53. In liberal social philosophy, perfectionism is the view that _____.

  a. only a perfect society is acceptable

  b. liberty is only possible in a perfect society

  c. liberty is the highest value a society can have

  d. the value of liberty is that people can reach their fullest potential

54. John Stuart Mill thought that _____.

  a. people should have the liberty to do whatever they want

  b. people should be restricted from doing anything immoral

  c. the only laws that should be enacted are those that everyone agrees on

  d. there should be no laws that only keep people from harming themselves

55. In a liberal society, _____.

  a. people should have the liberty to do whatever they want

  b. the government should not enact any laws that restrict freedom

  c. a justification must be given for any restrictions placed on freedom

  d. there will be only one political party in charge of government

56. **Which of the following situations would violate John Rawls's principle of justice?**

    a. A criminal being sentenced to death

    b. Two people being paid differently for doing the same work

    c. Laws being enacted to restrict people's liberties

    d. People working long hours for low pay

57. **If a certain kind of action is judged immoral, _____.**

    a. it will be made illegal

    b. it is because it harms others

    c. most people will agree that it is immoral

    d. it will probably be made illegal if it harms others

58. **The most common sort of argument against abortion states that it is wrong to _____.**

    a. kill

    b. kill innocent human beings

    c. undergo harmful medical procedures

    d. take someone's life against his or her will

59. **Mary Anne Warren defends abortion on the basis of _____.**

    a. a fetus's not resembling a person

    b. the fetus posing a threat to the mother's life

    c. a woman's absolute right to do as she pleases

    d. the needs of women with unwanted pregnancies

60. **Don Marquis thinks that his argument moves past the stalemate between the abortion opponent and defender because it _____.**

    a. conclusively establishes that a fetus is a person

    b. does not rely on establishing that a fetus is a person

    c. does not have to establish that killing is wrong

    d. shows why it is wrong to kill a person

61. **Judith Jarvis Thomson's defense of abortion shows that** _____.

   a. the fetus does not have a right to life

   b. abortion is always permissible for any reason

   c. there is no way to argue successfully that abortion is wrong

   d. a person does not have the right to his or her life being sustained at any cost

62. **Judith Jarvis Thomson thinks that abortion is wrong when** _____.

   a. contraception was used

   b. the pregnancy was intentional

   c. the pregnancy is at a late stage

   d. the fetus is not given anesthetic

63. **Abortion is legal because** _____.

   a. it is moral

   b. it is not harmful

   c. not everyone agrees on its morality

   d. if it were not, the population would grow too quickly

64. **Which of the following is *not* used as a basis for arguing against capital punishment?**

   a. Retributive justice does not require the death penalty.

   b. Equal justice cannot be used as the general basis for punishments.

   c. The death penalty may not work as a deterrent to crime.

   d. Criminals deserve a fair hearing in a court of law.

65. **The justice-driven motivation for capital punishment does *not* include which of the following?**

   a. The punishment ought to fit the crime.

   b. There must be a deterrent to violent crime.

   c. The crime of murder violates the ultimate value.

   d. Justice is the primary consideration in punishment.

66. One objection to the death penalty is that it may sometimes be used on the innocent. The defender of the death penalty should reply that _____.

    a. this happens so rarely as to be negligible

    b. this objection is based on an undue appeal to emotion

    c. this objection does not help us determine what the guilty deserve

    d. it is better for the innocent to be punished than for the guilty to be insufficiently punished

67. The defense of the death penalty that claims it is a deterrent to crime requires a commitment to _____.

    a. consequentialism

    b. duty-based ethics

    c. divine command theory

    d. a principle of equal justice

68. An opponent of capital punishment only has to argue that it is _____.

    a. too costly

    b. not necessary for justice to be served

    c. not an effective deterrent to crime

    d. harmful to society at large

69. A system of proportional justice requires that _____.

    a. punishments not be excessive

    b. no innocent person ever be convicted of a crime

    c. every suspect be given a fair hearing in a court of law

    d. crimes and punishments be ranked from least to most serious

70. A system of equal justice requires that _____.

    a. criminals get what they deserve

    b. the worst crimes be punished proportionally

    c. criminals be punished with the same crimes they commit

    d. only guilty criminals be sentenced with punishments

71. In defending the possibility of torture, the purpose of the ticking time bomb scenario is to _____.

    a. describe the kinds of torture that might be acceptable

    b. warn against the possibility that torture might be overused

    c. assume that a large number of lives may be saved by torture

    d. argue that torture is permissible for the same reason combat killing is

72. The argument that attempts to make an analogy between torture and combat killing is based primarily on _____.

    a. the person being tortured not being killed

    b. both of the situations involving the opportunity to defend oneself

    c. different rules applying from those that would ordinarily apply

    d. the person being tortured not being innocent

73. The main weakness in the argument that attempts to make an analogy between torture and combat killing is that _____.

    a. the situations are too different for an analogy to work

    b. it assumes that combat killing is morally acceptable

    c. it assumes that the methods of torture will not be too severe

    d. it requires that the setting of torture meet very specific conditions

74. The primary motivation for legalizing torture would be so that _____.

    a. it could be used whenever the need arises

    b. people will come to think that it is acceptable

    c. restrictions would be put on the kinds of torture that are permitted

    d. it would not happen more often than needed

75. Henry Shue says that torture is _____.

    a. a necessary evil

    b. the ultimate shortcut

    c. absolutely impermissible

    d. not something that civilized societies ever consider

76. One objection to euthanasia is that doctors have a duty not to harm. James Rachels's reply to this objection is that _____.

   a. doctors must harm to reduce suffering

   b. doctors sometimes harm inadvertently, but this is ethically acceptable

   c. killing in and of itself is never a harm, but someone's intentions can be

   d. killing is not a case of harming when a patient's death would be a good thing

77. The difference between active and passive euthanasia is _____.

   a. only of moral significance to utilitarians

   b. the difference between killing and letting die

   c. only of interest to doctors of terminally ill patients

   d. the difference between killing intentionally and killing inadvertently

78. The American Medical Association has a statement that opposes _____.

   a. keeping patients alive for as long as possible

   b. withholding treatment of terminal illnesses

   c. doctors bringing about the death of a patient

   d. too much pain medication being given to patients

79. To convince an opponent that active euthanasia is not immoral, the euthanasia proponent needs to establish that _____.

   a. less pain is better than more pain

   b. there is no moral difference between killing and letting die

   c. doctors do not have a moral duty to keep patients alive for as long as possible

   d. for a patient with a terminal illness who is in great pain, death would be a good thing

80. The main problem with accepting active euthanasia is that _____.

   a. the principle on which it is based would have to be accepted in other circumstances

   b. doctors would have to go against the recommendation of their profession

   c. it is not consistent with passive euthanasia

   d. it requires rejecting consequentialism

81. **Animal-rights activists mainly object to** _____.

   a. the use of animals in medical experiments

   b. animals being raised in farms and used as food

   c. animals being used without regard for their suffering

   d. the fact that humans use animals for their own purposes

82. **Animal suffering entails a decrease in the overall net utility only if** _____.

   a. the animals have a capacity for utility that is comparable to that of humans

   b. it does not result in an equal or greater increase in utility

   c. the animal suffering makes humans unhappy

   d. the animal suffering is unjust and undeserved

83. **What is utilitarianism's advantage over other normative bases for animal rights?**

   a. Utilitarianism is a normative theory that most people subscribe to anyway.

   b. Utilitarianism can serve as the basis for special concern for nonhuman animals.

   c. Utilitarians are the most influential ethicists who support animal rights.

   d. A utilitarian can accept any improvement in the treatment of animals.

84. **A normative theory besides utilitarianism that could be used as a basis for animal rights is** _____.

   a. the elimination of speciesism

   b. a duty not to cause suffering to any being

   c. maximizing happiness as much as possible overall

   d. taking into account any being's capacity for suffering

85. **Peter Singer thinks that speciesism is responsible for all of the following *except*** _____.

   a. keeping all humans alive even when they have no capacity for utility

   b. always treating a human life as more valuable than any number of animal lives

   c. treating most humans as though they have the greatest capacity for utility

   d. treating nonhuman animals, even higher apes, as though they had no capacity for utility

86. **Marginal utility is defined as the level at which people** _____.

    a. have only what they need to survive

    b. are not lacking in any physical comforts

    c. are above the poverty line for their society

    d. are in imminent danger of dying

87. **According to utilitarianism, which of the following causes a moral obligation to give in order to save lives?**

    a. Being geographically close to those in need

    b. Being personally involved with those in need

    c. Not being below the level of marginal utility

    d. Being above the level of marginal utility

88. **Utilitarianism can be used as the basis for arguing that someone who does not give to help the needy is, at worst, as morally bad as** _____.

    a. someone who kills the needy

    b. someone who stands by and lets a child drown

    c. people who have more than they need but do not give to those less fortunate

    d. people who do not want to know about the needs of people far away

89. **To save people's lives from starvation and disease, it is necessary** _____.

    a. to slow down all economic growth

    b. for everyone to sell all of their luxury possessions

    c. to convince the affluent that they are morally wrong not to help

    d. to give some resources that are not being used to sustain other people's lives

90. **How does Peter Singer's latest proposal about giving to save lives differ from his original proposal?**

    a. It involves fewer people being obligated to give.

    b. It is argued on the basis of traditional morality.

    c. It is meant to inspire more people to give.

    d. It is willing to settle for fewer lives being saved overall.

91. To most people, the term "reverse discrimination" means _____.

    a. doing the opposite of discrimination

    b. discrimination in favor of minorities

    c. discrimination in favor of the majority

    d. discrimination that has reversible effects

92. An argument in favor of affirmative action might be made on the basis of the difference principle in that _____.

    a. justice requires that those who are in similar situations be treated the same

    b. justice requires that those who are in different situations be treated the same

    c. it would be unjust to treat minorities differently on account of their race

    d. it would be unjust to treat minorities as though they are not in a disadvantaged position

93. If people are committed to consequentialism, they will view racial discrimination as _____.

    a. wrong in and of itself

    b. wrong when it leads to unfair disadvantages

    c. only defensible when it redresses past wrongs

    d. only defensible if it puts those of the majority at a disadvantage

94. Assuming that affirmative action succeeds in helping minorities, someone may still object to it on the basis that _____.

    a. racial discrimination is always wrong

    b. minorities are not disadvantaged

    c. minorities have the same capacities as anyone else

    d. subjecting the majority to disadvantages is unfair

95. Affirmative action may be thought *not* to be analogous to chemotherapy in that _____.

    a. chemotherapy does not always cure cancer

    b. chemotherapy disrupts the body's equilibrium

    c. affirmative action may not be necessary to achieve its ends

    d. affirmative action may not be sufficient to achieve its ends

96. **Which of the following is an example of a categorical imperative to a corporation regarding consumers?**

    a. Pay workers enough money so they will want to stay at their jobs.

    b. Pay a fair price for goods that are consumed.

    c. Do not exploit workers in foreign factories.

    d. Sell goods that consumers really want.

97. **Which of the following is an example of a categorical imperative to an employee regarding the corporation where he or she is employed?**

    a. Take personal time off work when needed.

    b. Do not use corporate resources to make your own money.

    c. If you want to earn more money, then you should work harder.

    d. Competent work must be rewarded with a commensurate salary.

98. **Which of the following is *not* an example of a corporation's observing ethical norms in favor of its employees?**

    a. Requiring employees to work a certain amount of hours per week

    b. Giving employees a certain number of vacation days

    c. Treating employees to holiday banquets

    d. Paying employees

99. **A corporation's responsibilities are not the same as those of its members because _____.**

    a. only a corporation can have social responsibility

    b. a corporation cannot be punished for its decisions

    c. a corporation makes decisions that are not the same as those of any of its members

    d. a corporation has responsibility for which its members do not have to answer

100. **The concept of social responsibility applies to corporations in cases when _____.**

    a. the corporation's profitability is at stake

    b. the public image of the corporation is at stake

    c. the corporation needs to keep its customers happy

    d. the corporation owes benefits to parties that make its business possible

Appendix

How to Write a Philosophy Essay

If you are taking an ethics or other introductory philosophy course, you will very likely be required to demonstrate your understanding of the material by writing an essay on some topic or other. Just as the subject matter of philosophy differs from any other subject, the way that philosophy is written is different from that in other subjects (see Chapter 1). The purpose of this appendix is to give some guidance in this area for those who are taking a formal ethics course and will need to write well in philosophy to be successful.

As covered earlier in various chapters in this book, philosophy seeks to expose and explain the foundational principles by which we reason about particular things we care about. This takes discussion much "deeper," beyond mere descriptions or information giving, than other subjects in the humanities. As a result, to demonstrate an understanding of philosophical material in written form, you have to be able to fully explain the material in your own words. When philosophers write philosophy, they understand that no matter what they write, even given a relatively narrow focus, more could always be said about that topic. But what they do write has to be such that as little as possible is taken for granted. The ability to explain things in this way is a discipline in and of itself, as was also explained in Chapter 1. In ordinary communication, all sorts of assumptions are necessary for participants to understand one another, but it's not normally necessary to state them all explicitly. Everyone shares and operates on the same basic assumptions in day-to-day life; a lot of common experience forms the background for our ordinary talk, such that "it's understood" already. In writing or talking or otherwise "doing" philosophy, however, your starting assumptions have to be made explicit and kept constantly in view. That way, you can reason about them and see what these starting assumptions (principles) lead to when you apply them to a particular topic. If you don't make your starting assumptions and prior commitments clear, you will just be stating your opinions; when you talk to people with different views on a subject, you will only be able to communicate about it by contradicting each other or "talking past each other"—that is, using terms in such different ways that you're not really even disagreeing but actually talking about entirely different things.

What all this means for writing philosophy in an examination situation is that you have to put yourself in the position of someone explaining the material to someone encountering it for the first time. *You* may know what you mean, in your own mind, because you've already studied the material, but what about your reader? More to the point, what about your instructor or another person grading your essay? Keep in mind the perspective of someone new to the material or yourself before you ever encountered it, and ask yourself, "Would he or she understand what I'm talking about?" This is also the way to answer the question of what your instructor is looking for as far as what grade you will receive. To get the best grade possible on a philosophy essay, you need to prove to the reader that you understand what is going on, in your own words, and are not just regurgitating certain words and phrases from your notes.

You can understand what all of this means in principle, but applying it specifically to philosophy may be another matter. When writing a philosophy essay, you may think you are explaining material when all you are really doing is *describing* or *telling*. Practice in writing philosophy essays is therefore very important to your ability to do it well. Ideally, you should write practice essays and ask your instructor or teaching assistant to critique them to see if you are on the right track and how your writing may be improved. Following are some examples of answers to a philosophy essay question. They have varying degrees of quality, and an explanation follows each one as to why it would receive the kind of grade shown. Comparing them may help you get a concrete idea of what a successful philosophy essay answer looks like.

A "C" Essay

Explain how ethical egoism defines the basis of the good. In so doing, explain why ethical egoism is consequentialist. What is the ethical egoist's primary argument against altruistic actions? Explain two of the biggest objections to ethical egoism.

Ethical egoism is a view according to which everyone should look after his or her own well-being. This means that each person has one life to live and has to live that life as best as he or she can. It is consequentialist because it says that the results of one's actions have to be beneficial to oneself in order for them to be good.

Ethical egoism requires that people do not act in the interests of others or commit acts of altruism. Acts of altruism don't benefit oneself, so ethical egoism has to say that they are forbidden. The highest value is one's own life, so the ethical egoist has to say that the only things that should be done are those that promote one's own life.

One objection to ethical egoism is that you cannot look after other people's interests, and yet most people think that helping others is good. Respecting other people's rights has to be a good thing, yet ethical egoism says it isn't. An ethical egoist can't do anything that benefits other people, just himself or herself, and most people would say that this is wrong.

Another objection is that it has to say that each person's own highest good is the only good. But what about other people's good? Other people should think that their highest good is the only good, so no one can really be right. There is no way to really tell that one's own good is the highest good, because no one can really say that one's own good is really in the best interests of everyone.

This essay answers, or at least addresses, every part of the question—so far, so good. But from the beginning, ethical egoism is poorly defined. The writer gives some things that are consistent with ethical egoism but does not say what is definitive about the theory. In "explaining" how the theory is consequentialist, the essay merely describes how consequentialism would define the good according to ethical egoism—it does not explain *why* ethical egoism is a form of consequentialism. The ethical egoist's "argument" against altruism is crudely and inaccurately presented: ethical egoism is compatible with acting in others' interests, provided that doing so also furthers your own interests. The first objection that is presented merely contradicts ethical egoism's thesis and states that common sense opposes it. The second objection is unclearly stated and insufficiently differentiated from the first objection.

A student might write an essay like this one if he or she simply studied all the bullet points from his or her notes. This student can expect no better than a C, pointing to the importance of *how* you take notes in philosophy; if you merely copy down all the slides, you may still not remember how one point connects to another. When listening to a philosophy lecture, it may be difficult to tell what is important, because the material is unfamiliar. But it is important to write down as much as possible of what is said; if the lecturer is fully explaining the topic and not digressing, *all* of it is probably important.

A "B" Essay

Explain how ethical egoism defines the basis of the good. In so doing, explain why ethical egoism is consequentialist. What is the ethical egoist's primary argument against altruistic actions? Explain two of the biggest objections to ethical egoism.

Ethical egoism is a view according to which the primary good is one's own well-being. It says that each person has one life to live, and so each person can only live his or her own life the best he or she can. Each person is best at looking after his or her own interests, and so that is the primary good for that person and not just doing good for others. Ethical egoism is a consequentialist theory in that it defines goodness of actions entirely in terms of the results of one's actions, the results being considered good if they advance one's own interests.

Ethical egoism requires that nothing be done that is not in one's own interests. Thus, it cannot allow altruism, actions that only benefit others. Since altruism by definition does not benefit oneself, ethical egoism concludes that it is not good. In acts of altruism, people are trying to do for others what they should have done for themselves, and this goes against each person's ability to further his or her own good.

One major objection to ethical egoism is its self-centeredness, which may make it actually unethical. Ethical egoism has to say that anything you do to further your own interest should be done. This means that if you can cheat and get away with it, you should do it. So it means that many of the kinds of actions we would think are unethical are actually morally obligatory. Regard for other people's rights per se has no place in ethical egoism; in fact, it has to say that it is morally wrong to regard other people's interests if it does not also advance one's own interests.

Another major objection is in how ethical egoism defines the good. Each person's good is that person's highest value. But this means that from each person's point of view, the highest value in the universe is one's own self. So everyone has to act as though they are the only being whose good is ethically good, but surely this cannot be correct. Usually we don't think of worthwhile relationships as being only those that are businesslike. Rather, if there's such a thing as love, people need to be able to look out for other people's interests purely for their own sake. But ethical egoism has to say that that is unethical, so there is reason to think that it must be wrong.

This essay gives a correct answer to every part of the essay question. Everything that is stated is correct as far as it goes. But it doesn't explain things to the extent needed to really teach the topic to someone with no prior exposure to it; that person would need to fill in the blanks and connect the dots a little to figure out exactly what is meant and implied. A person grading this essay would be able to tell that whoever wrote it has a general grasp of the subject matter but not necessarily a thorough or deep one. The essay could say more to demonstrate a full grasp of the ins and outs of the topic. It is a good essay— certainly better than the preceding C example—but not excellent, so it would receive a B.

An "A" Essay

Explain how ethical egoism defines the basis of the good. In so doing, explain why ethical egoism is consequentialist. What is the ethical egoist's primary argument against altruistic actions? Explain two of the biggest objections to ethical egoism.

Normative ethics is the part of ethical theory that tries to define the basis of the ethical good in order to explain what all ethically good actions have in common. A particular normative theory tries to give an answer as to what it takes for an action to be ethically good. Ethical egoism is a theory in normative ethics according to which the fundamental good for each person is his or her own well-being. Thus, ethical egoism says that actions that are morally good will be those that advance one's personal interests. This view is motivated by the conviction that each person has one life to live, and that therefore each person has sole responsibility for living his or her own life the best he or she can. Therefore, what each person does best, and better than anyone else does, is to look after his or her own interests. Ethical egoism says that these interests are defined in terms of long-term goods for the individual (as opposed to just whatever might bring immediate pleasure) and does not care about *how* those interests are furthered, just that anything that has the consequence of furthering one's own good should be done. Thus, it is a consequentialist theory—it defines goodness of actions entirely in terms of the results of one's actions, the results in the case of ethical egoism being good only if they further one's own personal interests.

Because ethical egoism defines the good according to each person's own interests, it cannot allow altruistic actions. Altruistic actions are those that are done purely for other people's sake and not for one's own benefit. Ethical egoism thinks this is wrong because it fails to do what each person does best, which is further his or her own interests. Ethical egoism does not require that one never do anything that benefits others. That is, if one promoted one's own interest and by doing so also benefited others—for example, starting a business and creating jobs as a part of that—that would be okay, according to ethical egoism. What ethical egoism does require is that nothing be done that is not in one's own interests. Since ethical egoism holds that furthering one's own interests is always obligatory, and altruism by definition does not benefit oneself, ethical egoism concludes that altruism is wrong, because it always involves failing to do what is obligatory. In fact, it says that altruism does not even help others, because it attempts to do what others are actually best at doing for themselves, so it keeps other people's ultimate good from being furthered either. Ultimately, ethical egoism sees altruism as wasting time and energy that could have been used to further one's own interest. Since ethical egoism says that for each person the highest value is that person's own life, any neglect of furthering that value is wrong—this is the primary objection to altruism from the standpoint of ethical egoism.

There some serious deficiencies in ethical egoism as an ethical theory. One of them is due to its self-interest combined with its consequentialism. Anything that furthers one's interest, according to ethical egoism, ought to be pursued. So suppose that someone is in competition with you for something that would significantly advance your interests, like getting a certain job or a promotion. Suppose further that you could knock this person off with a reasonable certainty of getting away with it. Ethical egoism says that this action would be a morally very good one. This seems to yield the wrong result, since most anyone would tend to think that such an action would be despicable. This is just an especially stark instance of the general problem that ethical egoism conflicts squarely with commonsense morality in thinking that you not only can but should step on other people if that's what it takes to reach your goals. Regard for other people's rights have no place in ethical egoism; in fact, ethical egoism would have to say that such regard per se is morally wrong. This seems completely backward.

Another big problem is from its combination of self-centeredness with the relative standard by which the ethical good has to be determined. Refer again to ethical egoism's primary value: each person's good is that person's highest value. But this means that from each person's point of view, the highest value in the universe is his or her own self! Consequently, each person must act as if he or she is the most important person in the world. Picture a world in which each person acted as if he or she were the most important person in the world. The results would be ugly, one can easily imagine. All this comes from the fact that, as a normative theory that is supposed to tell what kinds of actions are good, ethical egoism will give a different answer to each person. That is, the good can only be defined relative to each different person.

Ethical egoism is committed to the claim that we can only pursue relationships that are businesslike in the sense of being entered into for mutual benefit. Most people do get mutual benefit from their relationships, but they also genuinely care about other people's interests for their own sake. But ethical egoism says that this is wrong. In the end, if we didn't think it ethically permissible to care for others for their own sake, we couldn't have the most meaningful relationships we tend to have. And since such relationships do benefit our own interests, pursuit of ethical egoism could not even result in our interests being furthered, and so it would be self-defeating.

This essay, as compared with the one before it, goes into a lot more explanation of what is involved with ethical egoism to answer each part of the question, giving examples and delineating exactly what is and is not implied by the view under discussion. Of course, it is quite a bit longer than the other essays, but the length is necessary to explain things thoroughly. If you think you are overexplaining or stating the obvious, you are probably explaining things at the right level (not too much), as long as you are not just being repetitive and rambling. Go ahead and state all the "obvious" assumptions and implications of the view under discussion to demonstrate clearly that you understand what is involved; doing so on a consistent basis may well make the difference between a B and an A. It may not be necessary to go into quite as much length and detail as this example does, but doing so should be sufficient for an A. If it's a good grade you're after, you'll want to err on the side of overkill, since even if it's not a *necessary* condition for an A, it is likely to be a *sufficient* condition, and you'll want to focus on doing what's sufficient to bring about the desired results.

Glossary

antecedent: (Ch. 2) The part of a conditional that comes immediately after *if*. A true conditional with a true antecedent must have a true consequent. See also **conditional, consequent**.

applied ethics: (Ch. 1) The use of ethical reasoning toward a specific ethical issue. Arguments in applied ethics usually come from some particular standpoint in ethical theory. See also **argument, ethical theory**.

argument: (Ch. 1) An attempt to reason from certain facts and principles (premises) to establish the truth of a conclusion. See also **deductive argument, inductive argument, premise**.

categorical imperative: (Ch. 4) A proscription for action that requires that if everyone carried out the same kind of action for the same reason, the goal of the action could still be met. According to Immanuel Kant's normative theory, a categorical imperative is what provides norms for right action. See also **norm, normative ethics**.

conditional: (Ch. 2) A statement in the form of "if–then." The statement immediately following *if* is called the antecedent, and the statement immediately following *then* is called the consequent. A true conditional is such that if the antecedent is true, then the consequent in that case must also be true; a false conditional has a counterexample to it. See also **antecedent, consequent, counterexample**.

consequent: (Ch. 2) The part of a conditional that comes immediately after *then*. A true conditional with a false consequent must have a false antecedent. See also **antecedent, conditional**.

consequentialism: (Ch. 4) The normative theory that says an action is morally right only if its consequences are good overall. See also **normative ethics**.

counterexample: (Ch. 2) A true or possible case in which the antecedent of a conditional is true but its consequent is false, which proves the conditional false. See also **antecedent, conditional, consequent**.

deductive argument: (Ch. 2) An argument for which, if it is formally valid, the truth of the premises necessitates the truth of the conclusion. See also **argument, premise, valid**.

difference principle: (Ch. 6) The principle of justice that states that if one group of people is treated differently from another group, this must be justified by the existence of an appropriate difference between the two groups.

divine command theory: (Ch. 4) The normative theory that places the basis for morally good actions on the supposition that they are commanded by God (and that morally bad actions are those forbidden by God). See also **normative ethics**.

epistemology: (Ch. 1) The branch of philosophy that deals with the nature and conditions of knowledge.

error theory: (Ch. 5) In metaethics, the variant of nihilism that states that moral judgments are meant to refer to objective moral facts; there are no such things as objective moral facts; and therefore, all moral judgments are wrong. See also **metaethics, nihilism**.

ethical egoism: (Ch. 4) The normative theory that says it is always ethical to further one's own interests and unethical to do anything that is not to one's own benefit. See also **normative ethics**.

ethical theory: (Ch. 1) The collective term for the branches of ethics that deal with general and abstract issues about the nature and practice of ethics but not necessarily with any specific application. See also **applied ethics**.

ethics: (Ch. 1) The branch of philosophy that deals with the nature of goodness and the exercise of morally right actions.

eudaimonia: (Ch. 3) Literally "happiness" or "well-being"; in value theory, an objectively good state of well-being that is not defined in terms of subjective experiences. See also **value theory**.

expressivism: (Ch. 5) In metaethics, the variant of nihilism that states that moral judgments are essentially expressions of how we feel; there are no such things as objective moral facts; and therefore, unlike judgments of fact, moral judgments are never correct or incorrect. See also **metaethics, nihilism**.

fallacy: (Ch. 2) An attempt to make a valid inference in which the conclusion does not necessarily follow from the truth of the premises. See also **premise, valid**.

hedonism: (Ch. 3) In value theory, the view that subjective experiences of well-being are the ultimate value. See also **value theory**.

inductive argument: (Ch. 2) An argument for which the truth of the premises makes the truth of the conclusion extremely likely. See also **argument, premise**.

instrumental good: (Ch. 3) Something that is good because it can help bring about another good and not because it is good in and of itself.

intrinsic property: (Ch. 3) An inherent property of a thing; if you took away everything else in the world and the thing still had that property, the property would be intrinsic. See also **instrumental good**.

liberalism: (Ch. 6) The social and political philosophy that places a paramount value on liberty in society; different versions of philosophical liberalism give different accounts of what makes liberty valuable.

logic: (Ch. 2) A system of reasoning showing the necessary connections between statements and allowing one to make valid arguments. See also **argument, valid**.

marginal utility: (Ch. 12) The level of utility that includes the bare necessities of living (such as food, clothing, and shelter) and nothing more. See also **utilitarianism**.

metaethics: (Chs. 1, 5) The branch of ethical theory that examines the subject matter of morality itself and the nature of moral judgments to determine on what features of reality they are based. See also **ethical theory, metaphysics**.

metaphysics: (Ch. 1) The branch of philosophy that deals with questions about the nature of reality and its most general features.

modus ponens: (Ch. 2) The valid use of a conditional in which the truth of the consequent is inferred from the truth of the antecedent. See also **antecedent, consequent, valid**.

modus tollens: (Ch. 2) The valid use of a conditional in which the falsity of the antecedent is inferred from the falsity of the consequent. See also **antecedent, consequent, valid**.

moral agent: (Ch. 4) A person whose actions are such that he or she can be held morally responsible for the moral goodness or badness of those actions.

moral realism: (Ch. 5) The view that there are objective moral facts on which the truth or falsity of moral judgments depend and that hold true regardless of what anyone believes. See also **realism**.

nihilism: (Chs. 3, 5) Literally "nothingism"; in value theory, the view that there are no ultimate values worth pursuing; in metaethics, the view that there are no objective moral facts, so moral judgments are never true of anything. See also **metaethics, value theory**.

norm: (Ch. 1) A general standard of conduct that determines whether an action is morally good or bad.

normative ethics: (Chs. 1, 4) The branch of ethical theory that deals with the most general principles, or norms, that determine whether any action is morally right or wrong. See also **ethical theory, norm**.

premise: (Ch. 2) A part of the antecedent of an argument. The premises of an argument may be true or false independent of each other, but taken together they are supposed to entail the truth of the argument's conclusion. See also **antecedent, argument**.

realism: (Ch. 5) In metaphysics, the view that there is an objective reality independent of our thoughts about it and that our judgments are correct or incorrect based on whether they are true or false with regard to the objective facts. See also **metaphysics**.

relativism: (Ch. 5) In metaethics, the view that moral facts are specific to an individual or a culture; it is not possible to make moral judgments about an individual or culture that refer to moral facts that only apply outside that individual or culture. See also **metaethics**.

sentimentalism: (Ch. 5) The metaethical view that the content of our ethical views and judgments cannot be understood except in terms of the feelings we have about those things. See also **metaethics**.

sound: (Ch. 2) Describes a valid argument for which all the premises are true, guaranteeing that its conclusion is true. See also **argument, premise, valid**.

supererogatory: (Ch. 4) Describes an action that is morally good but not morally obligatory; a supererogatory act goes above and beyond what is required to be minimally morally decent.

utilitarianism: (Ch. 4) The main variant of consequentialism; it states that ethically good actions are those that best increase "utility," or happiness (that is, to the most beings, overall, that are capable of experiencing happiness or suffering). See also **consequentialism**.

valid: (Ch. 2) In logic, the description of a form of inference in which a necessary connection has successfully been demonstrated. A valid deductive argument is one for which, if all the premises are true, the conclusion has to be true also. See also **deductive argument**, **logic**.

value theory: (Chs. 1, 3) The branch of ethical theory that deals with questions of what is and what should be ultimately valued in life. See also **ethical theory**.

Bibliography

Annas, Julia. 1993. *The Morality of Happiness*. New York: Oxford University Press.

Blackburn, Simon. 2003. *Being Good: A Short Introduction to Ethics*. New York: Oxford University Press.

Bloomfield, Paul. 2001. *Moral Reality*. New York: Oxford University Press.

———. 2008. "The Harm of Immorality." *Ratio* 21:241–59.

Deigh, John. 2010. *An Introduction to Ethics*. New York: Cambridge University Press.

D'Arms, Justin, and Daniel Jacobson. 2000. "Sentiment and Value." *Ethics* 110:722–48.

Dworkin, Ronald. 1996. "Objectivity and Truth: You'd Better Believe It." *Philosophy and Public Affairs* 25:87–137.

Fish, Stanley. 1993. "How the Pot Got to Call the Kettle Black." *Atlantic Monthly*, November, 272:128–34.

Foot, Philippa. 1967. "Abortion and the Doctrine of the Double Effect." *Oxford Review* 5:5–15.

———. 2001. *Natural Goodness*. New York: Oxford University Press.

Friedman, Milton. 1970. "The Social Responsibility of Business Is to Increase Its Profits." *The New York Times Magazine*, September 13.

Gaus, Gerald, and Shane Courtland. 2010. "Liberalism." In *The Stanford Encyclopedia of Philosophy*, edited by E. N. Zalta. http://plato.stanford.edu/archives/fall2010/entries/liberalism.

Gibbard, Allan. 1990. *Wise Choices, Apt Feelings*. Cambridge, MA: Harvard University Press.

Harman, Gilbert. 1977. *The Nature of Morality*. New York: Oxford University Press.

Herman, Barbara. 1993. *The Practice of Moral Judgment*. Cambridge: Harvard University Press.

Kant, Immanuel. 1949. *Fundamental Principles of the Metaphysics of Morals*. Translated by Thomas K. Abbott. Upper Saddle River: Prentice Hall.

Lopez, Kathryn Jean. 2001. "Euthanasia Sets Sail: An Interview with Philip Nitschke, the Other 'Dr. Death.'" *The National Review Online*, June 5. http://old.nationalreview.com/interrogatory/interrogatory060501.shtml.

Luban, David. 2006. "Liberalism, Torture and the Ticking Bomb." *Harper's Magazine*, April, 11–16.

Mackie, J. L. 1977. *Ethics: Inventing Right and Wrong*. New York: Penguin Books.

Marino, Gordon, ed. 2010. *Ethics: The Essential Writings*. New York: Modern Library.

Marquis, Don. 1989. "Why Abortion Is Immoral," *Journal of Philosophy* 86:183–202.

McMahan, Jeff. 2009. *Killing in War*. New York: Oxford University Press.

Midgley, Mary. 1981. *Heart and Mind: The Varieties of Moral Experience*. London: Palgrave Macmillan.

Mill, John Stuart. 1978. *On Liberty*. Indianapolis: Hackett Publishing.

Mulligan, Thomas. 1986. "A Critique of Milton Friedman's Essay 'The Social Responsibility of Business Is to Increase Its Profits.'" *Journal of Business Ethics* 5:265–69.

Nathanson, Stephen. 1987. *An Eye for an Eye?: The Immorality of Punishing by Death*. Lanham, MD: Rowman & Littlefield.

Nietzsche, Friedrich. 2002. *Beyond Good and Evil*. Edited by Rolf-Peter Horstmann; edited and translated by Judith Norman. New York: Cambridge University Press.

Noonan, John T. 1970. *The Morality of Abortion: Legal and Historical Perspectives*. Cambridge: Harvard University Press.

Nozick, Robert. 1973. *Anarchy, State, and Utopia*. New York: Basic Books.

Pettit, Philip. 2007. "Responsibility Incorporated." *Ethics* 117:171–201.

Primoratz, Igor. 1989. *Justifying Legal Punishment*. Amherst, MA: Humanity Books.

Rachels, James. 1975. "Active and Passive Euthanasia." *New England Journal of Medicine* 292:78–80.

———. 1979. "Killing and Starving to Death." *Philosophy* 54:159–71.

Rawls, John. 1971. *A Theory of Justice*. Cambridge: Harvard University Press.

Shafer-Landau, Russ. 2010a. *The Fundamentals of Ethics*. New York: Oxford University Press.

———. 2010b. *The Ethical Life: Fundamental Readings in Ethics and Moral Problems*. New York: Oxford University Press.

Shue, Henry. 1978. "Torture." *Philosophy and Public Affairs* 7:124–43.

Singer, Peter. 1972. "Famine, Affluence, and Morality." *Philosophy and Public Affairs* 1:229–43.

———. 1993. *Practical Ethics*. New York: Cambridge University Press.

———, ed. 1994. *Ethics*. New York: Oxford University Press.

———. 2002a. *Animal Liberation*. New York: Ecco.

———. 2002b. "Unsanctifying Human Life." In *Unsanctifying Human Life*, edited by Helga Kuhse. New York: Oxford University Press.

———. 2009. *The Life You Can Save: Acting Now to End World Poverty*. New York: Random House.

Smart, J. J. C. 1956. "Extreme and Restricted Utilitarianism." *Philosophical Quarterly* 6:344–54.

Smith, Michael. 1994. "Realism." In Singer 1994.

Steele, Shelby. 1991. *The Content of Our Character: A New Vision of Race in America*. New York: Harper Perennial.

Thomson, Judith Jarvis. 1971. "A Defense of Abortion." *Philosophy and Public Affairs* 1:47–66.

———. 1976. "Killing, Letting Die, and the Trolley Problem." *The Monist* 59:204, 217.

Unger, Peter. 1996. *Living High and Letting Die: Our Illusion of Innocence*. New York: Oxford University Press.

Van Inwagen, Peter. 2002. *Metaphysics*. Boulder, CO: Westview Books.

Warburton, Nigel, and David Edmonds, eds. 2008. "Business Ethics," episode of podcast *Ethics Bites*. The Open University. http://www.open2.net/ethicsbites/business-ethics.html.

Warren, Mary Anne. 1973. "On the Moral and Legal Status of Abortion." *The Monist* 57:43–61.

Answer Key

CHAPTER 1 QUIZ

1. c   2. b   3. a   4. d   5. b   6. b   7. d   8. c   9. a   10. a

CHAPTER 2 QUIZ

1. d   2. a   3. c   4. b   5. d   6. c   7. d   8. b   9. c   10. a

CHAPTER 3 QUIZ

1. b   2. c   3. a   4. b   5. a   6. d   7. c   8. c   9. b   10. d

CHAPTER 4 QUIZ

1. c   2. b   3. a   4. d   5. c   6. d   7. b   8. a   9. b   10. c

CHAPTER 5 QUIZ

1. a   2. c   3. b   4. b   5. c   6. d   7. a   8. d   9. a   10. c

PARTS ONE AND TWO TEST

1. a   2. b   3. d   4. c   5. a   6. b   7. b   8. d   9. c   10. a
11. d   12. b   13. c   14. d   15. a   16. a   17. a   18. c   19. c
20. b   21. b   22. d   23. c   24. a   25. d

CHAPTER 6 QUIZ

1. a   2. a   3. b   4. c   5. d   6. b   7. c   8. c   9. d   10. b

CHAPTER 7 QUIZ

1. b   2. a   3. c   4. d   5. c   6. b   7. d   8. d   9. a   10. c

CHAPTER 8 QUIZ

1. d   2. b   3. b   4. c   5. a   6. c   7. d   8. c   9. a   10. d

CHAPTER 9 QUIZ

1. c   2. a   3. d   4. b   5. c   6. a   7. d   8. b   9. c   10. a

CHAPTER 10 QUIZ

1. b   2. a   3. d   4. d   5. c   6. c   7. d   8. c   9. a   10. d

CHAPTER 11 QUIZ

1. a   2. d   3. b   4. b   5. c   6. d   7. d   8. a   9. b   10. c

CHAPTER 12 QUIZ

1. c   2. c   3. a   4. b   5. d   6. d   7. c   8. b   9. a   10. d

CHAPTER 13 QUIZ

1. a   2. b   3. c   4. d   5. b   6. c   7. c   8. a   9. d   10. c

CHAPTER 14 QUIZ

1. d   2. c   3. a   4. c   5. b   6. d   7. b   8. a   9. c   10. d

PART THREE TEST

1. b   2. d   3. b   4. d   5. b   6. c   7. a   8. d   9. b   10. c
11. c   12. b   13. b   14. a   15. c   16. d   17. c   18. b   19. c
20. d   21. d   22. a   23. b   24. c   25. a

FINAL EXAM

1. b   2. c   3. a   4. d   5. c   6. a   7. b   8. b   9. d   10. c
11. a   12. d   13. c   14. d   15. b   16. a   17. d   18. b   19. c
20. a   21. d   22. b   23. c   24. c   25. d   26. c   27. b   28. a
29. d   30. b   31. b   32. c   33. c   34. d   35. a   36. c   37. d
38. b   39. a   40. d   41. b   42. a   43. c   44. c   45. d   46. a
47. d   48. b   49. c   50. a   51. b   52. a   53. d   54. d   55. c
56. b   57. d   58. b   59. a   60. b   61. d   62. b   63. c   64. d
65. b   66. c   67. a   68. b   69. d   70. c   71. c   72. b   73. a
74. a   75. b   76. d   77. b   78. c   79. b   80. a   81. c   82. b
83. d   84. b   85. c   86. a   87. d   88. a   89. d   90. c   91. b
92. d   93. b   94. a   95. c   96. d   97. b   98. a   99. c   100. d

Index